LIAR IN A CROWDED THEATER

LIAR
IN A
CROWDED
THEATER

Freedom of Speech

in a World of Misinformation

JEFF KOSSEFF

JOHNS HOPKINS UNIVERSITY PRESS

BALTIMORE

© 2023 Jeff Kosseff
All rights reserved. Published 2023
Printed in the United States of America on acid-free paper
2 4 6 8 9 7 5 3 1

Johns Hopkins University Press
2715 North Charles Street
Baltimore, Maryland 21218
www.press.jhu.edu

Library of Congress Cataloging-in-Publication Data is available.

ISBN 978-1-4214-4732-2 (hardcover)
ISBN 978-1-4214-4733-9 (ebook)

A catalog record for this book is available from the British Library.

Song lyrics for "Brain Damage," written by Jeff Bass, Mark Bass, and Marshall Mathers,
appear in chapter 4. Published by Eight Mile Style, LLC, and Martin Affiliated, LLC,
administered by Bridgeport Music Inc. Used with permission.

*Special discounts are available for bulk purchases of this book. For more information, please contact
Special Sales at specialsales@jh.edu.*

To the hundreds of midshipmen whom I've had the pleasure of teaching at the US Naval Academy. You constantly challenge me to think critically and to be a better scholar.

Contents

Note to the Reader

The views expressed in this book are mine only and do not represent those of the US Naval Academy, Department of the Navy, Department of Defense, or any other party. Although this book covers legal topics, it is not a substitute for legal advice from qualified counsel.

Because this book discusses legal battles over free speech, it includes language that some may consider to be offensive or inappropriate. The book contains this language to give an accurate and complete portrayal of the disputes.

LIAR IN A CROWDED THEATER

Introduction

Edgar Maddison Welch grabbed his AR-15 assault rifle and a loaded .38 caliber revolver and drove his Toyota Prius from Salisbury, North Carolina, to a specific destination: a pizza restaurant in the wealthy enclave of Chevy Chase in northwest Washington, DC.[1]

On the first Sunday afternoon in December 2016, the 28-year-old Welch walked through the front door of Comet Ping Pong with the assault rifle across his chest. Patrons and employees scrambled out the door as the man with the sandy beard walked toward the back of the restaurant and fired the rifle repeatedly. One employee had walked through the rear door to find Welch holding a rifle. The employee fled, and police soon arrested Welch.[2]

What could have motivated Welch to drive hundreds of miles to shoot up a pizza place?

A lie.

Welch had watched YouTube videos about "PizzaGate," an online conspiracy theory that claimed Democrats were operating a child sex-trafficking ring and performing satanic rituals in the Comet Ping Pong basement. The lie developed and spread on social media merely because the restaurant's owner had communicated with Hillary Clinton's campaign chairman, John Podesta, whose emails had been hacked during the 2016 presidential campaign. Despite a complete lack of support for the claims, Welch bought into the lies and was determined to put an end to the sex trafficking. "Raiding a pedo ring, possibly sacraficing [*sic*] the lives of a few for the lives of many," he texted to a friend two days before his trip to Washington.[3]

Falsehoods like PizzaGate tear through American life like a virtual tornado, swiftly spreading online. Some false speech comes in the form of disinformation campaigns that seek to upend American democracy. Other falsehoods ruin reputations, tear apart families, and destroy careers. Politicians routinely fib to voters. And US law shields much of this speech. The First Amendment, common-law safeguards, and statutes enacted by legislatures nationwide protect speakers and writers from criminal charges and civil claims arising from many types of allegedly false or misleading speech.

The Comet Ping Pong shooting and other incidents sparked by falsehoods have prompted many public officials and commentators to question whether the legal protections for false speech are too robust. A CBS *Sunday Morning* segment airing exactly two weeks after Welch entered Comet Ping Pong addressed the pizza restaurant shooting, Russian misinformation in the 2016 presidential election, and other harms caused by widespread falsehoods. Josh Earnest, then the White House press secretary for President Barack Obama, bemoaned the dissemination of fake news. His interviewer, Ted Koppel, asked whether the First Amendment remains relevant.

"I think it's always relevant, right?" Earnest said. "It's the foundation of our democracy. But one of the things that we accept as citizens of the United States are reasonable and responsible limitations on our constitutional rights. For example, I think most famously, the Supreme Court has said, you can't yell fire in a crowded theater, because that could pose a threat to the public."[4]

Fire in a crowded theater.

If you're discussing whether US law should protect false speech, there is a good chance that someone will say five words: "fire in a crowded theater." That person likely wants the government to regulate harmful speech, and justifies it by pointing out that the US Supreme Court said that you can never yell fire in a crowded theater.

Like much of the speech that those claiming fire in a crowded theater are trying to prohibit, the statement is not the complete truth. On a superficial level, the statement is incorrect because sometimes you *could* yell fire in a crowded theater without facing punishment. The theater may actually be on fire. Or you may reasonably believe that the theater is on fire. Or you are singing in a concert, and "FIRE" is one of your lyrics. Of course, there are scenarios in which intentionally lying about a fire in a crowded theater and causing a stampede might lead to a disorderly conduct citation or similar charge.

The real problem with the "fire in a crowded theater" discourse is that it too often is used as a placeholder justification for regulating any speech that someone believes is harmful or objectionable. Yet in reality, the Supreme Court has defined narrow categories of speech that are exempt from First Amendment protections and set an extraordinarily high bar for imposing liability for other types of speech. As the Supreme Court wrote in 2010, the United States does not have a "free-floating test for First Amendment coverage," and the free speech protections do not "extend only to categories of speech that survive an ad hoc balancing of relative social costs and benefits."[5]

"Fire in a crowded theater" is a derivative of a line in a 1919 Supreme Court opinion, *Schenck v. United States*. The case involved an appeal by a Socialist Party official of his conviction, under the Espionage Act of 1917, for distributing leaflets that criticized the military draft as a Thirteenth Amendment violation. The court unanimously rejected his appeal. Justice Oliver Wendell Holmes Jr. wrote that the First Amendment's protections depend on "whether the words used are used in such circumstances and are of such a nature as to create a clear and present danger that they will bring about the substantive evils that Congress has a right to prevent. It is a question of proximity and degree." To support his interpretation of the First Amendment, Holmes wrote that the "most stringent protection of free speech would not protect a man in falsely shouting fire in a theatre and causing a panic."[6] (Note that in Holmes's formulation, the theater was not necessarily crowded, the speech was false, and it caused a panic—three details that often are left out from current discourse.)

The crowded theater scenario was a hypothetical to support the low-burden "clear and present danger" test and the conviction of a military draft critic. And it probably wasn't even a hypothetical that Holmes had originally created. As law professor Thomas Healy documented in his excellent book about Holmes's free speech jurisprudence, Holmes likely had been inspired by a similar comparison in the record of another Espionage Act case that the Supreme Court was considering around the same time. During the trial of socialist Eugene Debs, prosecutor Edwin S. Wertz said that "a man in a crowded auditorium, or any theatre, who yells 'fire' and there is no fire, and a panic ensues and someone is trampled to death, may be rightfully indicted and charged with murder." As in *Schenck*, the "fire" hypothetical was persuasive, and the jury convicted Debs after six hours of deliberations.[7]

Although the Supreme Court has never had the occasion to adjudicate an actual dispute involving a person yelling fire in a crowded theater, the court did undercut some of the justification for Holmes's "clear and present danger" test. In a 1969 case, *Brandenburg v. Ohio*, the Supreme Court reversed the conviction of a Ku Klux Klan leader under Ohio's criminal syndicalism law, arising from the defendant's hateful speech at a rally. Rather than applying the original clear and present danger framework, the court set a much higher standard, writing that "the constitutional guarantees of free speech and free press do not permit a State to forbid or proscribe advocacy of the use of force or of law violation except where such advocacy is directed to inciting or producing imminent lawless action and is likely to incite or produce such action."[8] The more rigorous "imminent incitement" standard conflicts with Holmes's test, and two justices—Hugo Black and William Douglas—wrote concurrences in *Brandenburg* explicitly rejecting *Schenck* and its "clear and present danger" framework. A federal appellate judge summarized in 2020: "*Brandenburg* has thus been widely understood, starting with the two concurring Justices, as having significantly (if tacitly) narrowed the category of incitement."[9]

Yet the "fire in a crowded theater" enthusiasts persist, and they use the hypothetical to justify regulating a wide swath of harmful or objectionable speech without seriously evaluating the unintended consequences of giving the government more censorial power.[10] In recent years, many commentators and politicians have increasingly focused on misinformation and disinformation, such as election security lies, inaccurate claims about coronavirus safety measures, QAnon conspiracies, and other misrepresentations and falsehoods. Just as you cannot yell fire in a crowded theater, they argue, you can't say [insert false speech here].

But you often *can* utter or publish a falsehood without a regulator or court having the power to intervene, thanks to a long history of free speech precedent dating back to the founding of the United States. And these rights have not contracted; if anything, courts and legislatures have *expanded* protections for false speech over the years. Of course, US law does not protect *all* false speech. If a plaintiff meets the many stringent requirements for proving defamation, the defendant may be liable for damages. Regulators may oversee the claims that companies make about their products. Prosecutors may charge defendants with fraud, lying to government officials, and other crimes arising from false statements. There even are scenarios in which lying about a fire in a crowded theater could lead to liability. But the standards for holding speakers liable for false statements are high in the United States.

This book explains why courts have set such a high bar for protecting false speech, why we should not relax those standards in the face of serious threats, and how we can address those threats without defaulting to government censorship.

In part I, I explain why courts and legislators over the years have developed robust protections for false speech via landmark First Amendment rulings, common law, and statutes. (While much of the focus in modern free speech debates understandably is on the First Amendment, other legal safeguards supplement and expand protections for allegedly false or misleading speech.) The protections often hinge on the "marketplace of ideas" framework for free speech that Holmes developed just months after his theater hypothetical. The general thinking is that government regulation of speech is unnecessary because truth will prevail in the marketplace. The marketplace concept explains many reasons that US courts protect false speech, but it has some shortcomings and does not capture all the rationales for speech protection. Part I examines not only the marketplace theory but also other reasons, including self-governance, transparency, the recognition that we often do not know the "truth" with sufficient certainty, the need to hold people responsible for how they respond to speech, and the limited efficacy of speech regulations.

In part II, I outline concerns about modern falsehoods, including COVID-19 lies, spurious claims of election fraud, deep fakes, QAnon, and other conspiracies. While acknowledging that there are some extraordinary cases in which litigation and regulation are the appropriate solutions, I argue that some recent proposals to censor false speech far exceed the free speech strictures described in part I.

In part III, I explore ways other than regulation and litigation to blunt the harm of falsehoods and help promote the truth. We could better address false speech by empowering the subjects of falsehoods to effectively respond, providing online platforms with some breathing space to moderate harmful content, holding people accountable for how they respond to false speech, better informing the public and equipping them with media literacy skills to evaluate the veracity of claims, and restoring trust in institutions such as government agencies and the media.

A note about the coverage in this book: I often refer to "falsehoods" or "false speech" rather than "lies." I do so not to trivialize the harms of the speech, but because the book covers a wide range of utterances, from technically true but misleading statements to intentional and egregious, bald-faced lies, from innocent misstatements to intentional whoppers. There also is some disagreement as to the precise definitions of some key terms. For instance, *Merriam-Webster* defines "lie" as both "to make an untrue statement with intent to deceive" and "to create a false or misleading impression," with the former definition requiring a particular intent and the latter not. *Black's Law Dictionary* takes the latter approach, defining "lie" as "to tell an untruth; to speak or write falsely." *Oxford English Dictionary* defines "lie" as "to make a false statement with the intention to deceive," but as the *Stanford Encyclopedia of Philosophy* notes, that definition is "both too narrow, since it requires falsity, and too broad, since it allows for lying about something other than what is being stated, and lying to someone who is believed to be listening in but who is not being addressed."[11] Sometimes the legal protections apply only to certain types of false speech, such as unintentional falsehoods, and this book distinguishes between the different elements when relevant. This book also addresses opinionated statements that, while not necessarily asserting a false factual claim, can be highly misleading and are central to the modern debate about false speech.

Liar in a Crowded Theater is a defense of the robust protections for free speech that have long defined America. It is not an argument for absolute protections for false speech; while the First Amendment and other legal safeguards set a high bar for speech restrictions, that bar is not insurmountable, nor should it be. Few seriously argue that all false speech should be devoid of legal consequences, and I do not make that argument in this book. Nor do I argue that courts and legislators should *never* examine these free speech protections to deal with emerging and unanticipated threats; rather, I urge the greatest caution in doing so, and advocate a careful evaluation of the potential harms of curtailing free speech protections and consideration of why courts and legislators have long protected false speech. Finally, I do not seek to play down the very real challenges that modern false speech presents. Rather, I argue that lowering that bar for speech protections would not necessarily solve our current problems and could create even more hazards. I urge lawmakers, judges, and commentators to consider solutions other than reflexive regulation.

I do not pretend to have a magic cure to the substantial societal and political challenges presented by the rapid distribution of false and misleading speech. And I doubt that any solutions, regulatory or otherwise, would entirely address those challenges. The most realistic goal is to understand how the United States could reduce the pervasiveness and harms of falsehoods while staying faithful to our tradition of free speech.

PART I
Why the Law Protects Falsehoods

US legal protections for false speech are expansive. This is a feature and not a bug. In this part of the book, I explain why American law has evolved to protect so many falsehoods. The discussion includes, but goes beyond, First Amendment protections. It was not until the 2012 case of *United States v. Alvarez*, discussed in chapter 1, that the US Supreme Court clearly stated that false speech is not categorically exempt from the First Amendment. (But the court had provided at least some First Amendment protections for false speech dating back to 1964, when it set a high bar for defamation claims filed by public officials in *New York Times v. Sullivan*.)

The First Amendment only tells part of the story of the legal protections for falsehoods. The First Amendment was not incorporated to the states through the Fourteenth Amendment's due process clause until 1925.[1] And even before its incorporation, common-law rules protected some falsehoods—or potential falsehoods. State legislatures have supplemented those common-law and First Amendment protections with statutes that provide additional roadblocks for holding speakers accountable for allegedly false speech.

Free speech protections in the United States have evolved over more than two centuries; in the earliest years, they embraced the English view and focused more heavily on prior restraints that prevent speech from occurring,[2] but modern free speech protections also cover attempts to hold the speaker liable after the fact.[3] Thus many legal safeguards described in part I of this book involve not merely government prohibitions on speech, but also the use of the court system or other legal mechanisms to impose consequences for speech after it has occurred.

The next eight chapters explore not only when courts have protected allegedly false speech, but more importantly *why* they have done so. We begin this part with one of the most common metaphors for free speech: the marketplace of ideas. But that is just one of the reasons that courts and lawmakers have protected false speech.

Chapter 1

Marketplace

Any examination of legal protections for falsehoods requires a discussion of the marketplace of ideas, one of the most prominent theories of free speech in the United States over the past century. This chapter examines how the marketplace of ideas has shaped many legal rules that apply to false speech. It also explores the marketplace's many shortcomings, which help to explain why it is only one of several justifications for shielding falsehoods from lawsuits, regulation, and prosecution.

Justice Oliver Wendell Holmes Jr. most prominently articulated the modern marketplace of ideas framework in his dissent in *Abrams v. United States*, issued on November 10, 1919, about eight months after he wrote the infamously misinterpreted "fire in a theatre" line in *Schenck v. United States*. Holmes's views on free speech changed dramatically throughout 1919, as Thomas Healy thoroughly documented. Holmes spent time with legal scholars such as Zechariah Chafee Jr. and Harold Laski, who had recommended that Holmes read articles that present an expansive view of free speech rights.[1]

Abrams arose from the Espionage Act prosecution of five Russian immigrants who had distributed two circulars that criticized President Woodrow Wilson for sending troops to Russia. One circular, titled *The Hypocrisy of the United States and Her Allies*, stated that Wilson's "shameful, cowardly silence about the intervention in Russia reveals the hypocrisy of the plutocratic gang in Washington and vicinity."[2] Another pamphlet, printed in Yiddish and titled *Workers—Wake Up*, urged Russian immigrants to "spit in the face the false, hypocritic, military propaganda which has fooled you so relentlessly, calling forth your sympathy, your help, to the prosecution of the war."[3]

The defendants were indicted not for false speech, but for allegedly violating the Espionage Act. The indictment claimed, among other things, that the defendants conspired to "utter, print, write and publish disloyal, scurrilous and abusive language about the form of government of the United States," and to "utter, print, write and publish language intended to bring the form of government of the United States into contempt, scorn, contumely and disrepute."[4] After the defendants were convicted and sentenced to prison time of between 3 and 20 years each,[5] they asked the US Supreme Court to review their case. The defendants argued both that the evidence did not support Espionage Act convictions and that the Espionage Act violated the First Amendment.[6] "If the Constitution gives us the right of free speech and free press, then this right cannot be destroyed by the arbitrary decree of Congress, even though done in the alleged interest of the public welfare, and by calling the decree an Espionage Law, and even though the Courts concur that the decree is for the benefit of the public welfare," the defense lawyers wrote in their brief to the Supreme Court. "The right guaranteed in the Constitution was intended to enlarge intellectual opportunity as against abridgement either by prior restraint or subsequent punishment. The existence of the power to suppress any opinion is, in the long run, more destructive to human well-being than the ideas against which the power is exercised."[7]

The Supreme Court agreed to hear the case, and in a 7–2 vote, it affirmed the conviction. The majority provided little reasoning for its rejection of the defendants' constitutional challenge to the Espionage Act, writing that *Schenck* and other recent opinions "definitely negatived" such claims.[8]

Holmes, joined by Justice Louis Brandeis, issued a dissent. After questioning the sufficiency of the evidence for the convictions, Holmes focused on his First Amendment concerns. Holmes tried to square his dissent with the rulings in *Schenck* and other recent convictions.[9] "I do not doubt for a moment that by the same reasoning that would justify punishing persuasion to murder, the United States constitutionally may punish speech that produces or is intended to produce a clear and imminent danger that it will bring about forthwith certain substantive evils that the United States constitutionally may seek to prevent," he wrote. "The power undoubtedly is greater in time of war than in time of peace because war opens dangers that do not exist at other times."[10]

So far, this largely sounds like the Holmes who wrote *Schenck* earlier in 1919, though "clear and present danger" from *Schenck* has evolved to "clear and imminent danger." Rather than writing more about fires and theaters, Holmes shifted gears and began a discussion of the need to protect free speech. The "surreptitious publishing of a silly leaflet by an unknown man," Holmes wrote, would not present such a danger, and the government also would need to demonstrate intent to cause that harm. The government failed to meet that burden for these pamphlets, Holmes wrote. And even if the government could show the intent required by the statute, he wrote, a 20-year prison sentence was excessive. Although the defendants appeared to hold a "creed of ignorance and immaturity," the court should not have considered that in factoring the punishment.[11]

He followed this preliminary analysis with eight sentences that formed the basis for the modern marketplace of ideas framework, though his dissent did not use that phrase:

Persecution for the expression of opinions seems to me perfectly logical. If you have no doubt of your premises or your power and want a certain result with all your heart you naturally express your wishes in law and sweep away all opposition. To allow opposition by speech seems to indicate that you think the speech impotent, as when a man says that he has squared the circle, or that you do not care whole heartedly for the result, or that you doubt either your power or your premises. But when men have realized that time has upset many fighting faiths, they may come to believe even more than they believe the very foundations of their own conduct that the ultimate good desired is better reached by free trade in ideas—that the best test of truth is the power of the thought to get itself accepted in the competition of the market, and that truth is the only ground upon which their wishes safely can be carried out. That at any rate is the theory of our Constitution. It is an experiment, as all life is an experiment. Every year if not every day we have to wager our salvation upon some prophecy based upon imperfect knowledge. While that experiment is part of our system I think that we should be eternally vigilant against attempts to check the expression of opinions that we loathe and believe to be fraught with death, unless they so imminently threaten immediate interference with the lawful and pressing purposes of the law that an immediate check is required to save the country.[12]

To say that this was a shift from his *Schenck* opinion would be an understatement. In *Abrams*, Holmes recognizes that imposing criminal liability for unpopular or harmful speech is a tempting solution. But he suggests an alternative: testing those ideas on the free market. Holmes understands that society functions with "imperfect knowledge." He also is humble enough to recognize that his theory of the Constitution is an "experiment."[13]

Holmes was not the first person to advance a marketplace-based conception of free speech. As law professor Stanley Ingber noted in 1984,[14] the concept can be traced to English philosopher John Mil-

ton's 1644 address to Parliament. "And though all the winds of doctrine were let loose to play upon the earth, so Truth be in the field, we
do injuriously, by licensing and prohibiting, to misdoubt her strength,"
Milton said. "Let her and Falsehood grapple; who ever knew Truth
put to the worse, in a free and open encounter?"[15]

Also influencing Holmes's thinking during that time was philosopher John Stuart Mill's *On Liberty*, which Holmes read in the months
before he wrote the *Abrams* dissent.[16] Among Mill's objections to government censorship of purportedly false speech is the fallibility of
official judgments about whether speech is true. "Those who desire to
suppress it, of course deny its truth; but they are not infallible," Mill
wrote. "They have no authority to decide the question for all man-
kind, and exclude every other person from the means of judging. To
refuse a hearing to an opinion, because they are sure that it is false, is
to assume that *their* certainty is the same thing as an absolute certainty.
All silencing of discussion is an assumption of infallibility."[17] Mill also
saw danger in allowing censorship because false speech would be unable to compete with the truth: "[T]he peculiar evil of silencing the
expression of an opinion is, that it is robbing the human race; posterity
as well as the existing generation; those who dissent from the opinion,
still more than those who hold it." Mill continued, "If the opinion is
right, they are deprived of the opportunity of exchanging error for
truth: if wrong, they lose, what is almost as great a benefit, the clearer
perception and livelier impression of truth, produced by its collision
with error."[18]

As Vincent Blasi, a professor who specializes in First Amendment
law, described in one of the most engaging examinations of the marketplace metaphor, Holmes was guided particularly by Mill's first argument, a principle that became known as fallibilism, meaning that
"all propositions are subject to perpetual testing. And that process
of testing, whether it takes the form of systematic observation, controlled experiment, logical derivation, or probabilistic calculation, must
always hold out at least the possibility that prior understandings will

be displaced."[19] Although Holmes's theory relied on a hypothetical market, he did not use the phrase "marketplace of ideas." The earliest reference that Blasi could find (and I could not find an earlier one) was in a 1935 letter to the editor of the *New York Times*, in which the author wrote that if his preferred candidates did not run for president in 1936, "then their likes will issue not from a dark room at 2 o'clock in the morning, but as the result of men and ideas competing in the market place of ideas where public opinion is formed."[20]

In Blasi's analysis of Holmes's framework, the metaphor does not assume that the market will fix all problems with speech. Rather, Blasi writes, it is intended to combat impulses to censor. "It honors certain character traits—inquisitiveness, capacity to admit error and to learn from experience, ingenuity, willingness to experiment, resilience—that matter in civic adaptation no less than economic," Blasi wrote. "It devalues deference and discredits certitude, and in the process holds various forms of incumbent authority accountable to standards of performance."[21]

Holmes's dissent drew immediate attention, and some prominent opposition. Among the most notable was Northwestern University law professor John H. Wigmore's 1920 article in the *Illinois Law Review*, titled "*Abrams v. U.S.*: Freedom of Speech and Freedom of Thuggery in War-Time and Peace-Time." Wigmore directed particular ire at Holmes's statement about freely trading ideas on the market. "Very well," Wigmore wrote, "but does 'free trade in ideas' mean that those who desire to gather and set in action a band of thugs and murderers may freely go about publicly circularizing and orating upon the attractions of loot, proposing a plan of action for organized thuggery, and enlisting their converts, yet not be constitutionally interfered with until the gathered band of thugs actually sets the torch and lifts the rifle? Certainly not, they concede. Then where is the dead-line to be drawn at which Freedom of Speech does not become identical with Freedom of Thuggery? That is where the champions of freedom of speech give us no solution."[22]

Such criticism did not discourage Holmes and Brandeis from continuing to advocate for expansive First Amendment protections. "Fear of serious injury cannot alone justify suppression of free speech and assembly," Brandeis, joined by Holmes, wrote in a 1927 concurrence in *Whitney v. California*. "Men feared witches and burnt women. It is the function of speech to free men from the bondage of irrational fears. To justify suppression of free speech there must be reasonable ground to fear that serious evil will result if free speech is practiced. There must be reasonable ground to believe that the danger apprehended is imminent. There must be reasonable ground to believe that the evil to be prevented is a serious one."[23]

The Supreme Court's first explicit mention of "marketplace of ideas" came nearly 34 years after the *Abrams* dissent. In *United States v. Rumely*, the court affirmed the reversal of a conviction of an official of an organization that sold controversial books and refused to provide the names of purchasers to a congressional committee. The majority based its reversal on its interpretation of the committee's authorized powers. In a concurrence, Justice William O. Douglas addressed his First Amendment concerns with the conviction. "We have here a publisher who through books and pamphlets seeks to reach the minds and hearts of the American people. He is different in some respects from other publishers," Douglas wrote. "But the differences are minor. Like the publishers of newspapers, magazines, or books, this publisher bids for the minds of men in the market place of ideas."[24] Since then, the phrase "marketplace of ideas" has appeared in more than 1,500 federal and state court opinions, including more than 70 of the US Supreme Court.[25]

The marketplace of ideas framework addresses not only the supply side (the speakers) but also the demand side (the readers and listeners), by providing them with a right to *receive* speech. For instance, in 1965, the court struck down a law that restricted the mailing of "communist political propaganda" via the US Postal Service. "The dissemination of ideas can accomplish nothing if otherwise willing addressees are not free to receive and consider them," Justice William Brennan wrote in a concurrence. "It would be a barren marketplace of ideas that had only sellers and no buyers."[26] Two years later, the court struck down a New York law that prohibited state employees from being members of "subversive" groups such as the Communist Party. "The classroom is peculiarly the 'marketplace of ideas,'" Brennan wrote for the majority. "The Nation's future depends upon leaders trained through wide exposure to that robust exchange of ideas which discovers truth out of a multitude of tongues, [rather] than through any kind of authoritative selection."[27] In 1980, the court struck down a New York State regulatory order that prohibited electric utilities from inserting discussions of controversial policy issues in monthly bills. "If the marketplace of ideas is to remain free and open, governments must not be allowed to choose which issues are worth discussing or debating," Justice Lewis Powell wrote.[28]

The marketplace metaphor is not limited to debates about falsity, and in fact it has been more often used to address other speech restrictions. As law professor James Weinstein has aptly noted, in the first century after the *Abrams* opinion, "the Court most frequently invoked the marketplace of ideas rationale in cases concerning normative statements such as 'opinion' and 'ideas,' not factual assertions."[29] But how did the marketplace of ideas theory affect the ability of people to spread false factual claims?

The most clarity came from a lie that Xavier Alvarez told in 2007.

Alvarez's lie began soon after he was elected on November 6, 2006, by a 48-vote margin, to the Three Valleys Municipal Water District Board in the Claremont, California, area, despite not having the support of other board members.[30] In June 2007, the bespectacled Pomona resident, with a bushy dark mustache that practically devoured his face, was among a group of local officials who were on a tour of a Southern California Edison hydroelectric facility in the Sierra Nevada mountain range.[31] The century-old project, known as Big Creek, is a network of reservoirs and dams.[32] During a breakfast on the first morning of the tour, Alvarez met Melissa Anne Campbell, a Southern California Edison project manager who was helping to organize the trip. Her coworkers had told Campbell that Alvarez was a former marine, so she informed Alvarez that she, too, had served in the US Marine Corps. Alvarez said that he had served for 29 years, retiring at the rank of sergeant major, and that he spent 25 of his years in Marine Force Reconnaissance.[33]

But none of those stories were true. Not in the slightest. Alvarez never even served in the military. Having just met Alvarez, Campbell had no way of knowing that he had made all of this up. And his lies to her deepened later that day.

"Do you know who I am?" Alvarez asked Campbell on the bus ride to the hydroelectric plant.

Campbell said that she did not.

"I am a Congressional Medal of Honor winner," Alvarez said.[34] The claim was a particularly stunning one, as the Congressional Medal of Honor is the US military's highest honor. As of March 2022, only 66 of the roughly 3,500 Congressional Medal of Honor recipients were living.[35]

By Alvarez's account, his service during the 1979 Iran hostage crisis had led to his receipt of the medal. Campbell was thrilled to meet an actual Congressional Medal of Honor recipient, so she texted her husband, who searched online databases for information about Alvarez and came up empty. Because so few people have received the honor, and even fewer are still alive, he should have been able to easily find information about Alvarez. He texted back to his wife, informing her that he could not find any corroboration that Alvarez had received the Congressional Medal of Honor.[36]

Before dinner was served that night, Jeanetta Harris, a Southern California Edison employee who had overheard Alvarez's conversation with Campbell, asked if anyone in the room had a record of military service, and more than half of the people in the room stood up. Harris then told the audience that Alvarez had received the Congressional

Medal of Honor and other military decorations, and Alvarez stood up. At that point, Campbell showed her husband's text message to Roger Taylor, a Southern California Edison manager. After Campbell and Taylor confronted Alvarez, he told the same story that he had relayed on the bus, and said that he no longer wanted to discuss his military record.[37] While the guests were having drinks after dinner, Campbell and Taylor asked Alvarez which president had presented him with the Congressional Medal of Honor, and Alvarez replied that it was President Ronald Reagan. Alvarez claimed to have received the award because he was wounded during a raid while rescuing the US ambassador in Iran, when he had gone back to the embassy to save the US flag.[38]

To Campbell, the story sounded nearly identical to a scene in the movie *Rules of Engagement*. She asked Alvarez which unit he had belonged to at retirement, and he responded, "Delta," short for Special Forces Operation Delta, which Campbell knew was part of the army and not the marines. Alvarez told her that he did not like what she was doing. Campbell was confident that Alvarez was lying and walked away.[39]

The next day, Alvarez told other people on the trip that he was a Gulf War veteran who had served in Iran, and that he had also been a firefighter and a professional baseball player. And on a helicopter landing pad tour later that day, Alvarez said he had been on three Southern California Edison helicopters that had crashed. Campbell and her coworkers knew that this was a lie, as the only two major helicopter crashes in the company's history had led to the death of everyone on board. Campbell's supervisors realized that Alvarez was not telling the truth, but they warned her to stay away from the local water district board member. Soon after returning from the three-day trip, Southern California Edison suspended and then fired Campbell.[40]

Not only was Alvarez's lie an insult to all US soldiers who had risked their lives in service, but it also was a federal crime. The Stolen Valor Act, signed into law just months earlier, criminally prohibited people from falsely representing that they "have been awarded any decoration or medal authorized by Congress for the Armed Forces of the United States." The law was not explicitly limited to defendants who lied with a specified state of mind. Congress passed the law out of concern that some people falsely claim to have received the highest military honors. "These imposters use fake medals—or claim to have medals that they have not earned—to gain credibility in their communities," Senator Kent Conrad, the bill's author, said as he introduced the bill on the Senate floor on November 10, 2005.[41]

The Stolen Valor Act means that simply by uttering his lies about having received the Congressional Medal of Honor, Alvarez could face up to a year in prison. The Stolen Valor Act does not require any proof of the speaker's intent or of any harm that the lie may have caused. All that is needed to send someone to prison is proof of a lie about receiving a military decoration. But was Campbell's retelling of the Sierra Nevada trip sufficient proof of the lie? Perhaps it was, along with corroborating testimony from meeting attendees who heard Alvarez tell it. Fortunately for the Federal Bureau of Investigation, Alvarez would lie again, and this time the lie would be recorded.

On July 23, 2007, less than a month after the Southern California Edison trip, Alvarez attended a joint meeting of his water board and the neighboring Walnut Valley Water District Board at the Walnut Valley headquarters. At the start of the meeting, Edwin Hilden, a director of the Walnut Valley board, introduced Alvarez as a new member of the Three Valleys board. Alvarez asked if he should say "a little something about myself."

"If you want," Hilden replied.

"I'm a retired marine of 25 years," Alvarez said. "I retired in the year 2001. Back in 1987, I was awarded the Congressional Medal of Honor. I got wounded many times by the same guy. I'm still around." Alvarez said that after his military service, he received an engineering degree from California Polytechnic State University.[42]

About two months later, Alvarez's lie caught up with him. Based on his statement at the public meeting, federal prosecutors charged him with violating the Stolen Valor Act. The prosecution received attention in the local media, and acquaintances from the Pomona area soon told reporters of the extent of his lies about military service. Sid Sierra, who first met Alvarez about a decade earlier, said that Alvarez's frequent military stories earned him the nickname "Rambo" among some in the Mexican American Political Association. "He used to brag he was in Vietnam as a helicopter pilot, that he was shot down and that he and his buddies got the chopper fixed and got it back up [in the air]," Sierra told the *Los Angeles Daily News* at the time. Bob Kuhn, who served on the water board with Alvarez, told the newspaper that Alvarez had told stories of his military service. "He said he had Purple Hearts, that he was shot four or five times and that he won a Medal of Honor," Kuhn said. "He didn't do it in a boastful way, a braggadocio way, just very matter-of-factly." Alvarez, however, told the reporter that he never made the claim. "When you show up at these meetings, they introduce you," he told the newspaper. "Sometimes they want you to say what you have done for the community. . . . I must have been taken out of context."[43]

The problem for Alvarez is that the FBI had a recording. Rather than resting on the claim that he didn't lie, Alvarez's federal public defenders asked Judge R. Gary Klausner to dismiss the case on constitutional grounds. Alvarez's lawyers argued that the Stolen Valor Act violated the First Amendment because the law criminalized Alvarez's lie without requiring any evidence of intent, harm, or benefit to Alvarez. Political speech, Alvarez's lawyers argued, deserves the greatest protection under the First Amendment. "Falsehoods are not outside the realm of First Amendment protection, and therefore restrictions on false statements must be supported by a strong government interest and must be directly related to that interest," his lawyers wrote.[44]

Klausner, a Vietnam War army captain whom President George W. Bush appointed to the Los Angeles federal court in 2002,[45] did not think that the First Amendment protects lies such as Alvarez's. In a three-page order on April 9, 2008, Klausner denied Alvarez's motion to dismiss the criminal case, reasoning that Alvarez knew he was lying and intended to do so. "The content of the speech itself does not portray a political message, nor does it deal with a matter of public debate. Rather, it appears to be merely a lie intended to impress others present at the meeting," Klausner wrote. "Such lies are not protected by the Constitution."[46]

The next month, Alvarez pleaded guilty but reserved his right to challenge the constitutionality of the Stolen Valor Act.[47] Alvarez's fellow board members approved a resolution urging him to resign. Brian Bowcock, the board member who introduced the resolution, said that he received applause at a local restaurant because of his condemnation of Alvarez. In an affidavit submitted to the court before Alvarez's sentencing, Bowcock argued that Alvarez's lie was harmful. "His actions have eroded public confidence in our elected officials, outraged members of the community, and distracted the Board from the important work that it does, especially now as Southern California faces drought conditions," Bowcock wrote.[48]

At his sentencing hearing in the 22-story federal courthouse in downtown Los Angeles on July 21, 2008, Alvarez expressed remorse for his statements, which he chalked up to "incompetence," and said he had not intended to harm veterans. "I respect veterans very much," Alvarez said.[49] His lawyer urged Klausner to impose a light sentence of community service.[50] Klausner did not hide his disdain for Alvarez's lies when he imposed a $5,000 fine, probation, and community service.[51] The public ridicule that Alvarez had experienced, Klausner said, was not sufficient punishment. "This is a choice you made," Klausner told Alvarez. "You lived in a world, a make-believe world where you just make up stories all the time and that's your choice. And people are going to laugh at you obviously when they find out that you really don't, there's no credibility in anything you say."[52]

Alvarez appealed to the US Court of Appeals for the Ninth Circuit, requesting a ruling that the Stolen Valor Act's absolute prohibition of lying is unconstitutional. Representing Alvarez before the Ninth

Circuit was Jonathan Libby, who handled appeals for the Los Angeles federal defender's office. Among Libby's arguments for Alvarez was that the Stolen Valor Act's lack of a state-of-mind requirement rendered the law unconstitutionally overbroad. In other words, its scope was so broad that it encompassed speech protected by the First Amendment. "It applies not only to mistakes but to innocent bragging as well," Libby wrote in Alvarez's Ninth Circuit brief. "It includes satire. It would apply to a person who claimed he had received a military decoration while playing a role in a play or movie."[53]

The US government fought this challenge, arguing in its brief to the Ninth Circuit that "no protection exists for a deliberate lie, even in political speech."[54] Although the courts have provided limited protection to false speech in defamation cases, those rulings were intended to ensure unfettered debate about public issues, the prosecutors reasoned. For instance, requiring public figures to demonstrate actual malice in defamation cases is intended to prevent journalists from self-censoring out of fear of being sued. Such protections are unnecessary for lies about military honors, the government argued, because they are "not necessary to a free press, to free political expression, or otherwise to promote the marketplace of ideas."[55]

The case went to a randomly selected panel of three Ninth Circuit judges: Thomas G. Nelson, who was appointed by President George H. W. Bush in 1990, and President George W. Bush appointees Jay Bybee and Milan D. Smith Jr. (Full disclosure: I clerked for Judge Smith after he ruled on Alvarez's case.) At oral arguments on November 4, 2009, in the Ninth Circuit's Spanish colonial revival style courthouse in Pasadena, Libby pushed back on the government's argument that lies are not constitutionally protected. "People lie all the time, and I think all Americans believe that simply telling some of these lies are fully protected under the First Amendment," Libby said. "We tell lies to each other, sometimes to whoever will listen. We tell lies about personal facts about ourselves, about age, marital status, sexual orientation. These are all facts that people say all the time. Parents tell lies to their children. Santa Claus. The Easter Bunny. We try to make people feel better about themselves by lying."[56]

How else could the government protect the integrity of the Congressional Medal of Honor if it could not impose criminal penalties for lies about it? Smith asked. "There are only 94 living Medal of Honor recipients," Libby replied. "It is very easy for the government to publicize who these 94 individuals are." Such a response is in line with the "marketplace of ideas" approach; the government could fight lies such as Alvarez's by publicizing the names of the living recipients.

But the judges wanted to know how the public benefits from Alvarez's ability to freely lie about receiving the Congressional Medal of Honor. "All I can say is that the First Amendment, especially when read in the context of all of our rights under the Constitution, protects individual autonomy," Libby said. "And sometimes the protection of individual autonomy requires that we accept the right to be inaccurate and even to lie."

Two of the three judges agreed with Libby and ruled that the Stolen Valor Act was unconstitutional. Smith, joined by Nelson, used a heavily marketplace-based approach to reject the government's claim that false statements have no value at all. Perhaps Smith's largest barrier was the 1974 Supreme Court opinion in *Gertz v. Robert Welch*, where the court refused to require private figures to meet the high bar of actual malice to sue for defamation. The court wrote that the "erroneous statement of fact is not worthy of constitutional protection," and that false factual statements "belong to that category of utterances" that "are of such slight social value as a step to truth that any benefit that may be derived from them is clearly outweighed by the social interest in order and morality."[57] Smith rejected the government's claim that *Gertz* means that false statements receive no constitutional protections. "Rather, *Gertz*'s statement that false factual speech is unprotected, considered in isolation, omits discussion of essential constitutional qualifications on that proposition," Smith wrote.

Smith acknowledged that the government has the power to regulate some dangerous or harmful lies, such as fraud, but it does not have an absolute and general power to prohibit all lies, regardless of harm. "Satirical entertainment such as *The Onion*, *The Daily Show*, and *The Colbert Report* thrives on making deliberate false statements of fact," Smith wrote. "Such media outlets play a significant role in inviting citizens alienated by mainstream news media into meaningful public debate over economic, military, political and social issues."[58]

Because Smith determined that lies are not categorically exempt from the First Amendment, the court can only allow a content-based speech restriction like the Stolen Valor Act if it satisfies "strict scrutiny," an incredibly high legal standard in which the government must prove that the law advances a compelling interest, and it is narrowly tailored in achieving that interest. Smith acknowledged that the government might have a compelling interest in protecting the reputation of the military's highest honor, but the law was not narrowly tailored. As evidence, Smith pointed to Alvarez's very public exposure as a liar. "Here, Alvarez's lie, deliberate and despicable as it may have been, did not escape notice and correction in the marketplace," Smith wrote. "The preferred First Amendment remedy of 'more speech' thus was available to repair any harm."[59] Smith emphasized that he detested Alvarez's lies but that allowing the government to prohibit them would open the door to other, more nefarious speech restrictions. "We have no doubt that society would be better off if Alvarez would stop spreading worthless, ridiculous, and offensive untruths," Smith wrote. "But, given our historical skepticism of permitting the government to police the line between truth and falsity, and between valuable speech and drivel, we presumptively protect all speech, including false statements, in order that clearly protected speech may flower in the shelter of the First Amendment."[60]

Bybee dissented, asserting that the First Amendment historically had never protected lies. He wrote that the Supreme Court has only articulated limited cases in which protecting lies serves the public in-

terest, such as requiring public figures to prove actual malice in defamation cases.[61]

The federal government asked the Ninth Circuit to vacate Smith's
opinion and rehear Alvarez's appeal before a panel of 11 Ninth Circuit judges, known as an "en banc" review. Because a majority of active
judges failed to support the request, it was denied. Two judges issued
statements opposing the decision to deny rehearing. Smith and Chief
Judge Alex Kozinski wrote statements in support of the denial. Kozinski, a Reagan appointee, emigrated to the United States from Ro-
mania as a child with his parents, who survived the Holocaust.[62] While
often a staunch conservative, Kozinski was suspicious of providing the
government with excessive power to restrict civil liberties.[63] He would
resign his judgeship in 2017 amid former law clerks' accusations of sexual
harassment.[64] Allowing the government to prohibit any statements
only because they are false is "terrifying," Kozinski predicted. "If false
factual statements are unprotected, then the government can prosecute not only the man who tells tall tales of winning the Congressional
Medal of Honor, but also the JDater who falsely claims he's Jewish or
the dentist who assures you it won't hurt a bit," he wrote. "Phrases
such as 'I'm working late tonight, hunny,' 'I got stuck in traffic' and 'I
didn't inhale' could all be made into crimes."[65] To Kozinski, affirming
Alvarez's conviction would open the doors to criminalizing the quo-
tidian lies that are the foundation for daily life. His concurrence included one of the most extensive judicial statements about the value
of lies in everyday life, even if they are made with knowledge of
falsity:

> Saints may always tell the truth, but for mortals living means lying.
> We lie to protect our privacy ("No, I don't live around here"); to avoid
> hurt feelings ("Friday is my study night"); to make others feel better
> ("Gee you've gotten skinny"); to avoid recriminations ("I only lost
> $10 at poker"); to prevent grief ("The doc says you're getting better");
> to maintain domestic tranquility ("She's just a friend"); to avoid social

stigma ("I just haven't met the right woman"); for career advancement ("I'm sooo lucky to have a smart boss like you"); to avoid being lonely ("I love opera"); to eliminate a rival ("He has a boyfriend"); to achieve an objective ("But I love you so much"); to defeat an objective ("I'm allergic to latex"); to make an exit ("It's not you, it's me"); to delay the inevitable ("The check is in the mail"); to communicate displeasure ("There's nothing wrong"); to get someone off your back ("I'll call you about lunch"); to escape a nudnik ("My mother's on the other line"); to namedrop ("We go way back"); to set up a surprise party ("I need help moving the piano"); to buy time ("I'm on my way"); to keep up appearances ("We're not talking divorce"); to avoid taking out the trash ("My back hurts"); to duck an obligation ("I've got a headache"); to maintain a public image ("I go to church every Sunday"); to make a point ("Ich bin ein Berliner"); to save face ("I had too much to drink"); to humor ("Correct as usual, King Friday"); to avoid embarrassment ("That wasn't me"); to curry favor ("I've read all your books"); to get a clerkship ("You're the greatest living jurist"); to save a dollar ("I gave at the office"); or to maintain innocence ("There are eight tiny reindeer on the rooftop").[66]

After the federal prosecutors struck out in the Ninth Circuit, they asked the US Supreme Court to hear the appeal of the case. This was no longer just about whether Alvarez would pay a fine and perform community service. The nation's largest federal appellate court had struck down the Stolen Valor Act *and* made it more difficult for the government to impose consequences for false speech. But convincing the Supreme Court to review the Ninth Circuit's opinion would not be easy. Unlike federal circuit courts, the Supreme Court is not required to hear an appeal. The Supreme Court receives approximately 7,000 to 8,000 such requests each year and grants only about 1 percent of them.[67] In his request to the Supreme Court, US Solicitor General Donald Verrilli Jr., President Barack Obama's top advocate before the court, argued that the Stolen Valor Act "plays a vital role in safeguarding the integrity and efficacy of the government's military honors system."[68] Verrilli managed to persuade the court to hear the case. Alvarez's bloviation at a local water district meeting would allow the highest court in the United States to determine whether the First Amendment protects lies. And in an indication of the case's importance to the federal government, Verrilli, rather than one of his roughly 20 lawyers, argued the case himself.

The argument took place on the brisk morning of February 12, 2012, in the Supreme Court's grand courtroom. Verrilli, who had argued more than a dozen cases before the court, stood to begin. He kicked off the argument by telling the justices that the Stolen Valor Act is not broad but "narrowly drawn" and "carefully limited."[69] But he only got a few sentences into his argument before Justice Sonia Sotomayor interrupted. "General, may I pose a hypothetical," she asked slowly, not waiting for a response before presenting him with her scenario. What if a Vietnam War protester had held up a sign that stated, "I won a Purple Heart—for killing babies," when in fact that protester knew he had not won the military honor? Would that person be liable under the Stolen Valor Act?

"I think, Your Honor, it would depend on whether that was, that expression, was reasonably understood by the audience as a statement of fact or as an exercise in political theater," Verrilli replied. "If it's the latter, it's not within the scope of the statute, and it wouldn't be subject to liability."

Before Verrilli could complete his sentence, Sotomayor cut in. "Somewhat dangerous, isn't it, to subject speech to the absolute rule of no protection?" she asked. "Which is what you're advocating, I understand, that there are no circumstances in which this speech has value. I believe that's your bottom line."

"What I would say with respect to that, Your Honor, is that this Court has said in numerous contexts, numerous contexts, that the calculated factual falsehood has no First Amendment value for its own sake," Verrilli said.

Justice Anthony Kennedy jumped in. "Well, I'm—I'm not sure that that's quite correct," he began. At the time, Kennedy was the most moderate member of the court, often the "swing vote" that determined which side of an otherwise divided Supreme Court would prevail. He pointed to a page in the government's brief that claimed that false speech had no value. "I think it's a sweeping proposition to say that there's no value to falsity," Kennedy said. "Falsity is a way in which we contrast what is false and what is true."

Verrilli stressed that the Stolen Valor Act only "regulates a very narrowly drawn and specific category of calculated factual falsehood, a verifiably false claim that an individual has won a military honor."

Sotomayor questioned whether a lie about a military honor caused any harm outside the "emotional reaction" to that lie. "I too take offense when people make these kinds of claims, but I take offense when someone I'm dating makes a claim that's not true," Sotomayor said, prompting laughter throughout the packed courtroom.

"As a father of a 20-year-old daughter, so do I, Justice Sotomayor," Verrilli replied, before pointing more seriously to the harms to "the value of the medal in the eyes of the soldiers."

Unlike Verrilli, Jonathan Libby was not a regular member of the Supreme Court bar. This was Libby's first appearance before the justices, and he faced equally aggressive questioning from the justices. After Libby was four staccato sentences into his argument, Chief Justice John Roberts interrupted: "What is the First Amendment value in a lie, pure lie?"

"Just a pure lie?" Libby asked. "There can be a number of values. There is the value of personal autonomy."

"The value of what?" Roberts asked.

"Personal autonomy, that we get—," Libby said.

"What does that mean?" Roberts interrupted.

"Well, that we get to—we get to exaggerate and create—," Libby said.

"No, not exaggerate—lie," Roberts said, with more than a hint of exasperation in his voice.

"Well, when we create our own persona, we're often making up things about ourselves that we want people to think about us, and that can be valuable," Libby said. "Samuel Clemens creating Mark Twain. That was creating a persona, and he made things up about himself—"

"Well," Roberts said, his voice shooting up an octave, "but that was for literary purposes. No one is suggesting you can't write a book or tell a story about somebody who earned a Medal of Honor and it's a fictional character, so he obviously didn't. It just seems to me very different."

"Perhaps," Libby conceded, "but there are other things, in addition to the fact that people tell lies allows us to appreciate truth better."

Justice Samuel Alito jumped in, asking whether there is "First Amendment value in a bald-faced lie about a purely factual statement that a person makes about himself, because that person would like to create a particular persona? Gee, I won the Medal of Honor. I was a Rhodes Scholar. I won the Nobel Prize. There's a personal—the First Amendment protects that?"

"Yes, your Honor," Libby responded, "so long as it doesn't cause imminent harm to another person or imminent harm to a government function."

Justice Elena Kagan pointed out that the Supreme Court had said that the First Amendment may protect lies in an effort to prevent a chilling effect on truthful speech. "What truthful speech will this statute chill?" Kagan asked.

"Your Honor, it's not that it may necessarily chill any truthful speech," Libby replied. "I mean, it's—we certainly concede that one typically knows whether or not one has won a medal or not."

"So, boy, I mean, that's a big concession, Mr. Libby," Kagan said, noting that this meant that he needed to convince the court that its statement in *Gertz* was "puffery."

Later in the argument, Libby suggested that the government combat lies about military honors on the marketplace of ideas, such as by publicizing the names of people who actually received the honors.

Justice Antonin Scalia jokingly suggested that the government give a "Medal of Shame" to those who lied about military honors.

"Well, Your Honor—actually, that's certainly something the government could do," Libby said.

"Well, not under your theory, right?" Roberts replied. "I mean, it's still a sanction for telling something that you say is protected under the First Amendment, whether you get six months or a Medal of Shame doesn't matter under your theory."

"Well, there is a significant difference between a criminal sanction that puts someone in prison versus simply exposing them for what they are, which is a liar," Libby said. "And Mr. Alvarez, whether or not he in fact was sentenced to a crime, he still was exposed for who he was, which was a liar."

The Stolen Valor Act, Libby argued, is unconstitutional because it penalizes speech whether or not the lie caused harm or enabled the speaker to obtain anything of value. That prompted the justices to pepper Libby with questions about hypothetical lies, and whether the government could penalize the speakers. What if the speaker had lied to "get a date with a potential rich spouse," Alito asked. "Would that be enough?"

Libby tried to cobble together a response. "Your Honor, I think when it comes—when you get into the situation where you're getting something like a date, I do not know that—I certainly wouldn't consider that a *non de minimis* thing of value, but—"

"Some people might have a different opinion," Alito retorted, as the courtroom filled with giggles.

At some Supreme Court oral arguments, keen observers could predict which party has won over the justices. But at this argument, both sides confronted a good deal of skepticism from the bench. And the justices were indeed divided on the fate of Alvarez's case and the Stolen Valor Act.

Four months after oral arguments, six of the nine Supreme Court justices voted to uphold the Ninth Circuit's ruling for Alvarez, that the Stolen Valor Act is unconstitutional. Their reasoning was splintered, but the marketplace of ideas framed the justices' thinking.

Kennedy, writing for himself, Roberts, Sotomayor, and Ginsburg, wrote the plurality opinion, in which he emphasized that the government's argument that false statements are not constitutionally protected relies only on cases involving "defamation, fraud, or some other legally cognizable harm associated with a false statement, such as an invasion of privacy or the costs of vexatious litigation." The speech's falsity in those cases, he wrote, did not determine the outcome. "Our prior decisions have not confronted a measure, like the Stolen Valor Act, that targets falsity and nothing more," Kennedy wrote.[70]

Kennedy compared the Stolen Valor Act with Section 1001 of the federal criminal code, which prohibits people from making "any materially false, fictitious, or fraudulent statement or representation" to federal officials. The permissibility of this statute, he reasoned, "does not lead to the broader proposition that false statements are unprotected when made to any person, at any time, in any context." Likewise, Kennedy wrote, perjury statutes are constitutional not just because they cover false speech. "Perjury undermines the function and province of the law and threatens the integrity of judgments that are the basis of the legal system," he wrote.

Pointing to George Orwell's *1984*, Kennedy wrote of the dangers of giving the government broad authority to impose criminal penalties on lies no matter where, why, and to whom they were made. "Our constitutional tradition stands against the idea that we need Oceania's Ministry of Truth," Kennedy wrote. "Were this law to be sustained, there could be an endless list of subjects the National Government or the States could single out."

Because lies are not categorically exempt from the First Amendment, Kennedy reasoned, the Stolen Valor Act can only survive if it undergoes the rigorous level of scrutiny that the Ninth Circuit applied. And like the Ninth Circuit, Kennedy concluded that the statute could not meet that high standard. Key to Kennedy's ruling was the public attention and ridicule that Alvarez received for lying. "The remedy for speech that is false is speech that is true," Kennedy wrote. "This is the ordinary course in a free society. The response to the unreasoned is the rational; to the uninformed, the enlightened; to the straight-out lie, the simple truth."[71]

Kennedy followed that statement with a citation to Brandeis's 1927 concurrence in *Whitney v. California* and Holmes's *Abrams* dissent, driving home the importance of the marketplace of ideas. "The First Amendment itself ensures the right to respond to speech we do not like, and for good reason," Kennedy wrote. "Freedom of speech and thought flows not from the beneficence of the state but from the inalienable rights of the person. And suppression of speech by the government can make exposure of falsity more difficult, not less so. Society has the right and civic duty to engage in open, dynamic, rational discourse. These ends are not well served when the government seeks to orchestrate public discussion through content-based mandates."[72]

For a Supreme Court opinion to constitute a binding precedent, at least five of the nine justices must sign on. Only four justices supported the reasoning of Kennedy's ruling, though two more agreed with his conclusion. Justice Stephen Breyer, joined by Kagan, wrote a concurrence in which he agreed that the Stolen Valor Act is unconstitutional. But Breyer reached that conclusion by applying a less rigorous form of constitutional review. "The dangers of suppressing valuable ideas are lower where, as here, the regulations concern false statements about easily verifiable facts that do not concern such subject matter," Breyer wrote. "Such false factual statements are less likely than are true factual statements to make a valuable contribution to the marketplace of ideas. And the government often has good reasons to prohibit such false speech."[73]

Breyer also worried that enabling the government to prosecute false statements regardless of harm and state of mind increases fears of selective prosecution, such as "by prosecuting a pacifist who supports his cause by (falsely) claiming to have been a war hero, while ignoring members of other political groups who might make similar false claims."[74] Breyer recognized that the speech regulated by the Stolen Valor Act is not particularly valuable, but he concluded that the government failed to explain why it could not address the problem with counterspeech; for instance, Breyer predicted that "an accurate, publicly available register of military awards, easily obtainable by political opponents, may well adequately protect the integrity of an award against those who would falsely claim to have earned it."[75]

One argument that Kennedy failed to fully address in the plurality opinion was proposed most clearly in an amicus brief from Professors Eugene Volokh and James Weinstein. Rather than arguing that *all* false speech should be exempt from the First Amendment, they proposed treating "knowing falsehoods as categorically constituting a First Amendment exception," with some limits, such as for speech about government agencies and noncommercial lies about science or history.[76] Kennedy cited this amicus brief without explanation after his characterization of the government's argument "that false statements have no value and hence no First Amendment protection."[77] Yet the framework that Volokh and Weinstein proposed was not as sweeping, applying only to *knowing* falsehoods. Although Breyer did not explicitly address the amicus brief, he acknowledged that the Stolen Valor Act could "be construed to prohibit only knowing and intentional acts of deception about readily verifiable facts within the personal knowledge of the speaker, thus reducing the risk that valuable speech is chilled." Yet such a limiting principle is not enough to address his First Amendment concerns owing to the chilling effect on speech merely arising from the threat of prosecution:

> As written, it applies in family, social, or other private contexts, where lies will often cause little harm. It also applies in political contexts, where although such lies are more likely to cause harm, the risk of censorious selectivity by prosecutors is also high. Further, given the potential haziness of individual memory along with the large number

of military awards covered (ranging from medals for rifle marksman-
ship to the Congressional Medal of Honor), there remains a risk of
chilling that is not completely eliminated by *mens rea* requirements; a
speaker might still be worried about being prosecuted for a careless
false statement, even if he does not have the intent required to render
him liable. And so the prohibition may be applied where it should
not be applied, for example, to barstool braggadocio or, in the political
arena, subtly but selectively to speakers that the Government does
not like. These considerations lead me to believe that the statute as
written risks significant First Amendment harm.[78]

Three justices dissented, concluding that the Stolen Valor Act did
not violate the First Amendment. Lies about military honors inflict
"real harm on actual medal recipients and their families," wrote Alito,
joined by Scalia and Thomas. The Defense Department, Alito noted,
had stated that it could only build a database of people who won certain
military honors since 2001. "Without the requisite database, many efforts to refute false claims may be thwarted, and some legitimate
award recipients may be erroneously attacked," Alito wrote. "In addition, a steady stream of stories in the media about the exposure of imposters would tend to increase skepticism among members of the
public about the entire awards system. This would only exacerbate the
harm that the Stolen Valor Act is meant to prevent."[79] To Alito's mind,
the "counterspeech" in the marketplace of ideas would not be sufficiently
effective. Still, Alito acknowledged that some types of restrictions on
false speech would have an impermissible chilling effect on speaking
truthfully. "Laws restricting false statements about philosophy, religion, history, the social sciences, the arts, and other matters of public
concern would present such a threat," Alito wrote. "The point is not
that there is no such thing as truth or falsity in these areas or that the
truth is always impossible to ascertain, but rather that it is perilous to
permit the state to be the arbiter of truth." Unlike those unworkable

false speech restrictions, he wrote, the Stolen Valor Act "presents no risk at all that valuable speech will be suppressed."[80]

Alvarez left some questions open. None of the justices suggested that the First Amendment protects *all* false speech. Although the plurality, combined with the concurrence, stood for the general proposition that false speech is not categorically exempt from the First Amendment's protection, a majority of the court did not clearly identify how courts should analyze false speech restrictions. Particularly because the plurality and concurrence used different constitutional tests, it is hard to look at the *Alvarez* opinion and know exactly where the court has drawn the line for false speech. Indeed, a year after the opinion, Congress passed the Stolen Valor Act of 2013, which imposes criminal penalties on a person who "with intent to obtain money, property, or other tangible benefit, fraudulently holds oneself out to be" a recipient of a military honor.[81] As of 2022, the amended law has not been struck down as unconstitutional.

Underlying the entire prosecution of Alvarez—from the initial FBI investigation through the Supreme Court argument—was the implication that liars such as Alvarez are an inevitable by-product of free society. If we will allow a free flow of truthful speech, the theory goes, we must tolerate the occasional (or more than occasional) lie. And we should only prohibit lies if they fall within narrowly defined categories. Lies will happen. Even disgraceful lies.

Even Alvarez did not argue that his fabrications about receiving the Congressional Medal of Honor served any inherently noble purpose. But during the five years that his case was litigated, lawyers, judges, and the US Supreme Court agreed that the First Amendment requires us to tolerate even offensive lies such as Alvarez's claim to be a decorated war hero.

Alvarez's success in the nation's highest court was one of the most prominent examples of the marketplace of ideas approach to free speech. While free speech advocates hailed the ruling, it also drew criticism both for the result and the application of the marketplace theory. In a 2020 article, James Weinstein dissected the plurality, concurrence, and dissent, and criticized all three for an overreliance on the marketplace of ideas. "Rather than focusing on truth promotion and the marketplace of ideas, a free speech value at most weakly implicated by the Stolen Valor Act, it would have been far more useful if the Court had analyzed the law's effect on the autonomy and democracy bases for free speech," Weinstein wrote.[82]

Weinstein's criticism of the *Alvarez* opinions is part of a larger chorus of pushback to the marketplace of ideas theory that began long before Xavier Alvarez lied about his military honors. Understanding these criticisms is key to understanding that while the marketplace of ideas provides a partial explanation for protecting false speech, the theory has its limits and is not the only justification for these protections.

Some critics have rightly pointed out that the marketplace of ideas framework incorrectly assumes that all participants in the marketplace have equal ability to participate. As constitutional law professor Robert Sedler noted, the marketplace metaphor focuses on preventing government restrictions on speech, but it does not ensure equal access. "Things being what they are, the media and wealth interests obviously will have much bigger 'stalls in the marketplace' than the lone blogger or groups with limited resources," he wrote.[83] This was less of a concern to some of the judges who presided over Alvarez's case, as they considered the possibility of counterspeech that is produced by the federal government, such as a website that lists the names of actual winners of military honors. But counterspeech does not always come from such credible and powerful sources, and the falsehoods that require correcting might come from more powerful sources than a lone water district board member like Alvarez.

Women, racial minorities, and others may have a harder time competing in the marketplace of ideas. "Persons of color can easily become demoralized, blame themselves, and not speak up vigorously," legal scholars Richard Delgado and Jean Stefancic wrote in 1992. "The expense of speech also precludes the stigmatized from participating effectively in the marketplace of ideas. They are often poor—indeed, one theory of racism holds that maintenance of economic inequality is its prime function—and hence unlikely to command the means to bring countervailing messages to the eyes and ears of others."[84] To the extent that the majority has outsized access to participate in the marketplace of ideas, it will be more difficult for others to disseminate their countervailing speech.

The marketplace of ideas, at least as it is commonly interpreted, assumes that the one truth will prevail on the open market. But as described in chapter 5, in many cases it is impossible to identify a single objective truth, particularly in the early stages of a discussion as facts are just beginning to emerge. And that difficulty allows powerful speakers to shape the views of those who are already inclined to believe them. "That the marketplace reveals truth, or even the best solutions, is further belied by the lack of any consensus in this country on what is true or best," Professor Stanley Ingber wrote. "If the marketplace actually revealed truth, diversity and conflict presumably would diminish rather than increase. But because people's perceptions are based on their varying interests and experiences, their perceptions are not likely to be socially homogenized. Consequently, as long as people have differing experiences, there is little guarantee that any society can agree on what is 'true,' and diversity and conflict will likely persist."[85] Ingber correctly concluded that "it is difficult for a person to reject ideas, opinions, and positions as being false when they coincide with his own interests or when they appeal to his half-submerged prejudices."[86] That observation, which Ingber made in 1984, is as true if not more so today. If a partisan cable news outlet or social media commentator routinely spouts lies, it will be difficult to counteract those lies if the audience tends to avoid other sources of information.

Similarly, Ingber also criticized the marketplace of ideas framework for assuming that the audience was capable of understanding the substance of competing messages and responding rationally. "In order to gain acceptance by the public, the dissident must thus overcome both a socialization system that predisposes the public against unconventional perspectives, as well as a negative response to his message's packaging," Ingber wrote. "The marketplace is, therefore, skewed to afford status quo views greater opportunity for public exposure and acceptance. It is hardly likely that the public will give dissident views a 'rational' evaluation in this marketplace."[87] It is unclear, for instance, whether the marketplace would be fully effective in counteracting even Alvarez's lies about his military honors. While Melissa Campbell was diligent enough to check his story, it is quite possible that the average attendee at the water board meeting would not have scoured government databases to verify his claim. As I discuss in chapter 15 of this book, we could improve the marketplace of ideas by attempting to make the audience more rational and knowledgeable, such as by providing people with basic media literacy tools and ensuring that the audience has access to a robust and diverse media ecosystem.

The marketplace has evolved significantly from when Holmes wrote his *Abrams* dissent in 1919. As law professor Paul Brietzke observed, the market often is fragmented, and not the utopian vision of an open and inquisitive public square. "Producers often speak to make a profit, and they are usually very different people from the ostensible consumers, who often misunderstand or ignore the message, often lack a viable channel for communicating their response, and are often afraid to make fools of themselves by speaking up," Brietzke wrote.[88]

Brietzke made this observation in 1997, and his focus was on institutional media such as cable news. As the Internet has dramatically expanded since then, people may have more channels to participate in the marketplace. But some of the challenges that Brietzke observed have escalated in the past quarter century. This does not mean that the marketplace theory has no place in current discussions about free speech, but it is vital to consider how social media, artificial intelligence, algorithms, and other technologies have changed the marketplace. Indeed, even since the Supreme Court issued its *Alvarez* opinion in 2012, social media and other large platforms have played an increasingly important role in American discourse. This provides both opportunities for speech—such as the ability of individuals to more easily get their messages out when they previously would not have had a voice—as well as challenges—such as the potential for a handful of large companies to have an outsized and unfair influence on the marketplace for speech, and the ability of bad actors both domestically and abroad to easily disseminate falsehoods.

"Today's marketplace of ideas suffers from a host of serious problems that Holmes could never have anticipated when he championed this model one hundred years ago," Dawn Nunziato, a law professor who specializes in free speech, wrote in 2019.[89] Nunziato suggests reasonable solutions for platforms to begin to fix the marketplace of ideas in the Internet age, such as "by focusing on counterspeech remedies instead of censorship remedies in response to harmful speech."[90] Chapter 12 of this book examines how self-help and counterspeech could be more widely available to address some of the serious problems in the marketplace. This is particularly urgent, as the marketplace of ideas in the age of social media has great inequalities. While the First Amendment ensures that anyone can obtain a social media account, not all accounts have equal impact. In 2022, for instance, the most-followed celebrity Instagram accounts were those of soccer player Cristiano Ronaldo and singer Ariana Grande, with 272 million and 228 million followers, respectively.[91] These social media stars have far more ability to influence the marketplace of ideas than, say, a high school teacher in Los Angeles, a grocery store clerk in Peoria, or a stay-at-home parent in Maine.

We could attempt to fix many of the marketplace's shortcomings without further abrogating speech protections, as I outline in chapters 12 to 15. But the critics also are correct that while the marketplace of ideas framework provides a foundation for understanding why US law protects many falsehoods, it does not provide a complete justification. Indeed, if Holmes's argument for the marketplace of ideas was the only basis for protecting false speech, advocates of censorship might have stronger arguments for radical changes to the law. But the marketplace of ideas is *not* the only reason that courts and legislators prevent criminal and civil liability for many types of falsehoods. Statutes, the common law, and landmark First Amendment cases protect lies for many reasons beyond merely the belief that the marketplace will sort the true from the false. The first step in our trip beyond the marketplace begins with one of Holmes's most prominent intellectual critics of the twentieth century, Alexander Meiklejohn.

Chapter 2

Democracy

For more than a half century, courts have recognized that protecting free speech—including some false speech—is necessary for our democratic system of government. This is best reflected not in Oliver Wendell Holmes Jr.'s marketplace theory but in the writings of Alexander Meiklejohn, a philosopher who was president of Amherst College from 1912 to 1924.[1] In 1948, Meiklejohn published *Free Speech and Its Relation to Self-Government*, a series of lectures that articulated his views about the importance of free speech to enabling democratic government, as well as the weaknesses of Holmes's "clear and present danger" test and marketplace theory. Although "the winning of new truth" is vital, he wrote, that is not the primary purpose of the First Amendment. Rather, the First Amendment's main purpose "is to give every voting member of the body politic the fullest possible participation in the understanding of these problems with which the citizens of a self-governing society must deal."[2]

Under this approach, he wrote, the First Amendment's protections are broad: "It tells us that such books as Hitler's *Mein Kampf*, or Lenin's *The State and Revolution*, or the *Communist Manifesto* of Engels and Marx, may be freely printed, freely sold, freely distributed, freely read, freely discussed, freely believed, freely disbelieved, throughout the United States."[3] The purpose of such protection, Meiklejohn wrote, is not to defend the writer or publisher of the words. "We are saying that the citizens of the United States will be fit to govern themselves under their own institutions only if they have faced squarely and fearlessly everything that can be said in favor of those institutions, everything that can be said against them," he wrote. "The unabridged freedom of public discussion is the rock on which our government stands. With that foundation beneath us, we shall not flinch in the face of any clear and present—or, even, terrific—danger."[4]

Expanding on this perspective in a 1953 law review article, Meiklejohn argued that the First Amendment was intended to tear down government restrictions on political and religious freedoms. "Under the new Constitution," he wrote, "the people, now a corporate body of self-governing citizens, forbade their legislative agents to use, for the protection of the nation, any limitation of the religious or political freedom of the people from whom their legislative authority was derived."[5] Meiklejohn also distinguished between public and private speech. "The First Amendment does not protect a 'freedom to speak,'" he wrote in a 1961 article. "It protects the freedom of those activities of thought and communication by which we 'govern.' It is concerned, not with a private right, but with a public power, a governmental responsibility."[6]

Self-governance is not necessarily a complete replacement for the marketplace of ideas framework, but it can help to reconceptualize how we view free speech and the government's role. In a 2022 article, media law professor David Ardia made a compelling case for the shortcomings of the marketplace of ideas framework, but he did not advocate completely abandoning it. "We can take the core principle underlying the marketplace of ideas theory—that the government must be precluded from enforcing its view of what should and should not be subject to public discussion—as a starting point, but ultimately the Constitution requires more than the hands-off approach such a theory envisions," Ardia wrote. "What the Constitution requires is that government take an active role in ensuring that citizens are informed and capable of exercising their right of self-governance."[7] Among Ardia's suggestions to promote self-governance, which I discuss in chapter 15, are imposing robust transparency obligations on the government so that the citizenry has access to public information.

But how does self-governance theory relate to constitutional protection of falsehoods? This chapter describes how that reasoning led to strong protections from libel claims filed by public officials, as seen in the 1964 case *New York Times v. Sullivan*. And chapter 3 describes statutes and court rulings that give the media breathing space to inform the public about court proceedings, the police, and other high-profile public institutions and events. *New York Times v. Sullivan* was decided about nine months before Meiklejohn's death in December 1964. That summer, Meiklejohn told scholar Harry Kalven Jr. that the *Sullivan* decision was "an occasion for dancing in the streets."[8] *New York Times v. Sullivan* is among the Supreme Court's most robust protections for false speech, requiring public officials to prove "actual malice"—either knowledge of falsity or reckless disregard of falsity—for defamation claims. Although the court would later expand this requirement for public figure plaintiffs,[9] its origins are very much in the Meiklejohnian desire to foster self-government. But to fully understand *New York Times v. Sullivan*, it is necessary to assess how US courts have evolved in their approach to libel claims brought by politicians and other public officials. For decades, many courts were far less tolerant of falsehoods about the most prominent and powerful Americans, often refusing to tolerate innocent errors and placing the burden of proving truth on the defendants.

An illustration of the pre-*Sullivan* prevailing rule for libel claims by public officials can be seen in a dispute arising from an October 14, 1892, article in the *Cincinnati Post* about the race for the Democratic nomination for Kentucky's sixth congressional district, between lawyer Theodore Hallam and Colonel Albert S. Berry. The nomination was decided at a convention in Warsaw, Kentucky, beginning on September 27. Hallam's friends and delegates were transported to the convention on the steamboat *Henrietta*, and the food and drink was provided by the St. Nicholas hotel.[10]

The article, above the fold on the front page, carried the sensational headline:

BERRY PAID
Expenses of Theo.
Hallam
In the Sixth (Ky.) District
Contest
For the Nomination of a
Democrat for Congress

The article began, "The Berry-Hallam Congressional fight in the sixth Kentucky district is still on—that is to say, Banquo's ghost bobs up now and then to the annoyance of the Congressional nominee, Berry, and the mortification of the defeated candidate, Theo. F. Hallam."[11] Why, the newspaper asked, did the delegates ultimately side with Berry? The newspaper claimed to have the answer.

"Why, the champagne flowed off the decks so much that even the Henrietta was swimming in it," the newspaper quoted one delegate as saying. The paper reported that "Hallam and his crowd did all the feasting and the drinking." On the final day of the convention, Berry won the nomination. But the scandalous part of the article related to the $865.15 that the St. Nicholas charged for the food, wine, and cigars: the *Post* reported that the bill was made out to Berry. The newspaper reported that Berry and Hallam "had a quiet and confidential chat" on the last day of the convention. "Is Colonel Berry carrying out all and every of the promises he made?" the newspaper asked. "Ah, there's the rub."[12] The newspaper suggested that Berry paid the bill in exchange for Hallam's request that his delegates vote for Berry. "That bill is for 'dry' and 'wet' provisions ordered by Hallam, and disposed of by Hallam's supporters," the newspaper wrote. "Such generosity on the part of the victor to the vanquished is truly touching."[13]

Hallam sued the newspaper for libel. At trial, Hallam's witnesses alleged that the newspaper's reporter had telephoned the hotel, pretending to be Berry's son, and requested a copy of the bill. Hallam's witnesses claimed that another newspaper employee later asked the hotel to change the bill so that it was directed to Berry, but the newspaper presented evidence that tried to rebut those claims.[14] The judge instructed the jury that although Hallam was a political candidate, false factual allegations do not receive a special privilege in libel actions, so the newspaper could not avoid all liability by claiming good faith or probable cause.[15] In contrast, the judge instructed the jurors that "criticism and comment" about public officials, unlike false factual assertions, are conditionally privileged from libel claims, a protection known as the fair comment privilege.[16] This was a plaintiff-friendly approach, as it meant that the fair comment privilege only applied to opinions, and not assertions of fact. The jury found in favor of Hallam and awarded him $2,500, and the newspaper appealed to the US Court of Appeals for the Sixth Circuit.[17]

The appellate court affirmed the jury's verdict and the judge's instructions to the jury, including on the lack of privilege for factual claims about public officials. As the Sixth Circuit framed the newspaper's argument, "every one who has reasonable ground for believing, and does believe, that such a candidate has committed disgraceful acts affecting his fitness for the office he seeks, should have the right to give the public the benefit of his information, without making himself liable in damages for untrue statements, unless malice is shown."[18] The court disagreed with this argument. Privileges, the court reasoned, require a balancing of societal needs for the information against the private need to protect one's reputation.[19] Providing a privilege to the *Post* for its factual allegations about Hallam, the court wrote, would mean that "a man who offers himself as a candidate must submit uncomplainingly to the loss of his reputation, not with a single person or a small class of persons, but with every member of the public, whenever an untrue charge of disgraceful conduct is made against him, if only his accuser honestly believes the charge upon reasonable ground."[20]

The court acknowledged that political candidates "are often corrupt," and disclosing this corruption could benefit the public.[21] "But the danger that honorable and worthy men may be driven from politics and public service by allowing too great latitude in attacks upon their characters outweighs any benefit that might occasionally accrue to the public from charges of corruption that are true in fact, but are incapable of legal proof," the court wrote.[22] The Sixth Circuit predicted that its rule would not endanger press freedom. "No one reading the newspaper of the present day can be impressed with the idea that statements of fact concerning public men, and charges against them, are unduly guarded or restricted; and yet the rule complained of is the law in many of the states of the Union and in England," the court wrote.[23]

What was striking about the Sixth Circuit's reasoning was that it was at least partly driven by the concern that broader speech protection would discourage people from running for political office. One person who was not deterred from running for political office was the Sixth Circuit judge who wrote the opinion: William Howard Taft. Taft had served as solicitor general in Benjamin Harrison's administration before Harrison appointed him to the Sixth Circuit in 1892, just over a year before he wrote the opinion in favor of Hallam. Taft would eventually resign his Sixth Circuit judgeship in 1900 and become William McKinley's civil governor of the Philippine Islands and Theodore Roosevelt's secretary of war, before becoming president in 1909. He later would return to the judiciary, being appointed chief justice of the US Supreme Court by Warren Harding.[24] The *Hallam* opinion remained a proud accomplishment of Taft's. "We are preparing a law of libel with the view of curbing the extravagance of the newspapers here, and I have had occasion to refer to the case of *Post Publishing Company vs. Hallam* for a definition of privilege," Taft wrote in an

October 21, 1901, letter to University of Cincinnati Law School Dean Gustavus H. Wald, while Taft was serving as civil governor of the Philippine Islands.[25] Although Taft's opinion in Hallam's case did not explicitly refer to his experience as a public official, it reflected the concerns of someone who already had a taste of the public eye. But he was correct that his narrow approach—protective of the reputation of politicians—reflected the majority rule at the time. At least some judges were questioning whether Taft's approach was the wisest one.

The bold headline occupied the top of the left column on the front page of the *Topeka State Journal*'s August 20, 1904, edition:[26]

BLACK AND UGLY.
State School Fund Commissioners Force Questionable Deal.
Bonds Purchased by Which State Lost $32,000.

KEPT IN THE DARK.
Records Locked Up and Greatest Secrecy Observed.
Evidence of a Conspiracy by State Officers.

VALUATION IS RAISED.
Comanche County Brought to Standard by State Assessors.
Coleman Then Rules That This Is Basis to Be Taken.
Auditor Wells Forced to Register Bonds at Dead of Night.

The article began, "Appearances indicate that a conspiracy has been formed by which the school fund has been looted, and the facts point towards certain state officials as among the conspirators." The gist of the article was that state officials—including Secretary of State J. R. Burrow, Superintendent of Public Instruction L. L. Dayhoff, Attorney General Chiles Crittendon Coleman, and State Treasurer T. T. Kelly—had conspired for the state school fund to purchase $123,000 in Comanche County bonds in a manner that would cause the state school fund to lose more than $32,000. The newspaper alleged that the deal was brokered by former attorney general A. A. Godard, who stood to receive at least $8,000 in commissions. For the bond sale to go through, the newspaper alleged, the county's valuation needed to increase. This required Coleman to "make a new rule" that would enable a higher valuation, the paper alleged.

Taking particular offense to the story was Coleman, who had been elected Kansas attorney general in 1902 and was running for reelection just a few months after the article's publication. He sued the newspaper's publisher for libel in Shawnee County District Court in Kansas. At trial, the newspaper claimed that its article about public officials was privileged, meaning that it receives certain protections from liability even if the articles are false. Judge A. W. Dana took a fairly defendant-friendly approach to this claim, instructing the jury that an article is privileged if it is "published and circulated among voters for the sole purpose of giving what the defendant believes to be truthful information concerning a candidate for public office, and for the purpose of enabling such voters to cast their ballot more intelligently, and the whole thing is done in good faith, and without malice," even if "the principal matters contained in the article may be untrue in fact and derogatory to the character of the plaintiff." If the jury determines the privilege applies, Judge Dana instructed, "the burden is on the plaintiff to show actual malice in the publication of the article."[27] The jury found for the newspaper, and Coleman appealed to the Kansas Supreme Court.

Kansas's high court had little precedent to guide it in determining whether statements about political candidates receive special protection in defamation lawsuits. The US Supreme Court had yet to incorporate the First Amendment to the states. So Kansas Supreme Court Justice Rousseau Angelus Burch looked to the Kansas Constitution, which stated, "The liberty of the press shall be inviolate; and all persons may freely speak, write or publish their sentiments on all subjects, being responsible for the abuse of such right; and in all civil or criminal actions for libel the truth may be given in evidence to the jury, and if it shall appear that the alleged libelous matter was published for justifiable ends, the accused party shall be acquitted."[28]

Defining "liberty of the press" proved challenging for Burch. He found little help in English common law from the seventeenth century. Liberty of the press at the time, he wrote, "was then more theoretical than actual on account of the harshness of the law of libel and the manner in which that law was administered in the courts."[29] Nor did the colonial law provide much guidance. "Even the publication of general laws was forbidden by the magistrates, who yielded only after long and bitter struggles," Burch wrote. "Royal governors were instructed to prohibit printing, books were burned as offenders against the public welfare, and the school histories all tell about Governor [Berkeley's] boast that free schools and printing-presses were not allowed in Virginia."[30]

Although "liberty of the press" did not have a solid constitutional or common-law definition, Burch reasoned that the court should consider current societal needs to define the term. "The press as we know it today is almost as modern as the telephone and the phonograph," he wrote. "The functions which it performs at the present stage of our social development, if not substantially different in kind from what they have been, are magnified many fold, and the opportunities for its influence are multiplied many times. Judicial interpretation must take cognizance of these facts."[31] Burch did not suggest that "liberty of the press" meant an unrestricted freedom to publish anything. The government, he wrote, "may suppress the circulation of newspapers which, like the *Kansas City Sunday Sun*, of infamous memory, are devoted largely to the publication of scandals, lechery, assignations, intrigues of men and women, and other immoral conduct."[32]

Burch also recognized the need for subjects of media coverage to use libel law to protect their reputations. "A good reputation honestly earned is not only one of the most satisfying sources of a man's own contentment, but from a commercial standpoint it is one of the most productive kinds of capital he can possess," Burch wrote. "Therefore it ought to find guaranties of protection in the fundamental law along with those which guard the liberty of the press, and such is indeed the case."[33] But libel remedies are not unlimited, he wrote, and in cases involving public welfare, "the individual must frequently endure injury to his reputation without remedy."[34] In cases involving "matters of public concern, public men, and candidates for office," Burch reasoned, plaintiffs should have to demonstrate "actual malice," to sue for libel. "Under a form of government like our own there must be freedom to canvass in good faith the worth of character and qualifications of candidates for office, whether elective or appointive, and by becoming a candidate, or allowing himself to be the candidate of others, a man tenders as an issue to be tried out publicly before the people or the appointing power his honesty, integrity, and fitness for the office to be filled," Burch wrote.[35] Burch recognized that Taft had taken a far more reputation-protective approach in Hallam's case and had worried in particular that a press-friendly rule would discourage people from running for office.[36] Burch rejected this slippery slope argument, reasoning that in the states that provide more liberal protections for the press in libel cases, "men of unimpeachable character from all political parties continually present themselves as candidates in sufficient numbers to fill the public offices and manage the public institutions, and the conduct of the press is as honest, clean and free from abuse as it is in states where the narrow view of privilege obtains."[37]

What is "actual malice?" Burch defined it as "actual evilmindedness," and suggested how plaintiffs could establish it. "The proof is made from an interpretation of the writing, its malignity or intemperance, by showing recklessness in making the charge, pernicious activity in circulating or repeating it, its falsity, the situation and relations of the parties, the facts and circumstances surrounding the publication, and by other evidence appropriate to a charge of bad motives, as in other cases," Burch wrote.[38]

Even under this more press-friendly interpretation of libel law, Burch reasoned, newspapers still face limits. "The liberal rule offers no protection to the unscrupulous defamer and traducer of private character," he wrote. "The fulminations in many of the decisions about a Telamonian shield of privilege from beneath which scurrilous newspapers may hurl the javelins of false and malicious slander against private character with impunity are beside the question. Good faith and bad faith are as easily proved in a libel case as in other branches of the law, and it is an every-day issue in all of them."[39]

Still, Burch's opinion—and its requirement of actual malice—meant that Kansas provided far greater protection to inaccuracies about public officials than most other jurisdictions in the United States. As the *Harvard Law Review* noted the year after his opinion, the majority rule was that "although a candidate may be the object of fair comment and criticism based upon his known acts, the occasion is not privileged."[40] Although some other judges in the United States adopted views similar to those of Burch, it remained the minority view for more than a half century.[41] This would change in a big way in 1964, forever upending US defamation law.

New York Times v. Sullivan originated not from an article published in the *New York Times*, but from a full-page advertisement seeking contributions to the Committee to Defend Martin Luther King and the Struggle for Freedom in the South. Writer John Murray brought the advertisement to the *Times* on behalf of the committee, and *Times* advertising manager Vincent Redding approved it for publication, in part because the advertisement bore the names of dozens of people with good reputations.[42] The *Times* received about $4,800 to publish the ad on March 29, 1960.[43] Across the top of the advertisement were the words "Heed Their Rising Voices," a quotation from a recent *Times* editorial arguing for Congress to listen to the growing civil rights movement.[44]

The 10 paragraphs underneath the advertisement's headline detail the struggles that peaceful civil rights protestors faced throughout the South. "In Montgomery, Alabama, after students sang 'My Country, Tis of Thee' on the State Capitol steps, their leaders were expelled from school, and truckloads of police armed with shotguns and tear-gas ringed the Alabama State College Campus," the advertisement stated. "When the entire student body protested to state authorities by refusing to re-register, their dining hall was padlocked in an attempt to starve them into submission."[45] The advertisement also described harassment of King. "Again and again the Southern violators have answered Dr. King's peaceful protests with intimidation and violence," it stated. "They have bombed his home almost killing his wife and child. They have assaulted his person. They have arrested him seven times—for 'speeding,' 'loitering' and similar 'offenses.' And now they have charged him with 'perjury'—a *felony* under which they could imprison him for *ten years*."[46]

The advertisement prompted a retraction request less than two weeks later to the *Times* from Montgomery City Commissioner L. B. Sullivan. Although the ad did not name him, his responsibilities included oversight of the city police, so he believed that the allegations about the Montgomery Police Department's behavior were imputed to him, including the allegations that police "ringed" the college campus and that King was arrested.[47] Sullivan wrote that the publication charged him "with grave misconduct and of [*sic*] improper actions and omissions as an official of the City of Montgomery" and requested the *Times* to "publish in as prominent and as public a manner as the foregoing false and defamatory material contained in the foregoing publication, a full and fair retraction of the entire false and defamatory matter so far as the same relates to me and to my conduct and acts as a public official of the City of Montgomery, Alabama."[48] The *Times*'s outside counsel responded a week later. "We have been investigating the matter and are somewhat puzzled as to how you think the statements in any way reflect on you," the law firm wrote, stating that the

Times was continuing to investigate and "is always desirous of correcting any statements which appear in its paper and which turn out to be erroneous."[49] Later that month, Sullivan sued the *Times* and four signatories of the advertisement for libel.

The parties did not dispute that some claims in the advertisement were wrong. Among the errors in the two paragraphs: the song that the students sang (the "Star-Spangled Banner," not "My Country,'Tis of Thee"), the reason for the students' expulsion (because they demanded service at a courthouse lunch counter, not because they sang on the capitol steps), the portion of the student body that protested (most, but not all of them), the method of protest (a one-day boycott of attending school, not a refusal to register for classes), the level of police involvement (the police had been called to campus before but did not "ring" it), the number of times King was arrested (four, not seven), and whether King had been assaulted (although he claimed that he was assaulted while arrested for loitering, an arresting officer denied it).[50]

Indeed, the *Times* did print a retraction, but not at the request of Sullivan. Rather, on May 9, 1960, Alabama Governor John Patterson wrote to the *Times*, demanding it retract the advertisement to the extent that it reflected on him as the governor and ex officio chairman of Alabama's Board of Education. Later that month, the *Times* ran an article with the headline "Times Retracts Statement in Ad" and the subheading "Acts on Protest of Alabama Governor over Assertions in Segregation Matter." The piece described Patterson's concerns, explained that the advertisement was not prepared by the *Times* news department, and wrote that the *Times* "never intended to suggest by the publication of the advertisement that the Honorable John Patterson, either in his capacity as Governor or as ex-officio chairman of the Board of Education of the State of Alabama, or otherwise, was guilty of 'grave misconduct or improper actions and omission.'"[51]

Presiding over Sullivan's lawsuit was Alabama state court judge Walter B. Jones, an ally of Patterson and staunch supporter of Jim Crow laws. "The preservation of our country with all of its useful and worthwhile institutions, depends upon a strong White Race with a pure blood stream," Jones said in a 1957 speech in Selma, Alabama.[52] In a case related to Sullivan's, Jones prohibited integrated seating in his courtroom.[53] The jury consisted of 12 white men, and the local publicity surrounding the advertisement did not favor the *Times*. "It must be very disappointing to regular readers of the *New York Times*, one of the world's really great newspapers, to find it has been willing to lend its columns for such a page of falsehood as that published the other day and signed by money-beggars who want to defend such a despicable character as Martin Luther King in the courts and save him from the penalties of his derelictions," the *Alabama Journal* wrote on April 9, 1960.[54]

At trial, *Times* secretary Harding Bancroft explained why the paper granted Patterson's retraction request but not Sullivan's. "We did that because we didn't want anything that was published by The Times to be a reflection on the State of Alabama and the Governor was, as far as we could see, the embodiment of the State of Alabama and the proper representative of the State and, furthermore, we had by that time learned more of the actual facts which the ad purported to recite and, finally, the ad did refer to the action of the State authorities and the Board of Education presumably of which the Governor is ex-officio chairman."[55] Not surprisingly, Jones denied the *Times*'s request to dismiss and for a directed verdict. Jones instructed the jury that the statements at issue were "libelous per se," that "the law implies legal injury from the bare fact of the publication itself," and that "falsity and malice are presumed."[56] Jones told the jurors that they could award punitive damages despite a lack of actual damages and that "mere negligence or carelessness is not evidence of actual malice or malice in fact, and does not justify an award of exemplary or punitive damages."[57] Yet Jones declined to instruct the jurors that they must be "convinced" of malice based on "actual intent" to harm or "gross negligence and recklessness."[58] The *Times* argued that these instructions violated the First Amendment, an argument that Jones rejected.[59] The jury awarded

Sullivan the $500,000 in damages that he claimed in the lawsuit, and the *Times* appealed to the Alabama Supreme Court.[60] The state supreme court affirmed Jones, finding that his jury instructions were "a fair, accurate, and clear expression of the governing legal principles."[61] The court swiftly rejected the *Times*'s constitutional challenge, writing, "The First Amendment of the U.S. Constitution does not protect libelous publications."[62]

The *Times* asked the US Supreme Court to review the ruling. In its petition, the *Times* emphasized the need to limit defamation damages to allow public criticism of government officials. "If the judgment stands, its impact will be grave—not only upon the press but also upon those whose welfare may depend on the ability and willingness of publications to give voice to grievances against the agencies of governmental power," the *Times*'s lawyers wrote.[63] Sullivan's lawyers, however, painted a different picture: of a major news outlet defaming an innocent person. "The New York Times, perhaps the nation's most influential newspaper, stooped to circulate a paid advertisement to 650,000 readers—an advertisement which libeled respondent with violent, inflammatory, and devastating language," his lawyers wrote to the court. "The Times knew that the charges were uninvestigated and reckless in the extreme."[64] Sullivan's lawyers pointed to Taft's reasoning in *Hallam* that shielding publications for false factual statements would unfairly burden the reputations of politicians. "The Times cites no authority holding that the Federal Constitution accords it an absolute privilege to defame a public official," Sullivan's lawyers wrote. "The Times' policy arguments are equally pallid."[65]

The *Times* managed to persuade the court to take the case. In a footnote in its brief, the newspaper's lawyers pointed to *Coleman v. MacLennan* and a handful of other cases that required public officials to prove actual malice in defamation lawsuits. "Scholarly opinion, while describing as still a 'minority view' in libel law this requirement that a plaintiff officer or candidate prove actual malice, has favored it with substantial unanimity," they wrote.[66] In their amicus brief supporting the *Times*, the American Civil Liberties Union and New York Civil Liberties Union focused on *Coleman* and the handful of jurisdictions that adopted its broader view of the fair comment privilege, applying it not only to opinion but also statements of fact. "These courts hold that the rule of fair comment covers all critical statements about public officials, whether such statements are true or false, fact or comment, pointing out that the distinction between opinion and fact is difficult and confusing, and it does not better serve justice to attempt it," the groups wrote.[67] But they faced an uphill battle, as Taft's narrower protections in *Hallam* were the prevailing approach to public officials' libel claims.

Yet the court unanimously ruled for the *Times* (though three justices wrote or signed onto concurrences). The court found that the First Amendment requires public officials to demonstrate actual malice to recover damages in libel lawsuits. Writing for the court, Justice William Brennan acknowledged that the Supreme Court had repeatedly stated that the First Amendment does not restrict libel claims, though he differentiated those rulings. "None of the cases sustained the use of libel laws to impose sanctions upon expression critical of the official conduct of public officials," Brennan wrote.[68] Rather, he reasoned, the court had long settled the "general proposition that freedom of expression upon public questions is secured by the First Amendment."[69] This protection, he wrote, reflects a "profound national commitment to the principle that debate on public issues should be uninhibited, robust, and wide-open, and that it may well include vehement, caustic, and sometimes unpleasantly sharp attacks on government and public officials."[70]

Erroneous statements, Brennan wrote, are "inevitable in free debate," and therefore free expression requires "breathing space."[71] And a public official's concerns about reputational injury does not justify speech regulations, he wrote. "Criticism of their official conduct does not lose its constitutional protection merely because it is effective criticism and hence diminishes their official reputations," Brennan wrote.[72] Brennan pointed to the fierce opposition of Jefferson and Madison to the Sedition Act of 1798, which imposed criminal penalties on those who defamed federal government officials. "The right of free public discussion of the stewardship of public officials was thus, in Madison's view, a fundamental principle of the American form of government," Brennan continued.[73] The Supreme Court never opined on the constitutionality of the Sedition Act, as it expired in 1801, but Brennan noted that over the years both government officials and Supreme Court justices broadly agreed that the law violated the First Amendment.[74]

Although Sullivan's lawsuit did not involve the criminal penalties at issue with the Sedition Act, Brennan was just as concerned about the chilling effect on speech. "What a State may not constitutionally bring about by means of a criminal statute is likewise beyond the reach of its civil law of libel," Brennan wrote. "The fear of damage awards under a rule such as that invoked by the Alabama courts here may be markedly more inhibiting than the fear of prosecution under a criminal statute."[75]

That Alabama allows a libel defense of truth does not mitigate the concerns about chilling effects, Brennan wrote. He pointed to *Smith v. California*, an opinion that he wrote in 1959 that struck down a Los Angeles ordinance that penalized bookstores for selling obscene books, even if the booksellers were unaware of the offensive content.[76] "A rule compelling the critic of official conduct to guarantee the truth of all his factual assertions—and to do so on pain of libel judgments virtually unlimited in amount—leads to a comparable 'self-censorship,'" wrote Brennan. "Allowance of the defense of truth, with the burden of proving it on the defendant, does not mean that only false speech will be deterred."[77] Brennan noted that even in the *Hallam* opinion, Taft recognized that defendants could have trouble establishing factual truth. "Under such a rule, would-be critics of official conduct may be deterred from voicing their criticism, even though it is believed to be true and even though it is in fact true, because of doubt whether it can be proved in court or fear of the expense of having to do so," Brennan wrote. "They tend to make only statements which steer far wider of the unlawful zone."[78] These First Amendment concerns, Brennan reasoned, require public officials who sue for libel to show that the statements were made with "actual malice," which Brennan defined as "knowledge that it was false or with reckless disregard of whether it was false or not."[79]

To support the actual malice requirement, Brennan relied on Justice Burch's reasoning in *Coleman*, quoting extensively from it. Brennan noted that public officials who are sued for defamation receive similarly robust protections. "Analogous considerations support the privilege for the citizen-critic of government," Brennan wrote. "It is as much his duty to criticize as it is the official's duty to administer."[80] That the US Supreme Court heavily relied on a Kansas Supreme Court opinion from nearly six decades earlier shows the scarcity of courts that had imposed such a high bar for libel cases.

Three justices, however, wanted to provide even more robust protections. Justice Hugo Black, joined by Justice William Douglas, wrote that the *Times* had an "absolute, unconditional constitutional right" to publish the criticism, and the reversal of the judgment should not be conditioned on whether Sullivan demonstrated actual malice. "The requirement that malice be proved provides at best an evanescent protection for the right critically to discuss public affairs and certainly does not measure up to the sturdy safeguard embodied in the First Amendment," according to Black.[81] Justice Arthur Goldberg, also joined by Douglas, advocated for an absolute protection from lawsuits by public officials. "In a democratic society, one who assumes to act for the citizens in an executive, legislative, or judicial capacity must expect that his official acts will be commented upon and criticized," Goldberg wrote. "Such criticism cannot, in my opinion, be muzzled or deterred by the courts at the instance of public officials under the label of libel."[82] Although the *Sullivan* majority imposed a high burden for public official plaintiffs, it did not go as far as Black and Goldberg had urged, and did not entirely foreclose the possibility of a successful defamation lawsuit.

Still, *Sullivan* was a monumental development, providing robust First Amendment protections in libel law, an area where defendants had to rely on common-law doctrines like substantial truth and the opinion privilege. And the Supreme Court did not stop at protecting defendants from the claims of public officials. Three years later, the court expanded the actual malice requirement to cases involving "public figures" who are "involved in issues in which the public has a justified and important interest,"[83] though it refused to extend the protection to claims brought by purely private figures.[84]

While *Sullivan* is best known for requiring public official plaintiffs to establish actual malice, its second, equally notable impact, is placing the burden of establishing falsity on those plaintiffs. As legendary First Amendment litigator Floyd Abrams noted in a 2022 essay, until *Sullivan*, the general American rule in defamation cases was that the speaker had the burden of proving truth. "Based on the First Amendment, *Sullivan* flatly rejected that requirement of proof in American libel cases commenced by public officials," Abrams wrote.[85]

Meiklejohn had good reason to dance in the streets when the court issued the *Sullivan* opinion. While some judges, such as Burch, had long recognized the value of self-governance in free speech protections, their rulings were limited to state common law or state constitutions that only applied in particular jurisdictions. Brennan had taken Meiklejohn's philosophy and incorporated it into the First Amendment, where it would bind all US courts at the federal and state levels. As First Amendment scholar Lee Bollinger wrote, "*Sullivan* initiated a major theoretical and idiomatic avalanche, which Meiklejohn was thought to have precipitated."[86]

Brennan's rule still allows publishers to be subject to defamation judgments if the public officials meet the high bar of actual malice, and this is a less speech-friendly rule than Meiklejohn's absolutist view of First Amendment protections. "Some error could be tolerated, but lying and reckless reporting would threaten the integrity of the debate and thus the listener would not receive information vital to good governance," communications professors Gerald J. Baldasty and Roger A. Simpson wrote about *Sullivan* in 1981. "Such a provision would necessitate scrutiny of the behavior of individual journalists, and thus entail examination of the news process. The attempt to impose a measure of purity on the public debate added controls far more stringent than those of Meiklejohn, but the new fault standard was a logical development due to the Court's concern for the listener."[87] Indeed, in a lecture that he delivered at Brown University the year after the *Sullivan* opinion, Brennan pointed to Meiklejohn in describing his approach to deciding the case. "Some of the statements in the advertisement were not true," Brennan acknowledged. "The first amendment question was whether its protections nevertheless limit a state's power to apply traditional libel law principles, since the statements were made in criticism of the official conduct of a public servant. In other words, the case presented a classic example of an activity that Dr. Meiklejohn called an activity of 'governing importance' within the powers reserved to the people and made invulnerable to sanctions imposed by their agency-governments."[88]

When evaluating how and why courts protect falsehoods, it is not satisfying to look only at Holmes's marketplace of ideas. While that philosophy has surely driven many important court protections for free speech, it does not tell the whole story. Meiklejohn's views of free speech protection did not merely assume that the free market of ideas would sort the good from the bad. Rather, he viewed free speech protections as essential to preserving democracy. And those views underpinned the *Sullivan* decision. *Sullivan* contains some allusions to the marketplace, and even cites John Stuart Mill and John Milton. But marketplace theory does not fully explain the holding. Self-governance permeates the decision to hold public officials to a higher standard.

To get an idea of what American defamation law would be like without *Sullivan*, it is useful to compare it with the law of England. Although US defamation law originates from English common law, *Sullivan* marked a sharp divergence between the two countries. England does not have a similar actual malice requirement, and defendants still have the burden of proving truth. "There was never a single cultural or political moment to mark its start but, in the decades following *Sullivan*, London became the 'libel capital of the world' in which the aggressive and costly pursuit of libel claims by powerful people created a vast environment of self-censorship," First Amendment lawyers Dave Heller and Katharine Larsen wrote. "Scholars surmised that the common law created a 'structural chilling effect,' i.e., an environment where certain categories of news reporting—such as accounts of police misconduct—became 'no go areas' for fear of suit. Perversely, what flourished instead was celebrity gossip and scandal, which, even if deliberately false, could be paid for out of increased sales. In other words, tabloids could budget for payments of libel damages."[89]

Likewise, the Supreme Court of Canada held in 1995 that the Canadian Charter of Rights and Freedoms does not require *Sullivan*'s actual malice rule. The court reasoned that Canadian common law already provides defamation defendants with a number of defenses. "I simply cannot see that the law of defamation is unduly restrictive or inhibiting," Justice Peter Cory wrote for the court. "Surely it is not requiring too much of individuals that they ascertain the truth of the allegations they publish."[90] Although Canada's media have not been shuttered due to the court's rejection of an actual malice standard, it is difficult to measure the impact of the decision because the common law continued to develop after the 1995 decision to expand protections for fair comment and "responsible communications on matters of public interest."[91] Moreover, unlike the United States, the Canadian legal system often requires the unsuccessful litigant to pay many of the other side's litigation expenses.[92] The costs of losing a defamation lawsuit in Canada could discourage some potential plaintiffs from ever filing complaints.

While the *Sullivan* precedent has been vital to the US media over the past half century, it is not the only protection for reporting about public officials and other powerful institutions. As Michael Norwick of the Media Law Resource Center wrote in 2022, his group's research of news media litigation found that "actual malice was not the predominant reason that defendants were successful on dispositive motions, with other defenses such as substantial truth, opinion, the fair report privilege and the 'of and concerning' requirement collectively playing a much larger role in defendant success."[93] Indeed, the uncertainty about whether some plaintiffs qualify as "public figures" and "public officials," as well as the unpredictability of a finding of whether speakers acted with actual malice, means that defendants in defamation lawsuits cannot always rely on *Sullivan*. This uncertainty is compounded by the possibility of five Supreme Court justices agreeing to overturn *Sullivan*.

More than 30 states have bolstered the protections of *Sullivan* through laws that seek to prevent "strategic lawsuits against public participation," also known as SLAPP. These "anti-SLAPP laws" differ in coverage and strength, but they generally try to limit the use of defamation lawsuits and other civil actions to punish and chill speech about issues of public concern.[94] The laws generally allow defendants to challenge such suits early, placing a heavy burden of proof on the plaintiff, and often allow the plaintiff to recover legal fees.[95] In 2020, New York State went further and codified *Sullivan* in its anti-SLAPP law, requiring plaintiffs in covered cases to prove actual malice.[96] So even if the Supreme Court were to overturn *Sullivan*, defendants in defamation cases litigated under New York law still would have its protections. But many state anti-SLAPP laws are far weaker, some states do not have anti-SLAPP laws, and Congress has failed to adopt a federal anti-SLAPP law.[97] So the anti-SLAPP laws' procedural protections depend greatly on the court and state in which defamation suits are filed.

Limiting the liability from defamation claims filed by public officials and public figures is only one way that our legal system fosters the self-governance that Meiklejohn envisioned. Another protection— often codified in state statutes—provides an additional means for journalists to inform the public about powerful public institutions without fearing liability for an inadvertent error. And that protection again begins with Oliver Wendell Holmes Jr.

Chapter 3

Sunlight

Although Meiklejohn hailed the Supreme Court's adoption of the actual malice requirement in *New York Times v. Sullivan*, the opinion did not fully achieve his goal of protecting speech about matters of public concern. *Sullivan* focuses on the status of the *plaintiff*, not the subject of the coverage. A public figure may sue over a purely private matter, a situation that presumably would be of little worry to Meiklejohn. Conversely, a private figure might file a suit arising from a matter of great public concern, such as a court proceeding. Meiklejohn would expect the strongest protections in such a situation. "Under the public-speech theory, the public or private status of the plaintiff should bear no weight in judging the level of protection for the speech," communications professor Brian J. Steffen aptly wrote of Meiklejohn's philosophy.[1]

For the public to understand the workings of government agencies and powerful organizations, reporters and other commentators must be able to speak about their operations. US court opinions and statutes have long recognized the need to foster such discussion. The rationale—informing the public about public affairs—extends to various protections for reporting about false statements made by government agencies and other powerful figures, often in defamation cases. The general premise is that if media and others are held liable for reporting false speech that is uttered by the government or others that are central to society, they will be unable to inform the public about these vital institutions. These legal rules, which provide strong protections in defamation cases, include the fair report privilege, neutral reporting privilege, and the burden for private plaintiffs to prove falsity when suing the media over reporting on matters of public concern.

While the underlying goals of these protections are like that of the actual malice requirement in *Sullivan*, they operate not by setting a tougher standard for high-profile plaintiffs, but by determining the types of coverage in which the public has a particular interest in receiving. For instance, laws in the United States recognize that protecting some false speech is necessary for the public to understand the workings of courts, legislatures, and other government agencies. But what if government officials or litigants get their facts wrong?

Legal safeguards have long protected many government officials from defamation lawsuits based on what they say when carrying out their official duties, and these strong protections also apply to litigants or witnesses while they testify in court. But what about news media and other commentators who report on those government bodies? Should they face liability if the facts that they report are ultimately untrue? Consider, for instance, an arrest warrant for a local shop owner, alleging probable cause that he has committed murder. Imagine that the local newspaper reports accurately about the arrest warrant's allegations, but police later drop the charges after uncovering new evidence. The reporting likely devastated the shop's business. Should the shop owner be able to sue the newspaper for defamation?

State legislatures and courts have addressed that problem over more than a century, gradually adopting rules known as the fair report privilege, which provide strong—but not absolute—protection for reporting the official proceedings of government agencies and courts. And some courts have developed additional privileges and protections for discussion of similar newsworthy events, particularly if that discussion sheds light on the workings of the government. I consider these protections broadly to serve a function that is not fully captured in the leading free speech theories: public information.

An early justification for public information–based free speech protections came from Oliver Wendell Holmes Jr. Before President Theodore Roosevelt nominated him to the US Supreme Court in 1902, Holmes served for two decades on the Massachusetts Supreme Judicial Court. In 1884, Holmes decided a libel case brought by attorney Charles Cowley against the publishers and owners of the *Boston Herald*. The *Herald* accurately reported on a petition to remove Cowley from the Massachusetts bar.[2] The question for Holmes was whether the newspaper should be liable for publishing false claims contained in a petition. Holmes recognized that no binding Massachusetts law governed the case. Holmes looked to a 1799 English case, *Rex v. Wright*, which stated that "[t]hough the publication of such proceedings may be to the disadvantage of the particular individual concerned, yet it is of vast importance to the public that the proceedings of courts of justice should be universally known."[3] Holmes agreed, writing that the primary advantage "is the security which publicity gives for the proper administration of justice."[4]

Holmes linked the protection of the press from libel lawsuits to the public access to government proceedings. "It is desirable that the trial of causes should take place under the public eye, not because the controversies of one citizen with another are of public concern, but because it is of the highest moment that those who administer justice should always act under the sense of public responsibility, and that every citizen should be able to satisfy himself with his own eyes as to the mode in which a public duty is performed," Holmes wrote.[5] Holmes ultimately determined that the fair report privilege did not protect the newspaper because the court clerk returned the petition and it was not entered on the court docket, reasoning that "it is enough to mark the plain distinction between what takes place in open court, and that which is done out of court by one party alone, or more exactly, as we have already said, the contents of a paper filed by him in the clerk's office."[6]

Despite the newspaper's loss, Holmes's opinion set the foundation for the modern fair report privilege. Over the next century, more than 100 state court opinions nationwide would cite Holmes's opinion, often in creating their own protections for reports about public proceedings. While some state courts have adopted similar reasoning into their common law, in other states the legislatures have passed statutes that provide fair report privileges. The privileges protect not only coverage of court cases, but also coverage of legislatures and executive branch agencies. Although courts and legislatures generally only extend the privilege to "fair and accurate" reports of these government proceedings, they implicitly recognize that the privileges could extend to highly publicized factual allegations that are later proven to be false. Allowing such potential falsehoods, courts and legislatures have recognized, may be a necessary side effect of the openness that Holmes sought to foster. As Samuel Arthur Dawson wrote in a 1924 monograph about the fair report privilege, the protections are vital for democracy. "Without it the government could become despotic and work in obscure ways," Dawson wrote.[7] The privilege enables the media to publish information that matters to "the people in a free, self-governing society," law professor Kathryn Dix Sowle wrote in a 1979 law review article. "Without it, the law of defamation could subject the republisher to liability for reports concerning such matters as public trials, legislative debates, and the press conferences of public officials," she wrote.[8]

To see the evolution and breadth of the fair report privilege, it helps to look at another Massachusetts defamation case, filed more than 100 years after Cowley's. The lawsuit arose from a report to local police of a domestic disturbance in Townsend, Massachusetts, on May 11, 1997. The wife of Harry Yohe, a retired Green Beret, reportedly told police that her husband was threatening suicide, was heavily armed, and had been drinking and was on antidepressants. The police sent 30 vehicles, including a hostage negotiator and SWAT team, to Yohe's home, according to court filings. He was not in the house and was arrested at Fort Devens early the next morning. He was transferred to two hospitals for evaluations and soon released, with both hospitals failing to find evidence of suicidal ideation or intoxication.[9]

On May 14, 1997, the *Townsend Times,* published by Nashoba Publications, ran an article titled "Domestic Situation Turns Ugly." The article stated:

> TOWNSEND—Many local residents were alarmed Sunday night with the sight of up to 30 state police vehicles traveling through the streets of Townsend. Police Chief William May had called in the extra forces when a woman reported a drunk and suicidal husband in possession of deadly fire power and hundreds of rounds of ammunition.
>
> The domestic dispute between husband and wife began at about 7 p.m. on Mother's Day, stated May. Police were called at approximately 8:30 p.m. when the woman reported that she and her children had left the house with a drunk and suicidal husband still inside. The unidentified woman alerted police of the presence of two AK47s and 500 rounds of ammunition in the house, with her husband identified as a former soldier connected with special forces units.
>
> "He had been drinking all weekend," stated May. "She also told us that her older son was either in the house or on his way there . . . We determined that he was there."
>
> With the unidentified man in custody by midnight, police confirmed that he had been drinking. May stated it was his belief that the man was suicidal. No charges have been brought against him.
>
> The operation was secured at 4 a.m. Monday morning.[10]

The *Worcester Telegram and Gazette* published a similar article that week.[11] The reporters, who both interviewed May, based their stories on their interviews with him. Although the articles were accurate reflections of their conversations with May, the reporters did not do more reporting to verify the details, as they found him to be trustworthy.[12] May's statements to the reporters were based on the police report for the incident.[13] Yohe sued the two reporters, their newspapers, and May for defamation and intentional infliction of emotional distress. The case went to Judge Rya W. Zobel, whom President Jimmy Carter appointed to the federal court in Massachusetts in 1979. The newspapers argued that the claims against them were barred by the Massachusetts fair report privilege, which by that time "allows those who fairly and accurately report certain types of official or government action to be immune from liability for claims arising out of such reports." Massachusetts courts justify the privilege for three reasons: "1) the public has a right to know of official government actions that affect the public interest; 2) the only practical way many citizens can learn of these actions is through a report by the news media; and 3) the only way news outlets would be willing to make such a report is if they are free from liability, provided that their report was fair and accurate."[14] Applying this privilege, Zobel granted summary judgment for the newspapers, concluding that "[t]he report of Chief May, the person in charge of the relevant police department, was clearly an 'official' statement," and the evidence in the case shows "without contradiction that the newspaper stories accurately reported Chief May's statements."[15]

Yohe appealed the ruling to the US Court of Appeals for the First Circuit, arguing that the fair report privilege should not apply because the newspapers were reckless in their reporting about such serious claims. "The newspaper articles stated Yohe was suicidal, on drugs, alcohol and violent," his lawyers wrote in their appellate brief. "After coerced treatment in two hospitals, Yohe was released that evening within hours of both hospitals with no record of suicidal behavior, alcohol, drugs or being dangerous. After Yohe's release, the defendants [had] an opportunity to clarify these vicious accusations, but failed to do so."[16] The newspapers argued that Yohe's lawyers misinterpreted the test for the fair report privilege. "What Mr. Yohe fails to acknowl-edge is that the requirement of substantial accuracy refers to the ne-cessity that the media accurately report what government officials say and do, and *not to the accuracy of any statement that the officials may have made*," Nashoba Publications' lawyers wrote in their appeals brief.[17]

On February 26, 2003, the First Circuit affirmed Zobel's decision in favor of the newspapers, ruling that the fair report privilege applied to the statements. "The purpose of the privilege is to ensure that pub-lications may perform the important function of informing the public of actions taken by government agencies and officials," Judge Juan Tor-ruella wrote for the unanimous three-judge panel.[18] Under Massa-chusetts law, Torruella wrote, the fair report privilege protects the newspaper for a "rough-and-ready summary" of an "official action" that is "substantially correct."[19] Applying this standard, Torruella concluded that the privilege covers the newspaper articles. "The report of Chief May was clearly an 'official statement,' and the information in the articles was expressly and repeatedly attributed to Chief May," he wrote. "There is no dispute that the articles in question faithfully and accurately recounted May's official statement; the articles were, at a minimum, a 'substantially correct' summary of an official statement. There is also no evidence that the facts in either story were manipu-lated, enlarged or embellished upon by the reporters; had there been, the privilege might not apply."[20]

Although he acknowledged that the fair report privilege is not abso-lute, Torruella concluded that it still applied despite Yohe's allegations that the articles contained inaccurate information and the reporters failed to independently investigate those factual claims. For the pur-poses of the fair report privilege, Torruella wrote, "accuracy" means only "the factual correctness of the events reported and not . . . the truth about the events that actually transpired."[21] The plaintiff can only de-feat the fair report privilege, he wrote, by showing either "that the publisher does not give a fair and accurate report of the official state-ment, or malice," and Yohe failed to show either.[22] Torruella concluded his opinion by recognizing that May's statements about Yohe may have been at least partly inaccurate, and the newspapers may have spread those potential inaccuracies and harmed Yohe: "we cannot see how the challenged statements and articles constitute anything other than the legitimate and nondefamatory flow of information from a government official to an interested public."[23]

The opinion presents the trade-offs that states have made by adopting fair report privileges, either through common law or statute. The states recognize that the fair report privilege may lead to the publication of more falsehoods than otherwise would have been published, as the underlying government proceedings may not be entirely accurate. Yet the fair report privilege tolerates the potential for falsehoods owing to the overriding benefits of shedding light on public functions such as the police. Without the fair report privilege, the newspapers may have been far more reluctant to publish May's recounting of the police report and arrest. And beyond *Yohe v. Nugent*, the fair report privilege is crucial to public insight into other government functions, such as the judiciary. By protecting the media for coverage of judicial filings, indictments, and trials, the fair report privilege fosters a better public understanding of the judiciary and reduces the likelihood of improper actions such as prosecutorial misconduct.

The fair report privilege is limited to reports of government proceedings. What protections do the media and commentators receive for reports about accusations made by public figures and organizations that are not associated with government proceedings?

It depends on the jurisdiction. Some courts have adopted the "neutral reportage privilege" that extends fair report privilege principles to such allegations.[24] The reasoning behind the privilege elucidates the importance of protecting such reporting, even if it might lead to the spread of falsehoods. The privilege arose from the debate in the 1970s over the use of the insecticide DDT (dichlorodiphenyltrichloroethane), which environmentalists had long said harmed birds. Some scientists, including J. Gordon Edwards, argued against bans on DDT, reasoning that the chemical prevents starvation, crop destruction, and insect-borne diseases. They also pointed to the increase in bird sightings in the National Audubon Society's Christmas Bird Count. The Audubon Society argued that such citations were misleading because bird watchers were better skilled and there were more counters.[25] In the April 1972 issue of the Audubon Society's publication *American Birds*, editor Robert S. Arbib Jr. addressed the controversy:

> We are well aware that segments of the pesticide industry and certain paid "scientist-spokesmen" are citing Christmas Bird Count totals (and other data in AMERICAN BIRDS) as proving that the bird life of North America is thriving, and that many species are actually increasing despite the widespread and condemned use of DDT and other non-degradable hydrocarbon pesticides.
>
> This, quite obviously, is false and misleading, a distortion of the facts for the most self-serving of reasons. The truth is that many species high on the food chain, such as most bird-eating raptors and fisheaters, are suffering serious declines in numbers as a direct result of pesticide contamination; there is now abundant evidence to prove this. In addition, with the constant diminution of natural habitat, especially salt- and freshwater marshes, it is self-evident that species frequenting these habitats are less common than formerly.
>
> The apparent increases in numbers of species and individuals on the Christmas Bird Counts have, in most cases, nothing to do with real population dynamics. They are the result of ever-increasing numbers of birders in the field, better access to the Count areas, better knowledge of where to find the birds within each area, and increasing sophistication in identification.
>
> With increased local coverage by the press of Christmas Bird Count activities, it is important that Count spokesmen reiterate the simple and truthful fact that what we are seeing is [a] result of not more birds, but more birders. Any time you hear a "scientist" say the

opposite, you are in the presence of someone who is being paid to lie, or is parroting something he knows little about.[26]

With no factual support, Arbib claimed that some scientists were paid to lie. John Devlin, a nature reporter for the *New York Times*, asked Arbib which scientists were "paid liars." Arbib hesitated, and discussed the request with Audubon Society Vice President Roland Clement, who also cautioned against alleging that a particular scientist was a paid liar. Clement did, however, tell Arbib that Clement had recently written an article that named scientists who egregiously distorted the society's bird statistics. Clement told Arbib that he could provide those names, cautioning that they did not know whether these scientists were actually "paid liars" but only that they misinterpreted the society's statistics.[27]

Arbib said that he then provided the names to Devlin along with the warning that he had discussed with Clement, though Devlin said that Arbib did not provide such a warning when he gave the five names, including Edwards. He also said that Arbib represented that the five names were those to whom he referred in the April 1972 *American Birds* article. Devlin contacted the five scientists and reached three, all of whom strongly denied the allegations. On August 14, 1972, the *Times* published an article by Devlin titled "Pesticide Spokesmen Accused of 'Lying' on Higher Bird Count." The article began by quoting Arbib's claim that "[s]egments of the pesticide industry and certain 'scientist-spokesmen'" were "lying" about the bird statistics. In the sixth paragraph, Devlin named the five scientists, attributing them to an interview with Arbib. Devlin also summarized the denials from the scientists.[28]

Three of the scientists, including Edwards, sued the Audubon Society, the newspaper, Arbib, and Clement for libel. The case went before Judge Charles Miller Metzner, whom President Dwight D. Eisenhower appointed to the Manhattan federal court in 1959.[29] After years of discovery and a trial, the jury returned a verdict against the *Times* and Clement, and in favor of Arbib and the society. The *Times* asked Metzner to set aside the verdict, and he denied the request, concluding that the jury's findings, including that the *Times* published with actual malice, were reasonable. "It cannot be said that the Times knew that the statements in the story were false," Metzner wrote. "However, the jury was justified in finding clear and convincing proof from the evidence and the inferences to be drawn therefrom that the story of August 14 was published with reckless disregard of whether it was false or not."[30] The *Times* appealed the judgment to the US Court of Appeals for the Second Circuit. The case went before Second Circuit Chief Judge Irving Kaufman, a former federal prosecutor who was appointed to the court by President John F. Kennedy in 1961; Tom Clark, a retired US Supreme Court justice who had voted with the majority in *Sullivan*; and William J. Jameson, who was appointed to the US District Court for the District of Montana by President Eisenhower in 1957. (Although Clark and Jameson were not on the Second Circuit, they could hear cases there by designation.)

Writing for a unanimous panel on May 25, 1977, Kaufman reversed the judgment against the *Times*. "At stake in this case is a fundamental principle," Kaufman wrote. "Succinctly stated, when a responsible, prominent organization like the National Audubon Society makes serious charges against a public figure, the First Amendment protects the accurate and disinterested reporting of those charges, regardless of the reporter's private views regarding their validity."[31] Kaufman justified this finding based on the need for the public to learn about newsworthy statements. "The public interest in being fully informed about controversies that often rage around sensitive issues demands that the press be afforded the freedom to report such charges without assuming responsibility for them," he wrote.[32]

In laying out these principles, Kaufman was for the first time articulating the press's right to "neutral reportage," which is like the fair report privilege but not tied to a government proceeding. Like the fair report privilege, the neutral reportage privilege is not absolute. "Literal accuracy is not a prerequisite: if we are to enjoy the blessings of a robust and unintimidated press, we must provide immunity from defamation suits where the journalist believes, reasonably and in good faith, that his report accurately conveys the charges made," Kaufman explained. "It is equally clear, however, that a publisher who in fact espouses or concurs in the charges made by others, or who deliberately distorts these statements to launch a personal attack of his own on a public figure, cannot rely on a privilege of neutral reportage."[33] Applying this privilege to the scientists' lawsuit, Kaufman concluded that it protected the *Times*. "It is clear here, that Devlin reported Audubon's charges fairly and accurately," Kaufman wrote. "He did not in any way espouse the Society's accusations: indeed, Devlin published the maligned scientists' outraged reactions in the same article that contained the Society's attack. The Times article, in short, was the exemplar of fair and dispassionate reporting of an unfortunate but newsworthy contretemps."[34]

Kaufman recognized the "pain and distress" that the story caused the scientists, and he cautioned that his opinion is not an endorsement of such character attacks. "Nevertheless, we believe that the interest of a public figure in the purity of his reputation cannot be allowed to obstruct that vital pulse of ideas and intelligence on which an informed and self-governing people depend," Kaufman wrote. "It is unfortunate that the exercise of liberties so precious as freedom of speech and of the press may sometimes do harm that the state is powerless to recompense: but this is the price that must be paid for the blessings of a democratic way of life."[35] Kaufman effectively acknowledged that the neutral reportage privilege might protect the publication of falsehoods that could hurt their subjects. Yet he concluded that the First Amendment protects these falsehoods owing to the greater benefits to society arising from the coverage of public controversies. Also notable about his reasoning is that, unlike the fair report privileges that come from state statutes or common law, Kaufman derived the neutral reportage privilege from the First Amendment.

Floyd Abrams, the First Amendment lawyer who represented the *Times*, was quoted in the next day's edition of the newspaper as hailing the significance of this ruling. "Until this case, no court had made as clear the proposition that, when a journalist reports defamatory charges by one public figure against another, there can be no liability, regardless of the journalist's own views about the accuracy of the charges," Abrams said.[36] First Amendment scholars also welcomed the new privilege. "With more citizens becoming involved in important public issues such as economy, energy, education, and religion, it is important that the media be able, without fear of libel suits, to interview and quote business leaders, civic leaders, educators, and religious leaders in order to give the public a broader perspective on problems and to give all sides of the debate which up to now has been one-sided," Donna Lee Dickerson wrote in *Communications and the Law* in 1981.[37]

Although free speech advocates embraced the new privilege, many courts have refused to adopt it. A year after Kaufman's opinion, the US Court of Appeals for the Third Circuit concluded that the neutral reportage privilege contradicted Supreme Court precedent that defined actual malice that public officials and figures must show. "We therefore conclude that a constitutional privilege of neutral reportage is not created, as appellee would have us find, merely because an individual newspaper or television or radio station decides that a particular statement is newsworthy," the Third Circuit wrote.[38]

When courts have refused to recognize the neutral reportage privilege, they raise concerns about the ability of the media to report about public officials. One such case that drew national attention arose from an April 20, 1995, article in the *Chester County Daily Local*. The article, titled "Slurs, Insults Drag Town into Controversy," described attacks that William T. Glenn Sr., a councilman in the small Pennsylvania

town of Parkesburg, had launched at other members of the council
and the mayor. The article began:

> Councilman William T. Glenn Sr., the center of controversy at recent
> borough meetings, has called his colleagues "liars," "criminals,"
> "queers" and one a "shyster Jew."
>
> In a special meeting Wednesday night, Council President James B.
> Norton III moved to end fighting and name-calling among the
> disgruntled Council.
>
> It didn't work.
>
> The three-minute meeting was quickly adjourned after Norton
> read a statement, and Glenn began an onslaught of comments.[39]

Later in the article, the reporter summarizes Glenn's comments
about the other elected officials, including that Council President
James B. Norton III and Borough Mayor Alan M. Wolfe "are homo-
sexuals conspiring to remove [Glenn] from Council"; that Norton is
"crazy" and a "draft dodger"; that Glenn had caught the two colleagues
engaged in sexual acts and saw them "holding hands" while walking
in town; and that Glenn "detests queers and child molestors [*sic*]."[40]
The article quoted Wolfe as stating, "As he has done in the past, he is
creating stories," and Norton as stating, "If Mr. Glenn has made comments as bizarre as that, then I feel very sad for him, and I hope he
can get the help he needs."[41]
Wolfe and Norton sued the reporter, newspaper, and the newspaper's owner for defamation. At trial, the judge ruled that the neutral
reportage privilege was available regardless of whether the newspaper
article was published with actual malice, and the jury concluded that
the defendants were not liable owing to the privilege.[42] On appeal, the
Pennsylvania Superior Court reversed the trial court judge, reasoning
that a neutral reportage privilege did not exist.[43] The defendants appealed to the Pennsylvania Supreme Court, which agreed with the Superior Court that the First Amendment does not require the neutral

reportage doctrine because the actual malice requirement in *Sullivan* and its progeny provides a sufficient safeguard. "Accordingly, we conclude that the existing case law from the U.S. Supreme Court indicates that the high Court would not so sharply tilt the balance against the protection of reputation, and in favor of protecting the media, so as to jettison the actual malice standard in favor of the neutral reportage doctrine," the Pennsylvania Supreme Court wrote. "Rather, the U.S. Supreme Court has placed a burden (albeit a minimal one) on the media to refrain from publishing reports that they know to be false or that they published with reckless disregard of whether it was false."[44]

The Pennsylvania Supreme Court's rejection of the neutral reportage doctrine meant that a newspaper could face liability for accurately reporting on a dispute between two public officials if some comments made during the dispute are defamatory. While this might sound like a just result, it threatens the transparency that the privilege was intended to promote. The Parkesburg voters had a strong interest in knowing about Glenn's hateful comments not because of their potential veracity, but because they said a great deal about Glenn's character. The public also had an interest in knowing what was happening at council meetings. The Pennsylvania Supreme Court's ruling attracted swift criticism from editorial pages nationwide. "A newspaper can't reasonably be expected to resolve the truth of every allegation in the heat of the moment," the *Seattle Times* wrote in an editorial responding to the opinion. "It shouldn't withhold newsworthy accusations between public officials until it can prove who's telling the truth. The appropriate test is whether the newspaper reports responsibly—neutrally and accurately—allowing the public to decide whom to believe."[45]

The US Supreme Court never adopted or rejected the neutral reportage privilege, leaving it up to individual courts to decide. But in 1986, it used similar reasoning to make it more difficult for private figures to sue the media for defamation if the report involves a matter of public concern. In *Philadelphia Newspapers v. Hepps*, a Philadelphia businessman, his company, and franchisees sued the owner of the *Phil-*

adelphia Inquirer for a series of articles claiming that the businessman and companies were tied to organized crime and had influenced state government decision-making.[46] Because the plaintiffs were private figures, they only had to show that the newspaper negligently published false information, not that it acted with actual malice. But the parties disputed whether the plaintiffs had the burden of proving falsity. The Pennsylvania Supreme Court concluded that a Pennsylvania statute did not violate the First Amendment by placing the burden of establishing the truth on the defendant.[47] The burden of proof might sound like a legal technicality, but it can make all the difference in a defamation claim. Let's say that I posted on Yelp that a restaurant served me raw chicken, and the restaurant sued me for libel. If the burden of proof to establish falsity is on the restaurant, it would face a heavy lift to show that the chicken it served me weeks or months ago had been fully cooked. Yet if the burden is on me to show truth, I might not have any remaining evidence of the raw chicken.

In a 5–4 opinion, Justice Sandra Day O'Connor ruled that in speech about media coverage of matters of public concern, the First Amendment requires plaintiffs have the burden of proving falsity even if they are private figures. O'Connor recognized that in some libel cases, the truth or falsity of the claims might not be fully resolved, and the burden of proof will be vital to the outcome. "In a case presenting a configuration of speech and plaintiff like the one we face here, and where the scales are in such an uncertain balance, we believe that the Constitution requires us to tip them in favor of protecting true speech," O'Connor wrote. "To ensure that true speech on matters of public concern is not deterred, we hold that the common-law presumption that defamatory speech is false cannot stand when a plaintiff seeks damages against a media defendant for speech of public concern."[48]

The broader lesson from *Hepps* and the fair and neutral report privileges is that US law tolerates the publication of some false statements—even those that cause harm—in an effort to inform and educate the public about important public controversies. The protections stem from the Meiklejohnian commitment to fostering self-governance, just as the actual malice requirement of *Sullivan* does. Yet rather than protecting only the reporting about plaintiffs who are public figures or officials, the privileges more broadly provide for coverage of proceedings about which the public has an interest in learning.

Meiklejohn's focus on using free speech protections to foster democracy is best viewed as a supplement—rather than a counterweight—to Holmes's marketplace of ideas framework. They are not mutually exclusive reasons for protecting speech, including some speech that might be false. The US legal system protects false speech both because the law fosters a robust marketplace of ideas and because it seeks to promote and inform democracy. But these First Amendment theories capture only some of the reasons that the legal system protects false speech. These reasons are not neatly captured in legal theories, but in protections that courts and legislatures have chosen to provide to speech that may be true or false. The start of that journey begins with a case that was argued in the infancy of our modern democracy, by one of the nation's most prominent founders.

Chapter 4

Truth

Appreciating why the legal system protects some falsehoods requires an understanding of why the legal system values truth, and the evolution of the law's tolerance for at least minor deviations from that truth. While valuing truth sounds like a foregone conclusion, it was not always a given. Not only were defendants in criminal libel cases in England forbidden from using truth as a defense, but also an allegation that their statements were truthful could hurt their cases. Judges in England's Star Chamber in the 1600s developed a saying, "the greater the truth, the greater the libel."[1] Blackstone captured the traditionally limited British view of press freedom, writing that it "consists in laying no *previous* restraints upon publications, and not in freedom from censure for criminal matter when published."[2] That gradually changed as the British press became more adversarial to the Crown in the eighteenth century. "It was obviously not an adequate formula for free expression; among its other deficiencies, it did nothing to prohibit prosecutions for seditious utterances," David Lange wrote.[3] But the traditional view of the limits of press freedom—and the possibility of facing penalties for truthful statements—had already reached the colonies.

Perhaps the most influential early declaration of the benefits of truth in America came from Alexander Hamilton. At the turn of the nineteenth century, America's politics were divided between Hamilton's Federalists and Thomas Jefferson's Democratic-Republicans. Highly partisan newspapers emerged throughout America, arguing the causes of both sides.[4]

Those newspapers faced potential criminal liability merely for criticizing government officials. In 1798, Congress had passed the Sedition Act, which imposed criminal penalties for those who "write, print, utter or publish . . . any false, scandalous and malicious writing or writings against the government of the United States, or either house of the Congress . . . , or the President . . . , with intent to defame . . . or to bring them, or either of them, into contempt or disrepute; or to excite against them, or either or any of them, the hatred of the good people of the United States."[5] Jefferson and James Madison criticized the Sedition Act as unconstitutional, leading to the General Assembly of Virginia's passage of a resolution deeming the Sedition Act unconstitutional "because it is levelled against the right of freely examining public characters and measures, and of free communication among the people thereon, which has ever been justly deemed the only effectual guardian of every other right."[6] The Sedition Act's constitutionality was never tested in court, as Congress allowed the unpopular law to expire as Jefferson took office in 1801.[7]

Still, Jefferson also faced criticism from some journalists. Among the dedicated editors was Harry Croswell, a young Federalist who published the *Wasp*, out of the Hudson, New York, office of a larger Federalist newspaper. With a motto "to lash the Rascals naked through the world" and a pseudonym "Robert Rusticoat," Croswell proudly touted his willingness to sting with words. In his first edition, he noted that the *Wasp* "must therefore wade knee deep in smut before he can meet his enemies on their own ground."[8]

Two pieces in the *Wasp* would lead to his indictment for criminal libel. On August 12, 1802, the *Wasp* published "a few 'squally' facts," listing five actions of President Jefferson that the paper argued were unconstitutional.[9] "It would be an endless task to enumerate the many acts . . . in direct hostility to common sense and the constitution, of which the 'man of the people' has been guilty—These are facts," Croswell wrote in the article.[10] The second *Wasp* piece attracted even more attention. It involved James Callender, who was prosecuted and convicted under the federal Sedition Act in 1800 for publishing a pamphlet that attacked the character of George Washington and John Adams. After his release from jail and a falling out with Jefferson, Callender alleged that Jefferson paid him $100 while he was writing the pamphlet.[11] Croswell eagerly reported these allegations and drew some scandalous inferences. On September 9, 1802, Croswell published in the *Wasp*: "The charge is explicitly this:—Jefferson paid Callender for calling Washington a traitor, a robber, and a perjurer—For calling Adams, a hoary headed incendiary; and for most grossly slandering the private characters of men, who, he well knew were virtuous. These charges, not a democratic editor has yet dared, or ever will dare to meet in an open [and] manly discussion."[12] Jefferson had denounced Callender's pamphlet and argued that any gifts that he had provided were only "charity."[13]

Croswell was indicted for criminal libel in the New York State Court of General Sessions in Claverack in January 1803. His indictment was not under the federal Sedition Act, but New York common law, according to a 1964 book, *The Law Practice of Alexander Hamilton*, which used primary documents to reconstruct key moments of Hamilton's career, including the *Croswell* case.[14] Representing the state was not the district attorney, as is custom, but New York Attorney General Ambrose Spencer, a Jefferson ally whom Croswell had criticized in the *Wasp*.[15] After a number of pretrial disputes, Croswell was tried before New York Supreme Court Chief Justice Morgan Lewis at state circuit court in Claverack on July 11, 1803.[16] Croswell's defense attorneys, led by William W. Van Ness and Elisha Williams, asked Lewis to defer the trial until they could secure the testimony of Callender, who could speak to the truth of the claims in the article.[17] Lewis denied the request for a delay, reasoning that under the English common-law rule, the main factual question for the jury was whether Croswell published the libel.[18] The limited role of the jury came from a 1784 English opinion by Lord Mansfield in the *Dean of St. Asaph's Case*.[19]

The case went to trial before a jury the next day. Spencer called witnesses to testify as to the "truth of the innuendoes," which involved not the veracity of the allegations, but merely whether the article was about Jefferson and called his character into question.[20] After the close of arguments, Lewis instructed the jury that they were only charged with deciding whether Croswell published the piece and the truth of the innuendoes. The next morning, the jury returned a guilty verdict.[21] Croswell's lawyers asked the New York Supreme Court for a new trial, arguing both that the jury instructions were incorrect and that Croswell should have been able to introduce evidence of truth.[22]

The New York Supreme Court heard arguments on February 13 and 14, 1804. Lewis presided as chief justice, along with Justices James Kent, Brockholst Livingston, and Smith Thompson. Spencer had since been appointed to the state supreme court but did not hear the case (presumably because he had argued it at trial).[23] Although he was a sitting judge, Spencer argued the appeal for the government along with George Caines. Croswell's lawyers were Van Ness, Richard Harison, and Hamilton.[24] A primary goal of Croswell's defense was to argue that the *Dean of St. Asaph's Case* rule was incorrect, and that the jury had a far broader role in evaluating whether the publication was libelous.[25]

Prosecutor Caines argued that Lewis did not err in refusing to delay the trial for Callender's testimony, as evidence of truth was irrelevant in a libel defense. Indeed, Mansfield himself supposedly said, "the greater the truth, the greater the libel," the proposition that the accuracy of a statement can make it *more* defamatory because of the harm that it causes.[26] Under this rule, Caines argued, Callender's testimony on whether Jefferson actually paid him to write the comments about Washington would not help Croswell's defense. "The falsity therefore of the allegation is no part of the crime, because a truth may have the same effect, and having the same effect, is the same crime against which it is meant to guard," Caines said. "If then the falsity be not the offence, the truth cannot be the justification: for defences, like remedies, operate by contraries."[27]

Hamilton was the last of the five attorneys to present arguments to the New York Supreme Court. He focused on the need to protect the publisher's ability to publish truthful statements. "The Liberty of the Press consists, in my idea, in publishing the truth, from good motives and for justifiable ends, though it reflect on government, on magistrates, or individuals," Hamilton told the court. "If it be not allowed, it excludes the privilege of canvassing men, and our rulers."[28] Hamilton questioned the rule of the *Dean of St. Asaph's Case*, worrying that preventing the jury from considering evidence of truth could lead to abuse from appointed judges. "Let me ask whether it is right that a permanent body of men, appointed by the executive, and, in some degree, always connected with it, should exclusively have the power of deciding on what shall constitute a libel on our rulers, or that they shall share it, united with a changeable body of men, chosen by the people," Hamilton said.[29]

Hamilton urged the justices to reject Lord Mansfield's conclusion that criminal intent is enough to constitute criminal libel. "How can that be in itself criminal, which admits of a lawful excuse?" Hamilton asked. "Trespass is not in itself innocent," Hamilton analogized. "No man has a right to enter another's land or house. Yet it becomes in this latter case felony only in one point of view, and whether it shall be holden in that point, is a subject of Jury determination."[30] Under the common law that existed before Lord Mansfield's ruling, "the assertion of truth cannot be a crime," and "falsehood must be the evidence of the libel," Hamilton argued.[31] Hamilton pointed to a

1702 English criminal libel case, *Rex v. Fuller*, in which Hamilton said the judge "at every breath asked him, can you prove the truth[?]"[32] Hamilton was not arguing for all truthful statements to be immune from criminal libel prosecutions. He limited his arguments to defending truthful statements that were made "from good motives" and "for justifiable ends." This is known as the "truth plus" standard.[33] Under this interpretation, a defendant still could be held criminally liable for truthful statements if they were made with bad motives. But truth plus is more speech protective than the Star Chamber approach, which did not even allow the jury to consider truth as evidence.

Because Spencer—who had argued for the prosecution—would not decide the case, only four justices remained to vote as to whether to order a new trial. Chief Justice Lewis—who presided over the trial—was a fairly certain vote for the prosecution. That meant that all three remaining justices—Kent, Livingston, and Thompson—needed to vote in Croswell's favor to afford a new trial. Kent was a Federalist who was likely to vote in Croswell's favor, but Thompson and Livingston were both Jefferson allies.[34] Still, Kent at first seemed to convince Livingston and Thompson to support a new trial. But Lewis persuaded Livingston to reverse his vote, resulting in a 2–2 decision and a denial of a new trial for Croswell. Although this meant that Spencer and his prosecutors could have sought a judgment in Croswell's case, the dispute had kicked up such a public storm that they quietly dropped the case.[35]

The effect of Croswell's prosecution came not from the ultimate result, but the reasoning that Hamilton presented and Kent explained in his opinion in the case. Central to Kent's reasoning was that evidence of truth can help determine whether the defendant spoke with "malicious intent," which is a required element of criminal libel. "To shut out wholly the inquiry into the truth of the accusation, is to abridge essentially the means of defence," Kent wrote.[36] He emphasized that truth was not a defense in all types of libel charges, writing that "this doctrine will not go to tolerate libels upon private character,

or the circulation of charges for seditious and wicked ends, or to justify exposing to the public eye one's personal defects or misfortunes."[37]
After thoroughly describing English libel cases that supported his
point, Kent suggested that American law should place an even greater
emphasis on press freedom. "In England, they have never taken notice of the press in any parliamentary recognition of the principles of
the government, or of the rights of the subject, whereas the people
of this country have always classed the freedom of the press among
their fundamental rights," Kent wrote, pointing to statements of the
first American Congress, New York's Convention, and the US Constitution. The 1798 federal Sedition Act, he added, allowed the presentation of evidence of truth.[38] "And it seems impossible that they
could have spoken with so much explicitness and energy, if they had
intended nothing more than that restricted and slavish press, which
may not publish anything, true or false, that reflects on the character
and administration of public men," Kent wrote.[39]

Lewis wrote that after exhaustively reviewing English cases, he
could "now pronounce, with confidence, that it ever has been invari-
ably, and still is, the law of *England*, that the truth cannot be given in
evidence, as a justification in a criminal prosecution for a libel, at common law."[40] Lewis acknowledged that many have questioned whether
this rule is correct, and that even he'd had doubts. "But on reflection,
I have discarded the opinion, satisfied that truth may be as dangerous
to society as falsehood, when exhibited in a way calculated to disturb
the public tranquility, or to excite to a breach of the peace," he wrote.[41]

Although the New York Supreme Court's 2–2 split effectively prevented Croswell from receiving a new trial, Kent's opinion—based on
Hamilton's reasoning—was more enduring. The year after the split
opinion, William Van Ness, Hamilton's co-counsel and also a member of the New York State Assembly, persuaded the state legislature
to pass a criminal libel law that, among other things, allows a defendant "to give evidence, in his defence, [of] the truth of the matter
contained in the publication charged as libellous: *provided always*[,]

that such evidence shall not be a justification, unless, on the trial, it shall further be made satisfactorily to appear that the matter charged as libellous, was published with good motives and for justifiable ends."[42] The New York Constitution now contains a similar provision.[43] In other words, New York codified Hamilton's "truth plus" standard, ensuring that juries can consider truth but leaving the door open to criminal libel prosecutions for some truthful statements, if not made with good motives or for justifiable ends.

Throughout the 1800s, many other states passed laws that allowed for truth as a defense in both criminal and civil libel cases.[44] As First Amendment scholar Kyu Ho Youm wrote, *People v. Croswell* placed "an indelible mark upon the American libel law" and "gave truth an undenied prominence and relevancy as a defense to criminal libel."[45] Likewise, Marc A. Franklin wrote that *Croswell* "signaled the beginning of the end for the inadmissibility of truth."[46] Hamilton's arguments in Croswell's defense helped establish a value that we now take for granted: that the legal system values truth. Although Hamilton did not call for truth to be an absolute defense, his arguments and the later state legislation emphasized the role that truth must play in determining whether a defendant is guilty. More than 200 years after Croswell's trial, many states have repealed their criminal libel statutes. About 15 still have such laws on the books, but they are "rarely used," according to a comprehensive 2015 study by the International Press Institute.[47]

Libel disputes arise far more often in the civil context. Even in the 1700s and 1800s, courts in England and the United States were far more likely to recognize truth as a defense in civil defamation actions than in criminal cases.[48] And as the US Supreme Court provided constitutional protections in defamation cases beginning with *New York Times v. Sullivan* and extending to *Philadelphia Newspapers v. Hepps*, the plaintiff took on the burden of proving falsity (rather than the defendant having the burden of demonstrating truth).[49] In the years following *Croswell*, courts and legislatures did not devote much discussion to precisely what role truth would play in civil libel cases.[50] How much falsity would the common law tolerate?

The answer is in a concept known as "substantial truth."

Some truths are easier to identify than others. Consider this claim: "The last name of the author of this book contains seven letters." There is little room to argue that Kosseff contains anything but seven letters: K-O-S-S-E-F-F. Therefore it is a true statement. Now consider another statement: "The United States of America consists of only 24 states." That is not true, based on our knowledge of the geographic and political composition of the United States.

Yet even statements that are widely understood as true can be attacked for some ambiguities, such as this claim: "George Washington was the first American president." This is generally accepted as a true statement, as George Washington was the first president elected under the framework of the US Constitution. Yet during the First and Second Continental Congresses, starting in 1774, six men, beginning with Peyton Randolph of Virginia, held the largely ministerial title of "president." And beginning in 1781, after independence, and lasting for nearly eight years under the Articles of Confederation, ten men, beginning with Samuel Huntington of Connecticut, served as president of the Confederation Congress, also performing mostly ministerial functions.[51] Saying that George Washington was the "first American president" could be true if you interpret the statement to only mean the president under the Constitution that was ratified in 1788. But if you were to interpret "first American president" to include the leaders under the Continental Congress or Confederation Congress, the statement would not be true. A statement that is less susceptible to such challenges would be "George Washington was the first president of the United States of America," using the terminology from Article II of the Constitution.

Some statements may be objectively untrue, but courts may deem the error alone not enough to require a legal remedy. The line is not always clear. Imagine a newspaper reporting that a bank manager was indicted for allegedly embezzling $5 million, but in reality, the indictment claimed that he had only embezzled $4.8 million. Let's say that the manager sues the newspaper for defamation. Could the newspaper successfully argue that its reporting was true? What if he had only embezzled $4.2 million? $2 million? What if he was charged for embezzling $5 million but not yet indicted?

US courts have gradually come to protect not only precise truth in defamation cases, but also substantial truth. Judges have recognized that absolute precision often is impossible or impractical, and will avoid holding speakers liable as long as the "gist or sting" is substantially true.[52] The substantial truth doctrine stems in part from an understanding that errors are inevitable, and that the harms caused by minor discrepancies do not outweigh the chilling effect on speech that would arise if speakers were held to a standard of precision.

An early articulation of the substantial truth doctrine arose from a tragedy on May 31, 1889. The South Fork dam protected Johnstown, Pennsylvania, from the waters of Lake Conemaugh, a mile wide, two miles long, and sixty feet deep. That afternoon, the dam failed, and the entire city shook as debris and water swept across communities. The flood destroyed four square miles of Johnstown's downtown, and 2,209 died. More than 100 newspapers and magazines globally sent journalists to Johnstown to document the aftermath.[53] Among those publications was the *Pittsburg Times*. In its June 6, 1889, edition, the newspaper told the story of Joseph Jackson, a National Guard first lieutenant who was deployed to Johnstown in the wake of the flood.

Two *Times* correspondents reported that they observed a drunken Jackson, leaning on two younger privates and crying, "You just take me to a place, and I'll drink soft stuff." The correspondents reported that Jackson rebuffed the privates' requests for him to head back to the regimental quarters and "went staggering down the road to the line," where he encountered Peter Fitzpatrick, a local deputy sheriff who lost his family in the flood. The newspaper reported that Fitzpatrick told

Jackson that he could not pass through while drunk. Another man tried to help Fitzpatrick block Jackson, and a conflict arose between the men, according to the paper. The correspondent wrote that Fitzpatrick blocked Jackson from reaching for his pistol. "Then the privates got around him and begged him, one of them with tears in his eyes, not to report their officer, saying that he was a good man when he was sober," the paper reported. Fitzpatrick told them that if Jackson "does not go at once to his quarters, I'll take him there, dead or alive," the paper reported.[54] In the next few days, the newspaper published additional articles.[55] A colonel heard testimony from the newspaper correspondents, as well as women who testified on behalf of Jackson that he was not drunk. The colonel reportedly said, "Lieutenant Jackson will either have to stand a court-martial or resign his commission. One thing is certain, he can't remain in the regiment."[56]

Jackson sued the newspaper for libel in the Court of Common Pleas for Allegheny County. Although Jackson acknowledged that he had consumed alcohol, he objected to the paper's characterization that he was drunk. Jackson noted that there was no man named Fitzpatrick at the scene; the sheriff's deputy was reportedly named Kelly. And although he did not dispute that he was relieved and placed under charges, Jackson said he had not been arrested and his sword was not taken from him.[57] The case was tried in the courtroom of Judge Frederick Hill Collier, a former district attorney who had been a colonel in the Federal Army and was wounded in Gettysburg, later practicing law at a private firm and winning election to the bench in 1869.[58]

In his instructions to the jury, Collier said that the correspondents "had a perfect right" to present an account of the events that is "reasonably correct; not in every word, that is impossible; not in every particular, but, as to the substance they have a right to give a reasonably true and correct account of what they see and know there."[59] Collier told the jury that the article need not perfectly capture all the details, and instead the question was whether the articles were "a substantially true account of what happened there."[60] For instance, Collier emphasized that Jackson admitted to the truth of much of the newspaper reporting: "that he was under the influence of liquor; had taken four drinks of whisky that day while in uniform, as soon as he came there; that he had a scuffle with these people, and one of them struck him; that there were charges preferred against him; and that he was relieved." The newspaper could not be expected to be "correct in every word," Collier said, because "nobody could conduct a paper if that were so."[61]

The jury returned a verdict for the newspaper, and Jackson appealed to the Pennsylvania Supreme Court. The court voted to affirm Collier's instructions to the jury and the verdict. Writing for a unanimous court, Justice Henry Green summarized the evidence of the altercation and its aftermath, including Jackson's whiskey consumption and the punishments imposed on him. Although Jackson was never tried, Green wrote, his behavior was "certainly not that of a prudent and sober person," and the jury's finding for the newspaper was reasonable.[62] "It is true that in some particulars the statements in the published articles were exaggerated and sensational in their character, after the reprehensible manner of many, though not all, of the newspapers of the present day, but the effect of that kind of comment was fairly left to the jury as evidence of malice, and it was their function to decide upon its effect in the cause," Green wrote.[63]

Both Collier and Green recognized that the newspaper articles were not entirely accurate. But as long as the reporting was a substantially true and fair depiction of the altercation and aftermath, the judges concluded that the newspapers could not be held liable. Underlying both judges' statements was an assumption that perfect accuracy often is not attainable. The judges expected the newspaper reports to contain some inaccuracies, as some "truth" is on a sliding scale. Whether Jackson was drunk after consuming four whiskeys might be subject to some debate. Yet some of the alleged inaccuracies, such as the last name of the sheriff's deputy and whether Jackson had been arrested, are verifiable.

But even if some details were provably false, the judges were reluctant to impose liability unless those falsities made the general gist of the piece false. There was no dispute over the general gist: Jackson had been drinking, he got into an altercation with a sheriff's deputy, and he faced consequences with the National Guard. How far could speakers stray from the truth before they faced some liability for their statements? Courts would gradually set the boundaries for the substantial truth doctrine.

One of the highest-profile articulations of the rule involved a publication 110 years after the flood, 350 miles to the northwest of Johnstown.

In 1999, Marshall Bruce Mathers III, a 26-year-old from the Detroit area, suddenly became a household name. Better known as Eminem, his album *The Slim Shady LP* was released on Dr. Dre's record label in February 1999 and would sell more than 5 million copies in the United States alone.[64] Although the single "My Name Is" would get the most airplay, a lesser-known song on the album would land Mathers in court. In "Brain Damage," Mathers rapped about head injuries that he suffered at the hands of bullies while in school in Roseville, Michigan. The relevant lyrics from the song are as follows.

> Way before my baby daughter Hailie
> I was harassed daily by this fat kid named DeAngelo Bailey
> An eighth grader who acted obnoxious, 'cause his father boxes
> so every day he'd shove me in the lockers
> One day he came in the bathroom while I was pissin'
> And had me in the position to beat me into submission
> He banged my head against the urinal 'til he broke my nose
> Soaked my clothes in blood, grabbed me and choked my throat
> I tried to plead and tell him we shouldn't beef
> But he just wouldn't leave
> He kept chokin' me and I couldn't breathe
> He looked at me and said, "You gonna die, honky!"
> The principal walked in and started helpin' him stomp me

(*What's going on in here?*)

I made 'em think they beat me to death

Holdin' my breath for like five minutes before they finally left

Then I got up and ran to the janitor's storage booth

Kicked the door hinge loose and ripped out the four-inch screws

Grabbed some sharp objects, brooms and foreign tools

This is for every time you took my orange juice

Or stole my seat in the lunchroom and drank my chocolate milk

Every time you tipped my tray and it dropped and spilt

I'm getting you back, bully, now once and for good

I cocked the broomstick back and swung hard as I could

And beat him over the head with it 'til I broke the wood

Knocked him down, stood on his chest with one foot

Made it home, later that same day

Started readin' a comic, and suddenly everything became gray

I couldn't even see what I was tryin' to read

I went deaf and my left ear started to bleed

My mother started screamin', "What are you on, drugs?!

Look at you, you're gettin' blood all over my rug!" (I'm sorry)

She beat me over the head with the remote control

Opened a hole and my whole brain fell out of my skull[65]

Two months after the album's release, *Rolling Stone* published an article in which Mathers confirmed that DeAngelo Bailey was not a fictional character. "Motherfucker used to beat the shit out of me," Mathers was quoted as telling the magazine. "I was in fourth grade and he was in sixth. Everything in the song is true: One day he came in the bathroom, I was pissing, and he beat the shit out of me. Pissed all over myself. But that's not how I got really fucked up."[66] Mathers recalled to the magazine an incident at recess where Mathers had taunted one of Bailey's friends and said that Bailey "came running from across the yard and hit me so hard into this snowbank that I blacked out." The magazine reported that Mathers went to the hospital after his ear was bleeding, and quoted Mathers's mother saying that Mathers suffered a cere-bral hemorrhage and sporadically lost consciousness over five days.[67]

Bailey also spoke with *Rolling Stone* for the article. "He was the one we used to pick on," the magazine quoted Bailey as saying. "There was a bunch of us that used to mess with him. You know, bully-type things. We was having fun. Sometimes he'd fight back—depended on what mood he'd be in." The magazine asked about Mathers's story about going to the hospital, and Bailey reportedly told the journalist, "Yeah, we flipped him right on his head at recess. When we didn't see him moving, we took off running. We lied and said he slipped on the ice. He was a wild kid, but back then we thought it was stupid. Hey, you have his phone number?"[68] In the months after the album's release, Bailey thought it was "cool" that his name was in a rap song, told friends about it, and allowed publications to photograph him.[69] But his atti-tude about the song changed after he became the subject of jokes, such as being called an "old fat bully."[70] In August 2001, Bailey sued Mathers over both the song and the magazine article. At the time, Bailey had four children, none of whom lived with him, and was collecting trash for the city of Detroit.[71] The lawsuit claimed not defamation but a re-lated tort called false light invasion of privacy, in which the plaintiff claims that the "defendant broadcast to the public in general, or to a large number of people, information that was unreasonable and highly objectionable by attributing to the plaintiff characteristics, conduct, or beliefs that were false and placed the plaintiff in a false position."[72] The substantial truth doctrine applies to false light claims just as it does to defamation.

In a deposition for the case, Bailey recounted a different version of events than was depicted in the song. Bailey attended Dort Elemen-tary School with Mathers for one year, while Bailey was in sixth grade and Mathers was in fourth. When asked by Mathers's lawyer whether he "picked on" Mathers, Bailey said that he and his friends "joked" with Mathers. Bailey said that his friends did "bully-type things" such as pushing him down, and that Bailey "was just with them." When asked if he ever touched Mathers, Bailey said, "I might have bumped him or something. I mean actually physically hurt him, no."[73] But Bailey denied ever bumping into Mathers in the bathroom or hitting Mathers with his hand. Bailey said that it was his friend—and not Bailey—who flipped Mathers on the ice, but that Bailey did in fact lie and say that Mathers had slipped on the ice. Bailey said that he never threatened to kill Mathers.[74]

Mathers recalled a different version of events when he was deposed for the case, though his recollection did not hew directly to the song's lyrics. Mathers acknowledged that Bailey was not an eighth grader at the time, as his song claimed. Mathers also acknowledged that he did not know with certainty that Bailey's father boxes but said that "it was a rumor in the school."[75]

As to the song's claim that Bailey shoved Mathers into lockers each day, Bailey's attorney, Nicholas Hantzes, noted to Mathers that the elementary school did not have lockers. "Probably walls," Mathers replied.[76] Mathers said that the song's story about Bailey beating him in the bathroom was true "except for I don't know if he broke my nose, but it hurt."[77]

Mathers said that his only evidence of the bathroom incident was his own recollection. "I never went home and told anybody about that, my mother, because I knew my mother would go up to the school and he would just beat my ass worse," Mathers said.[78]

Mathers explained that the snowbank incident discussed in the magazine article—but not in the song—occurred after a friend of Bailey struck Mathers in the head with a snowball, causing Mathers to grab the child and push him against the wall. The child then told Bailey, Mathers said. "And DeAngelo came running, that's all I remember, came running, shoved me into a snowbank, and I remember blacking out for a little bit, I don't know how long," Mathers said. He went on to say that a girl named Angela woke him up.[79]

Hantzes pointed to Mathers's statement to *Rolling Stone* that "everything in the song is true."

"Are you disputing that you said that?" Hantzes asked.

"Disputing that everything in the song was true?" Mathers asked.

"Right."

"I was referring to being that there was a bully named DeAngelo Bailey that used to beat the shit out of me."

"But that's not what the song says," Hantzes replied. "The song says different than that."

"The song says, 'My mother beat me in the head with a remote control and my brain fell out of my skull,'" Mathers said. "So not everything in the song is—"

"True?"

"—true, right."[80]

Hantzes asked Mathers whether "it's a problem that you don't—that in the past you failed to differentiate between truth and reality in some of your songs?"

"Everything that I say in my music is not true," Mathers said. "Like everything, there's some things that are true, there's some things that aren't."[81]

Later in the deposition, Hantzes tried to get more clarity about some of the other statements in the song.

"And now the song also says that you retaliated along with the assistance of the principal against him," Hantzes said. "Is that part true?"

"That's ridiculous."

"Okay. So this whole part of the song here—"[82]

"Where I came back with the broomstick."

"Yeah."

"Yeah," Mathers said, "didn't happen."[83]

Mathers also said that Bailey had not taken Mathers's orange juice nor had Bailey tipped Mathers's tray, and that Mathers couldn't remember whether Bailey took his seat at lunch.

"Why is it that you didn't write about the incident that actually happened where you went to the hospital and you wrote in your song this thing that you never told anyone before until the incident on the playground?" Hantzes asked. "Why did you pick this?"

"Well, I could have kept it going, but in a song there's only so many bars you can do before—in a song you count bars and measures," Mathers said.

"Okay."

"If I would have depicted that it would have been a seven-minute song."[84]

Hantzes later asked Mathers whether it was fair to use Bailey's name in a song that contained some untrue statements.

"Yeah, I think it's fair," Mathers said. "You think it's fair he used to bully me every single day I came to class? The dude was twice my size. Do you think that's fair?"[85]

Besides the depositions of Mathers, Bailey, and others, the court record contains other evidence suggesting that the song might have been substantially true. Among the evidence was a 1982 negligence lawsuit that Mathers's mother filed on his behalf against the Roseville, Michigan, school district. The complaint alleged that Bailey attacked Mathers four times in 1981 and 1982. Among the allegations: On December 21, 1981, Mathers was "set upon, assaulted and battered by the same DeAngelo Bailey, inside a boys' restroom at said school, who did then and there beat, bruise, wound and ill-treat him," leading to injuries to Mathers's head, face, back, and legs. The lawsuit also alleged that a few weeks later, Mathers "was struck by a snowball containing a heavy object or piece of ice intentionally thrown at him by the same DeAngelo Bailey," and that Bailey then "beat, bruised, kicked, wounded, and ill-treated" Mathers while he was on the ground, leading to "severe and serious injuries," including a concussion and intermittent loss of vision and hearing.[86] In 1983, a judge dismissed the suit.

The song, Bailey's deposition, and Mathers's deposition and other evidence paint very different portraits. Yet there are at least some common threads among the different versions. We know that in the 1981–82 school year, Mathers was in fourth grade and Bailey was in sixth. We also know that Bailey's group of friends did "bully-type things" to Mathers. We know that Bailey had some level of physical contact with Mathers, though the extent of that contact varies greatly between Mathers's and Bailey's stories. Although Bailey asserts that Mathers's bathroom story is false, Mathers says that the injuries discussed in his song came from the recess snowbank altercation, which Bailey recalls (but says that he did not participate in). The 1982 complaint does not prove Mathers's version of the snowbank incident, but it does show that Mathers's mother alleged at the time that an incident involving Bailey had occurred. At the very least, there were some factual deviations from the incident as depicted in the song. The question for the court is whether these differences should trigger liability for Mathers, or if the substantial truth doctrine means that we must tolerate these inaccuracies.

The case went to Judge Deborah Servitto, a former Warren, Michigan, assistant city attorney who had served on the Macomb County state court for more than a decade.[87] After reviewing the evidence and the parties' arguments, Servitto granted summary disposition to Mathers, dismissing the case. Servitto issued an opinion on October 17, 2003, explaining her reasoning. In the lawsuit, Bailey claimed that four lines in the song placed him in a false light: (1) "so everyday he'd [Plaintiff] shove me in the lockers"; (2) "And [Plaintiff] had me in the position to beat me into submission"; (3) "he [Plaintiff] banged my head against the urinal 'til he broke my nose"; and (4) [Plaintiff] soaked my clothes in blood, grabbed me and choked my throat." Servitto wrote that she would only consider claims arising from lyrics that assert an "objectively verifiable event and provable as false." Most of those statements qualified, though the claim that Bailey beat Mathers into submission was "subjective," and the assertion that Bailey "broke" Mathers's nose might be viewed as a "figure of speech."[88]

For the factual claims, Servitto applied the substantial truth doctrine, which she wrote means that "the statement is not considered false unless it would have a different effect on the mind of the reader from that which the pleaded truth would have produced."[89] Servitto examined Bailey's deposition testimony, in which he acknowledged calling

Mathers names, bumping into him without consent, and being part of a group that did "bully-type things." She also considered that Bailey did not rebut many claims that Mathers made in his deposition, including that Bailey shoved him into walls.[90] "It is clear that the thrust or gist of the lyrics are that Plaintiff bullied Defendant, shoved Defendant into the lockers, and physically assaulted Defendant in the bathroom," Servitto wrote. "The uncontested facts demonstrate Plaintiff bumped Defendant in the hallway, did bully type things such as stealing Defendant's orange juice and knocking over his books, and was part of a group that assaulted Defendant. These uncontested facts demonstrate that Plaintiff essentially committed assault and battery on Defendant." Based on this analysis, she wrote, "a reasonable juror could not find that the facts as testified to by Plaintiff would have a different effect on the listener and/or reader of the lyrics contained in the song Brain Damage," and therefore the lyrics were substantially true. Servitto separately concluded that Bailey's statements and actions—including participating in media interviews—demonstrated that the lyrics were not "highly objectionable," a required element of false light claims.[91]

The opinion received significant media attention, and only partly due to the high profile of the defendant. In the final paragraph of the opinion, Servitto dropped a lengthy footnote that would place her opinion in a "universally understandable format."

> Mr. Bailey complains that his rep is trash
> So he's seeking compensation in the form of cash
> Bailey thinks he's entitled to some monetary gain
> Because Eminem used his name in vain
> Eminem says Bailey used to throw him around
> Beat him up in the john, shoved his face in the ground
> Eminem contends that his rap is protected
> By the rights guaranteed by the First Amendment
> Eminem maintains that the story is true

And that Bailey beat him black and blue

In the alternative he states that the story is phony

And a reasonable person would think it's baloney

The Court must always balance the rights

Of a defendant and one placed in a false light

If the plaintiff presents no question of fact

To dismiss is the only acceptable act

If the language used is anything but pleasing

It must be highly objectionable to a person of reason

Even if objectionable and causing offense

Self-help is the first line of defense

Yet when Bailey actually spoke to the press what do you think he didn't
   address?

Those false light charges that so disturbed

Prompted from Bailey not a single word

So highly objectionable, it could not be—

Bailey was happy to hear his name on a CD

Bailey also admitted he was a bully in youth

Which makes what Marshall said substantial truth

This doctrine is a defense well known

And renders Bailey's case substantially blown

The lyrics are stories no one would take as fact

They're an exaggeration of a childish act

Any reasonable person could clearly see

That the lyrics could only be hyperbole

It is therefore this Court's ultimate position

That Eminem is entitled to summary disposition[92]

To Servitto, it was sufficient that the evidence support the general
gist of the song: that Bailey had bullied Mathers. Even Mathers had
admitted that the song contained some departures from the events as
he had remembered them, but those differences were not large enough
for Mathers to face liability.

Bailey appealed to the Michigan Court of Appeals, arguing that Servitto was wrong to conclude that claims in the song and the magazine article were substantially true. "Since the Plaintiff has denied ever physically attacking the Defendant, it is impossible for the trial court to properly conclude that there was no question of fact as to whether the lyrics in the song 'Brain Damage,' and the statements in the *Rolling Stone* article were substantially true," Bailey's lawyers wrote in a brief filed with the appellate court.[93]

Although the appeals court did not use Servitto's colorful rhymes, the appellate judges affirmed her ruling for Mathers. Looking at the dictionary definition of "bully," the appellate court wrote that a "reasonable person could interpret the uncontested facts as indicating that plaintiff, individually and as part of a group, bullied defendant."[94] Both Servitto and the appellate judges agreed that Bailey's lawsuit failed because the song captured the general gist of the relationship between Mathers and Bailey, a gist that neither of them contested. To be sure, the accounts contained many discrepancies, and even Mathers admitted that some details about Bailey were false.

But our legal system tolerates those errors. Just as the Pennsylvania judges protected the *Pittsburg Times* despite its erroneous reporting about Jackson, the Michigan judges allowed Eminem to rap false allegations about Bailey, as long as the general story was substantially true. Why would our legal system allow Mathers to widely distribute a song that contains falsehoods about Bailey? Surely, Mathers is not a *Pittsburg Times* reporter who is documenting misbehavior of a member of the National Guard. Nor is he Harry Croswell, criticizing the most powerful person in the United States. Mathers is Eminem, one of the nation's most notorious musicians, mocking a Detroit sanitation worker to millions of fans.

Although Mathers is not a crusading journalist, he used his free speech rights to describe his experiences with bullying. In a *60 Minutes* interview more than a decade after the release of *The Slim Shady LP*, Mathers told Anderson Cooper that he had been bullied as a child and that rapping helped him earn respect.[95] By rapping about Bailey in "Brain Damage," Mathers conveyed his story to a wide audience, including children who may have been bullied. The substantial truth doctrine provided Mathers with the flexibility to tell that story. Recalling with precision every detail of bullying that occurred more than a decade ago would be challenging, if not impossible. And even if Mathers had precise documentation of the bullying he experienced in 1981–82, it is hard to imagine how he could fully and accurately convey every last detail within the rhyming structure of a rap. Even if Mathers wrote the song for a less noble reason, substantial truth protections would apply equally. The law does not grant free speech privileges only to those who are deemed sufficiently deserving of them. Such a system would allow courts—or legislators, or executive branch officials—to choose winners and losers. By establishing a baseline level of tolerance for minor inaccuracies across the board, the substantial truth doctrine provides speakers with the necessary breathing room to speak.

The substantial truth doctrine also underscores the reality that a consensus on one absolute truth is often unattainable. Recollections differ. Evidence disappears. People make honest mistakes. Oftentimes, the differences between accounts of an event do not matter much to the listener's general perception. The substantial truth doctrine also recognizes the difficulty of identifying one truth with complete precision. As the next chapter shows, courts also provide strong protections for statements that might seem likely to be false based on what we currently know at the time that they are spoken, but also have the potential of being vindicated as more facts surface.

Chapter 5

Uncertainty

The substantial truth doctrine protects defamation defendants by recognizing that it would be unrealistic and chilling to expect precise accuracy. Relatedly, in many cases outside the defamation context, defendants have been sued for publishing allegedly false information that has caused other harms, such as health problems. Courts often refuse to find publishers liable in such cases. They recognize that our understanding of truth evolves with knowledge, and knowledge evolves with time.

Imposing legal consequences through regulation, criminal prosecution, or civil liability is particularly challenging because a court or regulator may not have sufficient certainty as to the veracity of a statement at the time that the penalty is sought. More facts may need to surface, or there is little consensus over scientific methods. Oliver Wendell Holmes Jr. recognized this uncertainty in his famous 1919 dissent in *Abrams v. United States* when he wrote: "Every year if not every day we have to wager our salvation upon some prophecy based upon imperfect knowledge."[1] Philosopher Frederick Sontag traced the impact of Charles Darwin's work and other science on religious faith in concepts such as the existence of God. Sontag argued that Darwin's views still allowed for religious faiths but presented less certainty. Truth, Sontag argued, "should be divorced from an old, now-unreachable ideal of certainty. This does not mean that we must abandon truth to skepticism or to a debilitating relativism; we can maintain it as truth nevertheless, even though uncertain."[2]

The increasing willingness to recognize uncertainty illuminates the obstacles of regulation. It is one thing to merely deem a statement to be false; if the assessor is proven mistaken, they can reevaluate their claim of falsehood. But a government-sanctioned penalty—such as a fine, court verdict, or even imprisonment—can cause damage the minute that it is imposed, and reversing the damage often is difficult, if not impossible. The mere threat of legal consequences for speech that a government agency, legislature, or court deems to be "untrue" could prevent that speech from ever being uttered. Philosopher John MacFarlane has documented the realities of uncertainty in his many philosophical writings on "relative truth." He poses an example: the statement that "There will be a sea battle tomorrow." How do we evaluate that statement today? Do we say that it can neither be deemed true nor false, as we do not know today whether there will be a sea battle tomorrow? (MacFarlane calls that approach the "indeterminacy intuition.") Or do we evaluate whether the statement is true after tomorrow, at which point we will know whether a sea battle occurred? (MacFarlane calls this the "determinacy intuition.") MacFarlane argues that evaluating the truth requires consideration not only of the context in which the statement was made, but also of the context of the assessment and when the assessment is occurring. "It is failure to make room for this kind of context sensitivity that has left us with the traditional menu of unsatisfactory solutions to the problem of future contingents," MacFarlane wrote.[3]

Particularly when publications or broadcasts involve health and science topics, courts are willing to recognize that there may not be one enduring "truth," and acknowledge that our understanding of scientific truth and falsity evolves over time as we learn more. Among the most forceful articulations of this uncertainty came not from the US Supreme Court or a federal circuit judge. Rather, the principle is best voiced in a 1988 opinion from the Court of Common Pleas of Montgomery County, Pennsylvania, a small court on the northwest outskirts of Philadelphia.

The dispute arose out of *The Last Chance Diet*, written by Dr. Robert Linn and first published by Lyle Stuart Inc. in 1976. The book bills itself as a "protein-sparing fast program," which Linn wrote could help people lose up to 25 pounds in the first month. "Yes, stay on this protein-sparing fast and your weight loss can be twenty, fifty, one hundred pounds, whatever you need to lose," Linn wrote in the book's introduction.[4] People following Linn's diet consumed a prescribed liquid with amino acids that Linn developed called Prolinn, but did not eat any solid foods.[5] "There are no decisions to make," Linn wrote. "The decision not to eat—period—has already been made. There is no 'Well, a little of this won't hurt. I'll just eat less tomorrow.' You are not eating anything."[6] Linn warned that dieters must be under a doctor's supervision.[7]

Pennsylvania resident Patricia Smith bought the book in January 1977, and working with her doctor to follow the diet, lost more than 100 pounds. She died of cardiac failure in June 1977, and her family alleged that the death was due to the diet.[8] Smith's estate sued Linn, Lyle Stuart, her doctor, and companies involved with making the protein mix. By 1988, all defendants but Lyle Stuart had either settled or had their claims dismissed. The claims against Lyle Stuart arose from negligent publication, conscious and negligent misrepresentation, products liability, breach of warranty, and intentional infliction of emotional distress.[9]

The case against Lyle Stuart was heard by two Montgomery County judges: William W. Vogel, a former county commissioner who had served on the court since 1966,[10] and S. Gerald Corso, a former assistant district attorney.[11] After years of litigation and discovery, Lyle

Stuart asked Vogel and Corso for summary judgment dismissal of the lawsuit. In a September 30, 1988, opinion, Vogel granted the publisher's motion. As to the negligent publication and misrepresentation claims, Vogel wrote that he found "no cases that have directly held publishers liable based on the content of a publication."[12] Yet he cited many cases in which courts refused to hold publishers accountable for allegedly false or dangerous information. The First Amendment, Vogel concluded, applies to the publication of a diet book. "Clearly, *The Last Chance Diet* does not fall into any of the categories such as defamation, incitement, obscenity, fighting words or commercial speech which would lower the shield of First Amendment protection," Vogel wrote. "The First Amendment protects more than pure political speech, it protects speech on matters of public interest including political speech, science, morality and the arts, to name a few."[13]

Yet Smith's estate urged that the publisher should be liable because, before publication, a peer reviewer had warned that some of the information was "misleading and dangerous," according to Vogel. But Vogel rejected the idea that such claims overcome First Amendment safeguards. "The constitutional protection afforded to free speech is based on the idea that our society places utmost importance on the free flow and dissemination of ideas," Vogel wrote. "While acknowledging that certain ideas may be dangerous, unpopular or even harmful, the benefits to society in allowing an uninhibited exchange of ideas, even unpopular ones, far outweigh the ills such ideas might bear."[14] Vogel warned of the "Pandora's box" that such liability would open. "Placing publishers in fear of civil liability of an untold magnitude for publishing controversial, dangerous or even potentially harmful ideas would stifle the publication, broadcast and exchange of all but the most simplistic material," he wrote. "The fear of liability would eventually chill to a trickle the free flow of information so cherished by our society and protected by our constitution."[15]

That the peer reviewer disagreed with some of Linn's scientific claims, Vogel continued, should not increase the publisher's liability.

"Were publishers required to pick and choose between experts with regard to scientific publications (even those geared for the lay public), precious few scientific books or publications would reach the public," Vogel wrote. "Theories, especially scientific theories, frequently have groups of proponents and opponents. Often each claims the empirical data conclusively proves their theory correct and the other view inaccurate. It would be preposterous to relegate to publishers the responsibility of selecting the correct view."[16] Smith's estate appealed Vogel's ruling to the Superior Court of Pennsylvania, arguing that the book is "an incitement to immediate unreflecting action such as the action arising from shouting 'Fire!' in a crowded theater," an argument that the Superior Court swiftly rejected as "inapposite" when affirming Vogel's ruling.[17] Vogel was affirmed again in 1991 by the Supreme Court of Pennsylvania.[18]

Vogel's views from a 1980s dispute over a book apply with equal force to claims about medical misinformation on social media and the modern Internet. Throughout the COVID-19 pandemic, claims about the efficacy of masks or vaccines or social distancing proliferated on social media, sometimes contrary to what the scientific consensus was at the time. The unsupported claims were often dubbed "misinformation."[19] Yet under Vogel's reasoning, the First Amendment likely would prevent government regulation of such alleged misinformation. It is not for the regulators or the courts to determine the one absolute scientific truth. Such a task is often impossible, and it would chill discourse and scientific debate.

Our understanding of scientific truth evolves. Indeed, the COVID-19 pandemic was a lesson in the evolution of truth with time and data. In the earliest days of the pandemic, experts stated that COVID-19 spread mainly through droplets on surfaces and was not airborne. Public health advice therefore focused on washing hands and disinfecting surfaces.[20] As scientists learned more about the virus, the consensus on public health measures evolved.[21] Essential to the evolution in our conception of the "truth" about COVID-19 was the ability to have a free and open debate about the data. There is little doubt that some views might be better reasoned than others. Some views may sound objectively insane to anyone with background in the subject. Yet the First Amendment counsels strongly against using the force of government to ban or punish such analysis, no matter how misguided it is.

I found a copy of Linn's book and read it in one sitting. It advocates for what appear to be dangerous weight loss measures. In my layman's opinion, I cannot imagine that many nutritionists or physicians today would agree with such extreme measures. At least one expert in 1976 had concerns. And Smith's estate alleged that the diet led to cardiac failure. The dispute illustrates the nonbinary nature of the misinformation debate. The lawsuit arose not from a particular false statement of fact—such as an incorrect number—but from the allegedly false impression that the entire diet program was safe.

The Last Chance Diet is like so much information that is currently on the Internet and broadly dubbed "misinformation." Some scientists argued that the diet had questionable support, and it allegedly led to devastating health consequences for at least one reader. Indeed, some media reports have alleged that at least 60 people died after following *The Last Chance Diet*.[22] But three courts concluded that the First Amendment weighs strongly against the court system getting involved in the dispute over the veracity of the claims over this diet. The dismissal of the lawsuit was not a result of the court's assessment of the truth of the statements—Vogel did not even dare to make such an assessment. Rather, he concluded that the court has neither the ability nor the power to engage in such evaluation in the first place. Although Vogel's opinion in *Smith v. Linn* involved the claims against the book's publisher and not the author, law professors Dorit Reiss and John Diamond correctly noted that "there is a strong argument that some of the same concerns—that fear of litigation will lead creators of content to avoid publishing controversial materials, thus undermining vigorous debate on matters of public concern and the goals of the First Amendment—apply to authors."[23]

Smith v. Linn is not an outlier. For decades, courts across the country have hesitated to hold publishers responsible for information that allegedly led to tragic health consequences. Among the most prominent of such disputes stemmed from a mushroom-gathering excursion that Wilhelm Winter and his girlfriend, Cynthia Zheng, took on New Year's Day in 1988 in Marin County, California. They gathered about 60 pounds of mushrooms, and when they returned home, they sauteed some mushrooms and ate them with wine. But soon after, they both became sick, and the next day Zheng fell into a coma. Days later, they both required liver transplants. "I think another 12 hours and they'd both have been dead," their surgeon told the *Los Angeles Times*.[24] They had consumed the Amanita Phalloides, also known as the death cap, which is the deadliest type of mushroom.

Winter told the *Times* that he had long gathered mushrooms and used a book to guide him. "I relied on an encyclopedia, which is very elaborate," Winter said. "Either it let me down or I was being stupid. I haven't put my finger on it yet. But something went badly wrong because I normally don't eat mushrooms I don't know. I mean, I'm familiar with mushrooms and toadstools but this one I didn't know and I misdiagnosed it and that did it."[25] Winter was referring to *The Encyclopedia of Mushrooms*, which was first published by a British publishing company and then published in the United States by G. P. Putnam's Sons in 1979. The 280-page book, written by two plant biologists, contains hundreds of illustrations and descriptions of mushrooms that are found in the wild. "Strongly practical sections on habitat, collection and cooking are designed to help the mushroom-hunter and the cook know where and when to look for specimens, how to pick them and the most rewarding ways of preparing and cooking the edible species," the book jacket boasts.[26]

Winter and Zheng sued G. P. Putnam's Sons for negligence, negligent misrepresentation, false representations, breach of warranty, and products liability. The publisher asked the district court to dismiss the case on summary judgment, both because a book is not a "product" for the purposes of products liability and because G. P. Putnam's Sons did not owe a duty to readers of the encyclopedia.[27] Without determining whether Winter and Zheng actually relied on the book or whether it provided inaccurate information, the district court granted the publisher's motion. (The book does in fact include a picture of the Amanita Phalloides on page 168 with a long entry, starting with the statement that it is the "most poisonous fungus known to man," but the court did not need to wade into that factual dispute because it ruled that the publisher did not have any duty at all.)

Winter and Zheng appealed to the US Court of Appeals for the Ninth Circuit. They argued that a guidebook such as the encyclopedia is subject to products liability laws that ensure safety. "Books such as cookbooks, automobile repair guides, or guides to identifying mushrooms are not intended to be used merely as reading matter; they are intended to be used as reference tools in undertaking certain activities, and their content is designed to be relied on in undertaking those activities," they wrote in their brief to the Ninth Circuit.[28] The plaintiffs claimed that G. P. Putnam's Sons was misguided in arguing that the First Amendment bars products liability claims against book publishers. And like many others who sought to avoid First Amendment strictures, they turned to the crowded theater. "Application of First Amendment principles necessarily involves some balancing between the right of disseminating ideas, and the social cost of that dissemination, as exemplified by shouting fire in a crowded theatre," they wrote. "At issue here is the risk of inhibiting the dissemination of publications encouraging and instructing in the conduct of a potentially deadly activity by requiring that they be checked for accuracy or at least contain adequate warnings to the users. Balanced against this limited restriction is the protection of the purchasers of these publications from injury and death."[29] The plaintiffs argued that they stated claims under the other theories of liability as well.

The Ninth Circuit unanimously rejected this argument and affirmed the district court in a July 12, 1991, opinion. Writing for the three-judge panel, Judge Joseph Tyree Sneed III, appointed to the court by President Richard Nixon in 1973, wrote that products liability law is intended to hold manufacturers such as automakers strictly liable for dangerous products. While such liability for the written word might be tempting, Sneed acknowledged, the societal costs are different than imposing penalties for dangerous tangible goods. "We place a high priority on the unfettered exchange of ideas," Sneed wrote. "We accept the risk that words and ideas have wings we cannot clip and which carry them we know not where. The threat of liability without fault (financial responsibility for our words and ideas in the absence of fault or a special undertaking or responsibility) could seriously inhibit those who wish to share thoughts and theories."[30]

Sneed wrote that the plaintiffs were making an "illusory" distinction by suggesting that the court limit products liability to books that provide instructions on a dangerous physical activity. "Ideas are often intimately linked with proposed action, and it would be difficult to draw such a bright line," Sneed wrote. "While 'How To' books are a special genre, we decline to attempt to draw a line that puts 'How To Live A Good Life' books beyond the reach of strict liability while leaving 'How To Exercise Properly' books within its reach."[31] He acknowledged that some courts have found aeronautical charts to be subject to products liability law, but reasoned that such charts are "highly technical tools" and not comparable to a how-to book, which "is pure thought and expression."[32]

Sneed also rejected the plaintiffs' other claims, reasoning that publishers do not have a legal duty to verify whether their books are accurate. "A publisher may of course assume such a burden, but there is nothing inherent in the role of publisher or the surrounding legal doctrines to suggest that such a duty should be imposed on publishers," he wrote. "Indeed the cases uniformly refuse to impose such a duty. Were we tempted to create this duty, the gentle tug of the First Amendment and the values embodied therein would remind us of the social costs."[33] Sneed did not entirely rule out the possibility of liability based on the publication of false speech. In a footnote, he added that a "stronger argument might be made by a plaintiff alleging libel or fraudulent, intentional, or malicious misrepresentation, but such is not contended in this case."[34]

Had the Ninth Circuit imposed such a duty on publishers, it is unclear whether the outcome would have been any different, as the book did have at least some discussion of death cap mushrooms, and the plaintiffs would have the heavy burden of proving that their consumption of the death caps was caused by problems with the book. But the Ninth Circuit concluded that the First Amendment weighs against even forcing such an inquiry. Imagine if the Ninth Circuit had ruled differently, and publishers of how-to books were subject to the same liability as manufacturers of ladders and automakers. Publishers would need to review every possible scientific conclusion about the book's content and decide whether the book's author has gotten it right. While such an obligation might reduce the amount of unsupported claims in books, it also could be impossible given competing findings. The ultimate result would be a substantial chilling effect on speech, as publishers would fear the risk of making the wrong call.

Courts acknowledge uncertainty beyond instructional materials such as diet books and mushroom guides. The legal system provides speakers with wide latitude to take their best guesses based on available information. The law recognizes that many future events are unknown, and predicting them with certainty is difficult if not impossible.

Charles R. Cobb awoke early on June 1, 1997, and turned on the Weather Channel. Seeing no forecasts for bad weather or small craft warnings, the 58-year-old grabbed two life preservers and headed out for a fishing trip along the Florida Keys on his friend Mario Battistini's 12-foot aluminum boat.[35] The men were expected home at noon, but their failure to return by that evening prompted a sea and air search by the Coast Guard and Marine Patrol. The next morning, searchers discovered the washed-up bodies of both men. Cobb's family would later reveal that he was thrown from the boat during treacherous weather but survived for hours, thanks to his swimming and snorkeling skills, before drowning in the stormy seas. "With storms, going out in a little boat [such deaths] happen all the time," a Coast Guard spokesman told the *South Florida Sun-Sentinel.* "It definitely happens every year."[36]

Cobb's family and estate blamed the Weather Channel, suing the station for breach of contract, negligence, and gross negligence. The Weather Channel, the family alleged, "had information concerning the approaching adverse weather conditions but did not broadcast this information concerning Monroe County and the Florida Keys in a timely manner in order to allow effective precautions to be taken."[37]

Despite the tragic circumstances of his death—and the allegation that the Weather Channel provided a dangerously inaccurate forecast—a federal judge would ultimately dismiss the lawsuit, and an appellate court would affirm his decision.[38] While the lawsuit faced many problems, its failure highlights a primary reason that courts protect false speech in various contexts: Drawing the line between truth and falsity is difficult, often impossible, in the heat of the moment.

About a month after the lawsuit was removed from state to federal court in West Palm Beach, the Weather Channel moved to dismiss the claims. The station pointed to the "disastrous" impacts of holding it legally responsible for an inaccurate weather forecast. "Potentially every viewer of a hurricane forecast that inaccurately predicts where the hurricane will make landfall could sue the forecasters, recovering millions (or even billions) of dollars in hurricane losses," the station's lawyers wrote. "Those injured in a tornado or localized thunderstorm could sue the forecasters for failing to mention a localized disturbance on their national forecasts. Every viewer who watches television in the morning could seek recovery from the forecaster for omitting mention of a late afternoon storm that causes damage."[39]

Potential liability for failure to accurately forecast the weather, the station argued, could have a chilling effect. "Television stations would be forced to consider abandoning weather predictions," the station's lawyers wrote. "Networks such as the Weather Channel could determine to close up business rather than face potentially unlimited liability and burdensome litigation for allegedly failing to predict the future accurately."[40] Such chilling effect raises First Amendment concerns, they wrote, quoting from a New Jersey federal court's dismissal of an emotional distress lawsuit against a newspaper for inaccurate reporting: "Accuracy in news reporting is certainly a desideratum, but the chilling effect of imposing a high duty of care on those in the business of news dissemination and making that duty run to a wide range of readers or TV viewers would have a chilling effect which is unacceptable under our Constitution."[41]

The plaintiffs responded that a specialized cable television station that provides "crucial emergency information" should not receive the same First Amendment protections as some other media. And what if the First Amendment did apply to the Weather Channel? The plaintiffs' lawyers reverted to the old fallback argument for regulating speech: the crowded theater. "The comment of Mr. Justice Oliver Wendell Holmes could be recalled that you cannot yell 'fire' in a crowded theater because this creates a clear and present danger of a panic-related stampede and trampling of patrons," the plaintiffs' lawyers wrote. "On the other hand, if the theater is actually burning, does the management have the right to simply remain silent and not activate the fire alarm or fire extinguishing system[?] Likewise, if there is a clear and present danger of severe weather, can the Weather Channel merely remain silent and attempt to hide behind the First Amendment?"[42] Setting aside the obvious problems that the lawyers did not fully quote Holmes, the analogy falls short. In "falsely shouting fire in a theatre and causing a panic," the shouter in Holmes's hypothetical caused harm by sharing a falsehood. The lawyers for Cobb's family extended that logic to the Weather Channel's alleged *failure* to provide certain information that might have prevented the accident.

But should the Weather Channel be legally required to accurately forecast the weather? After all, a number of rapidly changing factors inform a forecast. The plaintiffs' lawyers argued that such an expectation is reasonable. "This is a very hi-tech 1998, not past years, and the Defendant is named *the* Weather Channel because there is no other organization or agency in its league," the lawyers wrote. "This case involves possession of vital information and remaining silent or simply not bothering to process and distribute available information as well as negligence in formulating its forecasts which is well within the Weather Channel's very advanced capacity."[43] But could the "very advanced capacity" of the Weather Channel be expected to provide a sufficiently precise forecast? And just how accurate is the forecast expected to be? We wouldn't expect the Weather Channel's high- and low-temperature forecasts to consistently be exactly the same numbers as those that are recorded. What about a difference of five degrees? Could the Weather Channel face liability if it rains on a day when the station predicted a 25 percent chance of precipitation? What about a 5 percent chance? In other words, how inaccurate can a statement be before the courts will impose liability? The judge deciding the case was James C. Paine, whom President Jimmy Carter appointed to the southern Florida federal court in 1979. Paine was known to local lawyers for his relative impartiality on the bench, though he received some attention in 1991 when he called for the legalization of some drugs.[44]

In a short opinion, Paine dismissed the Cobb family's lawsuit, reasoning that imposing such a duty would "chill the well established first amendment rights of the broadcasters."[45] An inaccurate prediction, Paine wrote, should not lead to liability. "Predicting possible future events whose outcome is uncertain is not an exact science for which a broadcaster should be held liable," he wrote.[46]

Paine was not the first judge to confront this issue. He pointed to a 1986 opinion from the US Court of Appeals for the First Circuit that reversed a judgment against the National Weather Service in a negligence lawsuit brought by the representatives of a fisherman who died in a storm. "A weather forecast is a classic example of a prediction of indeterminate reliability, and a place peculiarly open to debatable decisions, including the desirable degree of investment of government funds and other resources," the First Circuit wrote. "Weather predictions fail on frequent occasions. If in only a small proportion parties suffering in consequence succeeded in producing an expert who could persuade a judge, as here, that the government should have done better, the burden on the fisc would be both unlimited and intolerable."[47] In both cases, the plaintiffs at least brought credible claims that the deceased might have avoided their fates had the weather predictions better reflected what would actually happen in the future. The protections for predictions and forecasts are intended to create breathing space for scientists to use their best efforts to predict the future based on the information available. These safeguards implicitly recognize that some forecasts will be less accurate than others, and they implicitly accept the consequences of that inaccuracy.

Judges could have taken a different course, holding forecasters liable if their predictions caused harm. This likely would have led to fewer services like weather forecasts. Under such a legal regime, would the Weather Channel predict the weather to millions of viewers, knowing that the occasional incorrect forecast is inevitable? Judges are willing to provide forecasters with sufficient protection to avoid this chilling effect.

Relatedly, many of the statements that are dubbed "misinformation" are not statements of fact. They are opinions, sometimes based on questionable reasoning or factual assumptions. Throughout US history, dating to the hyperbolic colonial pamphlets, writers and speakers have freely, loudly, and sometimes dangerously hurled opinions and invectives to accomplish their political goals. While these opinions often leave much to be desired and can even lead people down dangerous paths, the law provides strong protection for opinions, as chapter 6 reveals.

Chapter 6

Opinion

Some of the most controversial speech does not purport to make a factual claim, though it may have dangerous consequences. Courts have provided broad protections for opinions, even if the subject of the speech believes that it is terribly unfair and could lead listeners to draw false conclusions.

American founders cautioned against laws that restrict the expression of opinions, even those that might be unpopular or against national interests. For instance, speaking out in 1794 against a House resolution that criticized Pennsylvanians for rebelling against a whiskey tax, then-congressman James Madison said on the House floor that "opinions are not the objects of legislation."[1] Even abhorrent opinions, the founders recognized, were a product of a free society. In an 1811 letter, Thomas Jefferson wrote that "to the principle of union I sacrifice all minor differences of opinion. [T]hese, like differences of face, are a law of our nature, and should be viewed with the same tolerance."[2] And by establishing truth as a defense in *People v. Croswell* and its aftermath as described in chapter 4, Alexander Hamilton paved the way for strong judicial protections of even controversial opinions. The First Amendment "presupposes that right conclusions are more likely to be gathered out of a multitude of tongues, than through any kind of authoritative selection," Judge Learned Hand famously wrote in 1943.[3] The US Supreme Court captured the tolerance for even abhorrent opinions in a 1974 opinion. "Under the First Amendment there is no such thing as a false idea," Justice Lewis Powell wrote. "However pernicious an opinion may seem, we depend for its correction not on the conscience of judges and juries but on the competition of other ideas."[4]

This willingness to allow the free flow of opinions has shaped US discourse. From the rancorous political pamphlets of colonial America to the yellow journalism of William Randolph Hearst and Joseph Pulitzer, media outlets have long sensationalized and blustered. Cable television news is perhaps the highest-profile modern journalism that relies more heavily on opinion than fact. With MSNBC and CNN on the left and Fox News, One America News Network (OAN), and Newsmax on the right, cable news viewers tend to watch and trust the channels most in line with their partisan beliefs.[5] Robust First Amendment protections have been key to this opinion-centric journalism.

The dichotomy between fact and opinion was key to a dispute that began with a July 22, 2019, article in the *Daily Beast* that reported that while he was a reporter for One America News, Kristian Rouz also freelanced for Sputnik News, which the Russian government finances. The article claimed that "Kremlin propaganda sometimes sneaks into Rouz's segments on unrelated matters, dropped in as offhand background information," and cited two examples to support its claim. The article also quoted a former Federal Bureau of Investigation agent as saying, "This completes the merger between Russian state-sponsored propaganda and American conservative media. . . . We used to think of it as 'They just have the same views' or 'They use the same story leads.' But now they have the same personnel."[6]

That evening, MSNBC host Rachel Maddow aired a three-and-a-half-minute segment based on the *Daily Beast* article. With an image of the article on the screen behind her, Maddow said:

> [P]erhaps the single most perfectly formed story of the day, the single most like sparkly story of the entire day is this scoop from reporter Kevin Poulsen at "The Daily Beast" who has sussed out that Trump's favorite more Trumpier than Fox TV network, the one that the president has been promoting and telling everyone they should watch and is better than Fox, turns out that network has a full time on air reporter who covers U.S. politics who is simultaneously on the payroll of the Kremlin. What?[7]

Maddow stated that "at the same time [Rouz] works for Trump's favorite One America News team, he is also being paid by the Russian government to produce government-funded pro-Putin propaganda for a Russian government funded propaganda outfit called Sputnik."[8] Maddow discussed the Russian interference in the 2016 US election and the role of Sputnik, and that Sputnik was registered in the United States as an agent of a foreign power. Maddow then stated:

> [A]mong the giblets the news gods dropped off their plates for us to eat off the floor today is the actual news that this super right wing news outlet that the president has repeatedly endorsed as a preferable alternative to Fox News. . . . We literally learned today that that outlet the president is promoting shares staff with the Kremlin.
>
> I mean, what? I mean, it's an easy thing to throw out, you know, like an epitaph in the Trump era, right? Hey, that looks like Russian propaganda. In this case, the most obsequiously pro-Trump right wing news outlet in America really literally is paid Russian propaganda. They're [sic] on air U.S. politics reporter is paid by the Russian government to produce propaganda for that government.[9]

Less than two months later, One America News owner and operator Herring Networks sued Maddow, MSNBC, and its corporate parents for defamation in California federal court. In its complaint, Herring acknowledged that Rouz, who was born in Ukraine, wrote freelance articles for Sputnik News, but that he "chose the topics and viewpoints of the articles" that he produced for Sputnik.[10] The complaint noted that Maddow is a liberal who is "obsessed" with conspiracies about Trump and Russia. "Her obsession is so pronounced that even other media outlets have called her out for her lack of journalistic integrity," Herring's lawyers wrote.[11] The crux of the complaint focused on Maddow's statement that One America News "really literally is paid Russian propaganda." In reality, Herring said, OAN "is not paid by the Russian government," and the network "has taken no money outside the Herring family whatsoever. None of OAN's content comes from the Russian government."[12] Maddow's statement, Herring wrote in the complaint, "amounts to a charge of treason and disloyalty to the United States of America."[13]

The case was assigned to Judge Cynthia Bashant, a former federal prosecutor whom President Barack Obama appointed in 2014. The defense was led by Theodore Boutrous Jr., one of the nation's top litigators. The defendants moved to dismiss the case under California's anti-SLAPP law (recall that SLAPP stands for "strategic lawsuits against public participation"), which allows early dismissal of lawsuits arising from defendants' exercise of their free speech rights, unless the plaintiff can show "that there is a probability that the plaintiff will prevail on the claim."[14] The defendants wrote that Herring will not succeed because the case arose from Maddow's expression of her opinion, and defamation lawsuits must hinge on a false factual statement.[15]

One barrier for such a defense is the 1990 US Supreme Court case *Milkovich v. Lorain Journal*.[16] The case involved a defamation lawsuit arising from an Ohio newspaper sports columnist's claim that a high school wrestling coach had lied about a fight at a wrestling match.[17] The Supreme Court refused to recognize "a wholesale defamation

exemption for anything that might be labeled 'opinion.'"[18] The court
reasoned that the relevant question is whether the speaker knew of particular facts that led to the statement. "If a speaker says, 'In my opinion John Jones is a liar,' he implies a knowledge of facts which lead to
the conclusion that Jones told an untruth," Chief Justice William
Rehnquist wrote for the majority. "Even if the speaker states the facts
upon which he bases his opinion, if those facts are either incorrect or
incomplete, or if his assessment of them is erroneous, the statement
may still imply a false assertion of fact. Simply couching such statements in terms of opinion does not dispel these implications; and the
statement, 'In my opinion Jones is a liar,' can cause as much damage
to reputation as the statement, 'Jones is a liar.'"[19]

Rehnquist outlined two ways in which a statement could be protected opinion. First, at least in cases involving media reporting on issues of public concern, statements must be "provable as false before
there can be liability under state defamation law." Second, statements
are opinion if they cannot "reasonably be interpreted as stating actual
facts," allowing breathing room for "imaginative expression" and "rhetorical hyperbole" that Rehnquist concluded "has traditionally added
much to the discourse of our Nation."[20] Rehnquist wrote that the Ohio
newspaper's article was not pure opinion, as it was "not the sort of loose,
figurative, or hyperbolic language which would negate the impression
that the writer was seriously maintaining that petitioner committed
the crime of perjury," and the "general tenor of the article" did not "negate this impression."[21]

The defense lawyers in the Maddow case argued that under the
Milkovich standard, Maddow's comments were pure opinion.[22] They
also urged the court to disregard Herring's focus on the word "literally," which the defendants said is mere hyperbole.[23] To support its position that Maddow's statement was a factual statement, Herring's
response included a 20-page analysis of the sentence by Stefan Th.
Gries, a linguistics professor. After an extensive analysis, Gries concluded that it is likely that "the broad overall and specific context of

the utterance and its specific linguistic characteristics would lead an average viewer towards considering the statement a statement of fact." His analysis relied heavily on the development of the use of the word "literally" and its "juxtaposition with *really*," which Gries concluded "would lead an average viewer to (i) adopt the strongest possible interpretation that the context (Maddow's contextualizing remarks) allows for and (ii) accept that as a statement of fact that Maddow emphasizes and to whose truth she strongly commits herself."[24] Herring also submitted a comment that One America News received via its website on the evening that Maddow's report aired. "You are a propaganda tool for Russian oligarchs," the commenter wrote. "True justice would be for everyone at OANN to be sent to the Russian gulag for 20 years."[25]

Because of the COVID-19 lockdown, Judge Bashant held a telephone hearing on the motion to dismiss on May 19, 2020. Bashant began the hearing by telling the lawyers that the real question in the case is whether Maddow's statement, when viewed in context, was one of opinion or fact. Boutrous urged Bashant to dismiss the case because the statement "was both true, and it's a classic example of nonactionable opinion based on truthful disclosed facts."[26]

Bashant asked whether Maddow's statement is "susceptible to different constructions," meaning that it is a question for a jury to decide. No, Boutrous replied, because it is a statement of opinion based on facts as disclosed in the *Daily Beast* article. Boutrous also challenged the plaintiff's claim that Maddow accused it of treason. "What the plaintiffs are trying to do is put words in Ms. Maddow's mouth," Boutrous said. "She did not say that they committed treason. Even if she had, it's in a rhetorical, hyperbolic way."[27]

Herring's lawyer, Amnon Siegel, challenged Boutrous's assertion that Maddow was merely stating an opinion. "I think the fundamental problem is that she does not make it clear that she's giving an opinion when she states very clearly and very firmly that One America News is really literally paid Russian propaganda," Siegel said. "That's not an equivocal statement. That's not a statement—it's not couched in any way. It's not framed in any way."[28]

When Siegel mentioned the linguistic analysis, Bashant interrupted him to say that the opinion was not "very helpful," both because she did not think she should consider such evidence at an early stage and because his statements were "largely irrelevant, frankly."[29]

Siegel replied that Bashant could consider the report at this stage of the litigation, and argued that Gries's report was important because "he says that the term 'really literally' based on his research almost always precedes an actually true statement."[30]

Siegel's arguments failed to persuade Bashant. Three days after the hearing, she issued a 17-page order granting the defendant's request to dismiss the case. Examining the "totality of the circumstances," Bashant concluded that Maddow's statement was one of opinion and not fact. Key to Bashant's ruling was the context in which Maddow supplemented the *Daily Beast* article with her "colorful" opinions. "Viewers expect her to do so, as it is indeed *her* show, and viewers watch the segment with the understanding that it will contain Maddow's 'personal and subjective views' about the news."[31] Bashant considered Maddow's laughter and statements such as "I mean, what?" to interpret the context in which she provided the commentary. "For her to exaggerate the facts and call OAN Russian propaganda was consistent with her tone up to that point, and the Court finds a reasonable viewer would not take the statement as factual given this context," Bashant wrote.[32]

Herring appealed the dismissal to the US Court of Appeals for the Ninth Circuit, the appellate court for the western United States. The judges hearing the case were Milan D. Smith Jr., an appointee of President George W. Bush who had written the 2010 opinion protecting Xavier Alvarez's right to lie; John B. Owens, an appointee of President Barack Obama; and Eduardo C. Robreno, a federal district court judge from Pennsylvania who was sitting on the Ninth Circuit by designation. The judges held virtual oral arguments on July 27, 2021.

Much of Siegel's argument was devoted to a back-and-forth with Judge Smith, who appeared skeptical. "I think you referred to her as a liberal commentator, and basically spinning things to the left and so on," Smith said. "Wouldn't that color how we and the 'reasonable viewer' should look at what was said? Wouldn't it be viewed as spin, if you will?"[33]

Siegel agreed that he had portrayed Maddow as liberal but did not think that converts the statement to one of opinion. "The context does not negate the impression that there, at that point, Ms. Maddow was making a statement of fact," Siegel said.[34] That Maddow "sprinkles in some commentary," Siegel said, does not change that conclusion. "So yes, Ms. Maddow's political views are relevant, but let's also remember her own statements are certainly relevant too," Siegel said.[35]

Judge Robreno noted that the "really literally is paid Russian propaganda" line was followed by a statement explaining the payments that the reporter received from the Russian government. "So what's wrong with that?" Robreno asked. "It's an opinion based upon a disclosed fact. Maybe the fact is wrong, but it is disclosed."[36] Siegel again cautioned against the assumption that the statement was one of opinion, pointing to ambiguity in the statement about the reporter.

Boutrous generally received more welcoming questions, and he used his argument time to stress the free speech values inherent in dismissing the case. "It's well within the breathing space of the First Amendment for Ms. Maddow or someone who was watching the show to say, 'You know, if you do that, you are Russian propaganda. I think you are Russian propaganda,'" Boutrous said. "Viewers could disagree with that and say, 'Well, it's different.' But that's a perfectly in-bounds opinion and observation here."[37]

A few weeks after oral argument, the panel unanimously affirmed the dismissal of Herring's lawsuit. Writing for the three judges, Smith concluded that because Maddow's statement was opinion and not fact, Herring did not show that it had a reasonable probability of succeeding.[38] In support of this conclusion, Smith pointed to the context of the remarks by Maddow, to whom Herring referred as a "liberal television host." Smith also considered the tone with which Maddow presented the segment. "Maddow's gleeful astonishment with *The Daily Beast*'s breaking news is apparent throughout the entire segment," he wrote. "Thus, at no point would a reasonable viewer understand Maddow to be breaking *new* news. The story of a Kremlin staffer on OAN's payroll is the only objective fact Maddow shares."[39]

Smith also concluded that Maddow's tone was hyperbolic and an "obvious exaggeration," supporting the argument that it was one of opinion: "In comparison to the undisputed facts that Maddow reports, the contested statement was particularly emphatic and unfounded: Maddow went from stating that OAN employs a Sputnik employee to stating that OAN reports Russian propaganda," Smith wrote.[40] Although Smith agreed with the district court that Maddow's statement, standing alone, was "susceptible of being proven true or false," on balance he concluded that the hyperbolic context supports a finding that Maddow's statement was one of opinion, and not the basis for a defamation lawsuit.[41] "Maddow's statement is well within the bounds of what qualifies as protected speech under the First Amendment," Smith wrote. "No reasonable viewer could conclude that Maddow implied an assertion of objective fact."[42]

Smith's ruling is in line with more than a century of precedent in libel lawsuits that arise from opinions. While factual claims are valid subjects of libel suits, generally critics cannot face punishment for merely stating their opinions. Of course, there is not always a clear line between a factual allegation and opinion. Maddow's commentary—though hyperbolic and politically slanted—may have left the impression with at least some viewers that OAN broadcasts propaganda that is paid for by the Russian government. OAN's argument that she should defend the merits of the defamation claim was not entirely unavailing.

Yet imagine the consequences if commentators could face lawsuits not only for false factual allegations but also for unpopular opinions. Politicians, companies, and so many others could stifle critics and often prevent them from even speaking. The opinion defense—while imperfect—provides critics with the breathing room to comment on facts and allegations without fearing ruinous defamation verdicts. Protecting opinions reflects a trade-off that tolerates some implications that might lead to false impressions.

The rationale that allowed Maddow to avoid liability for her comments about OAN extends beyond standard defamation lawsuits. In claims arising from disputed scientific conclusions, courts hesitate to second-guess scientists and may find that their conclusions are statements of opinion that are not subject to litigation.

Such a claim was the focus of a dispute that arose from a study of two leading types of nonhuman surfactants, which are biological materials used to line the lungs of infants who are born with deficiencies in natural surfactants. (A surfactant deficiency could lead to lung failure and death.)[43] Two of the largest makers of nonhuman surfactants, ONY Inc. (maker of Infasurf) and Chiesi Farmaceutici S.p.A. (maker of Curosurf), had long disputed which company's products were more effective. In particular, they disputed the relative mortality rates of each product, as well as the "length of stay," which is the number of days that infants stay in the hospital after receiving each surfactant.[44] Chiesi hired medical doctors to analyze and present data about the relative efficacy of Curosurf and Infasurf. At pediatric medical conferences in 2007, the doctors presented findings claiming that the mortality rate of patients given Curosurf was 20 percent lower than that of patients given Infasurf, and that the length of stay associated with Curosurf was 15 percent shorter than that of Infasurf. The doctors, working with a Chiesi employee, also published findings based on Chiesi's database in a September 2011 article in the *Journal of Perinatology*, titled "Mortality in Preterm Infants with Respiratory Distress Syndrome Treated with Poractant Alfa, Calfactant or Beractant: A Retrospective Study."[45]

ONY claimed that the article contains several inaccurate statements, including that Infasurf "was associated with a 49.6% greater likelihood of death" than Curosurf; that Curosurf treatment "was associated with a significantly reduced likelihood of death" when compared with Infasurf; and that this "large retrospective study of preterm infants with [respiratory distress syndrome] found lower mortality among infants who received [Curosurf,] compared with infants who received [either Infasurf or another competing surfactant,] even after adjusting for patient characteristics such as gestational age and [birth weight], and after accounting for hospital characteristics and center effects."[46] ONY also argued that by failing to include the length-of-stay data presented by Chiesi's researchers in 2007, the article masked the likelihood that the study was comparing patients with different health characteristics. (This is because factors that may cause the mortality rate to be higher may also lead to shorter lengths of stay, and vice versa.)[47] ONY claimed that one of the two peer reviewers recommended against publication, but the editor-in-chief of the journal ultimately decided to publish it.[48] Chiesi and the distributor and marketer of Curosurf, Cornerstone Therapeutics, highlighted the article in a press release. The journal denied ONY's retraction demand but published letters from ONY that rebutted the article.[49]

In December 2011, ONY filed a lawsuit in federal court in Buffalo, New York, against Nature America, which publishes the journal, as well as Chiesi, Cornerstone, and others involved in the research, asserting various state and federal claims relating to false and misleading trade practices and tortious interference with business contracts.[50]

The case went to Judge William M. Skretny, a former prosecutor appointed by President George H. W. Bush in 1990. In May 2012, Skretny granted the defendants' motion to dismiss the lawsuit. The state and federal laws involving false or misleading trade practice claims differ in scope, but all center on false or misleading factual assertions. Skretny reasoned that these causes of action do not apply to "statements of opinion," and ONY's claims "are based upon the conclusions of the authors published in an academic article in a scientific journal."[51] Similar to the dispute between OAN and Maddow, Skretny noted that key to resolving the claim is "whether the Article sufficiently states the facts on which these conclusions are based or whether it impermissibly implies that the conclusions reached are supported by additional information not afforded the reader." Skretny noted that the readers of peer-reviewed journals tend to be specialists in the field and generally understand the issues in the articles.[52] Evaluating the entire article, Skretny concluded that "the average reader would perceive these statements as debatable hypotheses rather than assertions of unassailable fact." For instance, the article's statement that Infasurf is associated with a "significantly greater likelihood of death" than Curosurf is a "non-actionable hypothesis based upon limited and articulated facts."[53]

ONY appealed to the US Court of Appeals for the Second Circuit, arguing, among other things, that Skretny incorrectly concluded that the "greater likelihood of death" statement was one of opinion. "Evaluated through the lens of the average reader, the Article clearly states that the use of Infasurf results in more deaths than Curosurf," ONY's lawyers wrote. "Indeed, the average reader would be surprised to learn that the authors of a scientific article are doing no more than expressing mere subjective 'opinion' based upon detailed (and presumably provable and reproducible) statistical analysis in reporting a 'greater likelihood of death.'"[54]

ONY failed to convince the Second Circuit that Skretny was incorrect. On June 26, 2013, a unanimous three-judge panel affirmed the dismissal. Writing for the panel, Judge Gerard E. Lynch acknowledged that "the line between fact and opinion is not always a clear one," pointing to *Milkovich*, in which the Supreme Court concluded that the columnist's assertion that the wrestling coach had lied was not one of pure opinion.[55] Lynch noted that science articles do not easily fit into the binary fact/opinion categories. "Indeed, it is the very premise of the scientific enterprise that it engages with empirically verifiable facts about the universe," Lynch wrote. "At the same time, however, it is the essence of the scientific method that the conclusions of empirical research are tentative and subject to revision, because they represent inferences about the nature of reality based on the results of experimentation and observation."[56]

Peer-reviewed academic journals, Lynch observed, make their authors' conclusions available to other experts, who can conduct further research and respond to those conclusions. "In a sufficiently novel area of research, propositions of empirical 'fact' advanced in the literature may be highly controversial and subject to rigorous debate by qualified experts," Lynch wrote. "Needless to say, courts are ill-equipped to undertake to referee such controversies. Instead, the trial of ideas plays out in the pages of peer-reviewed journals, and the scientific public sits as the jury."[57] Lynch did not completely rule out the possibility of liability arising from a claim in a scientific article. He noted that ONY did not allege that the researchers had fabricated the data on which the article was based. "Rather, plaintiff alleges that the inferences drawn from those data were the wrong ones, and that competent scientists would have included variables that were available to the defendant authors but that were not taken into account in their analysis," he wrote. "But when the conclusions reached by experiments are presented alongside an accurate description of the data taken into account and the methods used, the validity of the authors' conclusions may be assessed on their face by other members of the relevant discipline or specialty."[58] Lynch was not discounting the possibility of a highly flawed conclusion in a scientific article. But by broadly couching these conclusions as non-actionable opinion rather than actionable factual assertions, Lynch is recognizing the inability of courts to do a better job at assessing the veracity of scientific conclusions.

Like the Ninth Circuit in *Maddow*, the Second Circuit highlighted the importance of protecting opinions. Even though those opinions may not be terribly well founded, it is more dangerous for a judge or other government official to arbitrate which opinions are permissible. And as chapter 7 shows, courts also protect alleged falsehoods because they recognize that the speakers should only bear part of the responsibility for the harms stemming from their speech.

Chapter 7

Responsibility

As discussed in the previous two chapters, courts often are reluctant to adjudicate disputes about the veracity of speech. Courts do impose liability for false speech in some narrow situations, such as defamation, fraud, and perjury. But they also recognize that some factual claims are up for debate and ill-suited for adjudication or regulation. Courts also provide broad protection for opinions, even those that are terribly misguided.

A related rationale for protecting false speech is that courts expect the recipients of speech to exercise their own discretion. This concept was implicit in law professor Martin H. Redish's self-realization theory of free speech. According to Redish, this theory encompasses two interpretations: "development of the individual's powers and abilities" and "the individual's control of his or her own destiny through making life-affecting decisions."[1] While the theory focuses on speakers, it also considers the interests of the *recipient* of speech. With this approach, Redish writes, "the motivation of the speaker may be irrelevant, as long as the individual's faculties are developed by the *receipt* of information whether it be opinion or fact."[2]

Still, frequently in debates over free speech, the focus is on the obligations of the speaker. But underlying many rulings that protect allegedly false speech is the court's expectation that readers and listeners bear at least some responsibility for how they react to speech. This is particularly true when the claim involves not defamation or another reputational harm to the plaintiff, but an allegation that the defendant's false speech contributed to the plaintiff's decision to take an action that caused harm to the plaintiff.

In other words, should the speaker be fully responsible for all harms caused by their falsehoods? Or should the burden be on the consumer of the speech? To answer these questions, many courts look to a case involving an error made during the deadline pressures of breaking news reporting. Yet this mistake took place not on social media, a newspaper website, or even a blog. It occurred more than a century ago, on a news ticker service that Dow Jones & Co. provided to stock brokerages.

The investment world was eagerly awaiting the outcome in *Eisner v. Macomber*, a case in which the US Supreme Court was considering whether the Sixteenth Amendment allows the federal government to tax certain stock dividends. The outcome could have an enormous impact on trading stocks whose dividends are not paid out in cash but in more ownership of the company. That is why Newark, New Jersey, investor Gaston Jaillet acted quickly when this headline came across his broker's Dow Jones ticker service at 12:09 p.m. on March 8, 1920: "STOCK-DIVIDENDS—ARE INCOME WASHN—SUPREME COURT HAS RULED THAT STOCK DIVIDENDS ARE INCOME THEREFORE TAXABLE 12 09 PM."[3]

Stock and bond prices plummeted on the news, as investors—including Jaillet—sold quickly in reaction to the headline.[4] This was a logical reaction, as the Supreme Court's ruling threatened to boost the costs of holding certain stocks.

But there was a problem: the Supreme Court had actually ruled that pro rata dividends are *not* subject to federal taxation. As Supreme Court

Justice Mahlon Pitney wrote in the concluding paragraph of the majority opinion in *Macomber*: "we are brought irresistibly to the conclusion that neither under the Sixteenth Amendment nor otherwise has Congress power to tax without apportionment a true stock dividend made lawfully and in good faith, or the accumulated profits behind it, as income of the stockholder."[5]

Dow Jones issued a correction 45 minutes after its initial report: "STOCK DIVIDENDS NOT TAXABLE WASHN— ANNOUNCEMENT THAT THE LOWER COURT WAS UPHELD IN THE STOCK DIVIDEND CASE CORRECTS THE FIRST ANNOUNCEMENT THAT THESE DIVIDENDS ARE TAXABLE 12 54 PM."[6]

This correction was of little comfort to Jaillet, who said that his quick sales of stocks at low prices cost him $2,218.75 (the equivalent of more than $30,000 in 2022).[7] Two days later, he sued Joseph Cashman, in his capacity as treasurer of Dow Jones, for negligence. In the complaint, Jaillet's lawyers wrote that the *Macomber* decision "was of the greatest importance in the determination of the value of stocks, bonds and securities and said decision had been anxiously awaited for many months, and it was well-known to this defendant that its report thereof would have a material effect upon the stock markets of the country, wherein said stocks, bonds, and securities were dealt."[8] After Jaillet filed his lawsuit, Dow Jones issued a public statement that chalked up the error to the reporter's reading a complex court opinion on deadline. The reporter had prepared a bulletin before the ruling and would add the word "not" depending on the outcome. "The first impression that the reporter and many others received was that the lower court had been reversed, and therefore stock dividends were taxable, and the word 'not' was stricken out," the company wrote.[9]

Jaillet failed to persuade trial court Judge John M. Tierney to impose liability for this error. In May 1921, he dismissed the case, reasoning that Dow Jones did not owe a legal duty to present accurate information to Jaillet. Although everyone has a "moral obligation" to speak truthfully, Tierney reasoned, outside of particular cases such as breach of contract or defamation, the law does not create liability for false speech. "Theoretically, a different rule might be logically adopted, but as a matter of practical expediency such a doctrine seems absolutely necessary," Tierney wrote.[10] Tierney reasoned that Jaillet lacked "privity"—or a legally recognized relationship—with Dow Jones. "He is but one of a public to whom all news is liable to be disseminated," Tierney wrote. "His action can be sustained only in case there was a liability by the defendant to every member of the community who was misled by the incorrect report. There was no contract or fiduciary relationship between the parties, and it is not claimed that the mistake in the report was intentional."[11]

Jaillet appealed to the Appellate Division, New York's intermediate appellate court, which affirmed the dismissal without explanation.[12] He appealed again to the Court of Appeals, New York's highest state court. In their brief to the court, his lawyers emphasized that Dow Jones relied on its reputation for accuracy in selling its ticker service. "The defendant does not wish to assume the reputation of speaking lightly and in a manner which will not induce persons to act on the ticker's information," they wrote. "If it were the argument of the defendant that its service is not to be regarded with seriousness, it would not enjoy at the present time the attention of the financial world."[13] This esteemed reputation of Dow Jones and the widespread reliance on its ticker service, Jaillet argued, means that it should have a duty to readers under negligence law. "The reaction of the trader to a stock ticker report reduces his mental reaction to a mere instinctive purchase or sale on the strength of the report," his lawyers wrote. "Since the essence of the transaction on the stock market is speed, the reasoning process of the stock broker and the customer must necessarily yield to an impulsive decision."[14] Expecting the financial community to scrutinize every ticker service report for accuracy would destroy the value of the service, Jaillet argued. "In this respect it differs materially from an ordinary newspaper which boasts of no specialty in announcing technical news, and which the ordinary prudent man does not consult as a guide for his financial investments," he wrote. "The ticker's report would be then merely suggestive that some event had happened, leaving the exact result open to question."[15]

In its brief to the New York Court of Appeals, Dow Jones argued that the losses were caused by Jaillet's choice to sell the stocks. Jaillet's losses, the company wrote, are different from those of a plaintiff who was hit by a car. "It is simply a case where, the negligence of the defendant having created a false impression in the mind of the plaintiff, the latter proceeded to take affirmative and quite unnecessary action thereon, which action directly resulted in his financial loss," the company wrote.[16] Dow Jones focused on Jaillet's contributions to the harms that he alleged to have suffered. "Exactly how or why he lost money does not appear from the complaint, but a man who instantly sells his stock on an unverified advance report is on the face of things grossly negligent," Dow Jones wrote. "That his act was the cause of his losses cannot be doubted. Without his sales he would have suffered no loss."[17]

This was a matter of New York negligence common law, not a lofty constitutional case (the First Amendment did not even appear in the briefs, as the US Supreme Court would not incorporate First Amendment free speech protections to the states until 1925). The briefs of both sides were filled with centuries-old tort precedent, but they boiled down to whether the speaker should be liable for harm caused by indisputably false speech on which someone else relied. The New York Court of Appeals ruled for Dow Jones on January 30, 1923. It summarized the trial court's opinion in one paragraph but did not explain its reasoning for affirming.[18] Despite the lack of reasoning from New York's high court, Jaillet's unsuccessful lawsuit has been cited by dozens of courts nationwide, often involving troubling circumstances in which a plaintiff was seriously harmed by relying on allegedly inaccurate information. The result is almost always the same: protecting the speaker, with an implication that the plaintiff had the burden to avoid the harm caused by the false speech.

The headline stretched across seven of the eight columns of the front page of the April 12, 1932, *Albuquerque Journal*: "FORMER GOV-ERNOR CURRY DIES." The subheads below were just as clear:

SUDDEN DEMISE
AT HILLSBORO
SHOCKS STATE;
FUNERAL TODAY
Unpretentious Services,
Burial in Community
Cemetery, for Man Who
Was Prominent in N.M.
WAS ROUGH RIDER AND PHILIPPINE EXECUTIVE
Named Territorial Governor by President Roosevelt;
Elected to Congress at
First State Election

Below these headlines was a seven-paragraph Associated Press article, reporting that former New Mexico governor George Curry's death was "brought about by natural causes, though it came unexpectedly."[19]

George Curry was alive and well. But his son, Clifford Curry, said that he went into shock after reading the article and suffered a heart attack, rendering him incapable of working. Clifford's wife, Angelita, said that she also experienced physical shock after reading the article, and the child she gave birth to a few months after the article suffered injuries as a result of her shock. They sued the newspaper for $13,592.[20] The defendants moved to dismiss, arguing that the complaint did not allege that the newspaper knew that it was untrue, that the complaint did not allege that the newspaper intended to injure the Currys or acted with malice, and that the injuries should not have been anticipated. (It is not clear from the remaining court records how the substantial error ended up on the newspaper's front page.) The state trial court agreed with the newspaper and dismissed the case.[21] The Currys appealed to the New Mexico Supreme Court, pointing to the maxim *res ipsa loquitur*, the thing speaks for itself. "The defendants' publication of the untrue statement of George Curry's death was an act of negligence, ... unjustified, unexcused and unexplained by the defendants under the maxim 'res ipsa loquitur'; and such negligent wrongful act, wrongfully invading plaintiffs' right of security and resulting in injury to the plaintiffs, was a tort," the Currys wrote in their brief to the New Mexico high court.[22] They argued that they need not show an intent to harm or malice, and that the alleged damages "are such as a reasonable person ought to have anticipated might result" from the incorrect publication.[23]

These arguments failed to persuade the New Mexico Supreme Court, which unanimously affirmed the dismissal on May 3, 1937. Writing for the court, Justice Charles Rufus Brice began the analysis section of his opinion with long quotes from the trial court's opinion in *Jaillet v. Cashman* and noted that the two New York appellate courts affirmed the dismissal without explanation. "The New York courts evidently assumed that the legal principles supporting their conclusion that no such right existed, in the absence of a contract, fiduciary relationship, or intentional injury, were so well established that it was unnecessary to more than state the conclusion without giving reason or authority therefore," Brice wrote. "We might well follow this example; but appellant's exceptionally good presentation of their case, and apparent abiding faith that a cause of action has been stated, impels us to give our reasons for sustaining the judgment of the district court."[24]

Reviewing English common law and some early US court precedent, Brice concluded that speakers generally can only be liable for negligent falsehoods if they owe a duty of accuracy to the listener or reader.[25] "No attempt has been made by any American court, nor will be by us, to state rules which will apply generally to all conditions or circumstances, which will authorize a recovery for damages resulting from false words negligently written or spoken, and in the absence of contract, malice, intentional injury, or other like circumstance," Brice wrote.[26] Brice also looked to other courts that have held that emotional distress caused by negligent conduct generally only leads to liability if it was caused by the plaintiff fearing injury to himself, not out of fear of injury to someone else. "The same rule should apply to this case," he wrote. "The wrong, if any, was done to Governor Curry, not his relations or friends. That emotional distress may follow from acts of negligence it is quite apparent, but no more than to a mother who witnesses the negligent killing of her child, in which case the consequential damages cannot be recovered."[27] Unlike the judges in *Jaillet*, Brice acknowledged the free speech implications under the First Amendment and an analogous section of the New Mexico constitution. "The common law (and as we have seen, the English law of today) does not recognize, as actionable, injuries resulting from negligently spoken or written words," Brice wrote. "To what extent, if any, the liberty of the press and speech as we understand it, is involved, we need not decide."[28]

As courts took increasingly expansive views of First Amendment protections throughout the twentieth century, the *Jaillet* rule evolved from one of common law to a constitutional protection. This can best be seen in another lawsuit against Dow Jones, filed more than six decades later, in the same court where Gaston Jaillet sued the company. In 1986, Dow Jones's core business still was gathering and distributing news, but it had long since expanded beyond news ticker services at stock brokerages. About 200,000 people connected their computer modems to telephone lines and dialed up to Dow Jones News/Retrieval, which offered "timely" and "accurate" news for $3 per minute.[29] Among the subscribers was Elridge Daniel, an investor and law student at the time. On the service, he read about a Canadian oil company's restructuring and relied on the report. But the news item failed to note that the prices it reported were in Canadian dollars, he claimed. He alleged that omission harmed him, and he sued Dow Jones for negligence.[30]

The case went to Judge Lewis R. Friedman of the Civil Court of the City of New York, Special Term, a former Manhattan prosecutor who had recently taken the bench.[31] Dow Jones was represented by Robert D. Sack, a renowned media lawyer at Gibson, Dunn & Crutcher who would become a federal appellate court judge in 1998. Dow Jones moved for summary judgment, arguing that Daniel failed to state a valid claim. The case led to one of the first written opinions on record to address the liability of a computerized information service.

Friedman apparently recognized the importance of the case, beginning his opinion with commentary about the changes in delivery of information. "Early in this century, news, transmitted by radio and telephone, became available to subscribers through dedicated news tickers and to the public by 'extra' editions of newspapers," Friedman wrote. "Widely available radio and television made news known to the public within minutes of its occurrence. In the last few years, instantaneous news has become available to subscribers with access to a microcomputer and a telephone, even at home."[32] Daniel's claim, Friedman wrote, requires an assessment of whether these technological changes require new legal rules. "Do modern techniques for delivering the news change the rules applicable to its providers?" Friedman asked.[33]

He began his legal analysis by recounting *Jaillet*. "The rationale of the holding was that unless the scope of liability was limited, the publisher of news might become liable to an undefined, infinite class of news readers," Friedman wrote.[34] Since the *Jaillet* opinions, Friedman wrote, courts have continued to hold that speakers are not responsible for negligent misstatements unless they had a "special relationship" with the plaintiff.[35] Daniel argued that his contract for services from Dow Jones created this special relationship, but Friedman held that more than a mere purchase is necessary to establish a duty. "There is no functional difference between defendant's service and the distribution of a moderate circulation newspaper or subscription newsletter," Friedman wrote. "The instantaneous, interactive, computerized delivery of defendant's service does not alter the facts: plaintiff purchased defendant's news reports as did thousands of others. The 'special relationship' required to allow an action for negligent misstatements must be greater than that between the ordinary buyer and seller."[36]

Unlike *Jaillet*, which was dismissed based on tort common-law principles, Friedman's dismissal of Daniel's claims also considered the First Amendment implications. "The First Amendment guarantees that society will be able to receive news limited, if at all, only by the most carefully imposed, narrowly constructed, finely drawn, restraints in areas such as copyright, defamation, unfair competition, incitement and obscenity," Friedman wrote.[37] Friedman rejected Daniel's argument that the Dow Jones service receives the lower level of First Amendment protection given to commercial speech. "News services, whether free to the public, as are television or radio, or more expensive, specialized media, such as defendant's computerized data base, are instruments for the free flow of all forms of information, and should be treated as unquestionably within the First Amendment's guarantee of freedom of the press," Friedman wrote.[38] Just like Jaillet more than a half century earlier, Daniel was unable to hold Dow Jones accountable for allegedly inaccurate information. The undertone of the ruling is that Daniel is responsible for decisions that he makes, even if they were based on inaccurate information that Dow Jones provided.

Judges also recognize that placing too much responsibility on speakers—and not enough responsibility on the recipients—could discourage recipients from acting prudently and lead to unnecessarily harmful consequences. Consider, for instance, the case of Lauren Rosenberg. On January 19, 2009, the Los Angeles resident was in Park City, Utah, and needed directions for a roughly two-mile walk. She said that she used the Google Maps service on her Blackberry for walking directions. She claims that although she requested walking directions, Google directed her down State Route 224, a sidewalk-free rural highway with high-speed traffic.[39] While walking the route, she said, she was hit by a car and suffered "severe permanent physical, emotional, and mental injuries," and incurred medical expenses and other damages of more than $100,000.[40] She sued the driver and Google in Utah state court. Among her claims against Google were that it was negligent by failing to satisfy its "duty to exercise reasonable care in providing reasonably safe directions" and by failing to warn her of the dangerous conditions.[41] Google moved to dismiss the complaint, pointing to cases such as the unsuccessful lawsuits against the Weather Channel and the publisher of the *Encyclopedia of Mushrooms*, described in chapter 5. "Just as the publishers and broadcasters in all these cases owed no duty to the readers who read their publications and viewed their programming, the First Amendment prohibits holding that Google has a legal duty to every member of the public who reads walking directions published on Google Maps," Google's lawyers wrote.[42]

Judge Deno G. Himonas agreed with Google and dismissed the claims against the company on May 27, 2011. In concluding that Google did not owe a duty to Rosenberg, Himonas examined standard questions in negligence claims and reasoned that although some harm to Rosenberg was "reasonably foreseeable," Google did not have a "special relationship" with Rosenberg and her injury was unlikely.[43] Most interesting in his analysis, however, were the "policy considerations" that Himonas believed weighed strongly against Google having a duty to Rosenberg. Imposing a legal duty on Google to investigate the safety of every route on Google Maps, he wrote, would "impose an onerous burden" on the company. Even Rosenberg's argument that Google should have warned users of potential dangers, Himonas wrote, would be overly burdensome. Such a rule, he wrote, would mean that "Google might have to investigate and warn about any foreseeable risks along every route, which might include negligent drivers, drunk drivers, dangerous wildlife, sidewalks or roads in disrepair, lack of lighting, and other risks that may only exist during certain times of day."[44] The potential benefits to public safety, Himonas wrote, do not justify these burdens. He noted that Utah law requires pedestrians to yield to vehicles while crossing the street and to take other reasonable steps to watch for traffic. "To impose the duties suggested by Rosenberg would reduce, if not eliminate, the duties already imposed on pedestrians," Himonas wrote. "Thus, while imposing a duty on Google would make Google responsible for its own negligent actions, it would serve to diminish the responsibility that pedestrians have for their own safety, which does not serve the goal of making individuals accountable for their own errors."[45]

Himonas's reasoning was in line with the decisions dating back to *Jaillet*. But it was particularly noteworthy in that it examined not only the unfairness of placing all responsibility for harms of allegedly false speech on the speakers rather than the recipients, but also because it recognized that such a legal framework often is not the most effective way to deal with a problem. As the next chapter explains, many judges have recognized that regulations and liability for false speech often are ineffective tools.

Chapter 8

Efficacy

Perhaps you've read chapters 1 through 7 and still aren't sold on the value of legal protections for many types of false speech. The harms caused by misinformation, you reason, are simply too great, and far outweigh the intrusions on free speech that would come from more regulation.

There is one more reason that courts hesitate to impose regulations or liability for false speech: It often is not terribly effective. Censorship regimes may block some lies. But it is rare that government regulations can effectively block all or even most false speech, and in doing so they may also prevent a great deal of true speech with little benefit. And judges and regulators very well may err in deciding whether a statement was truthful.

One argument for the general inefficacy of censorship came from Alexis de Tocqueville in his two-volume book *Democracy in America*. In it, de Tocqueville acknowledged that some may wish to "correct the abuses of unlicensed printing" by subjecting the writer to a jury trial. But de Tocqueville predicted that "if the jury acquits him, the opinion which was that of a single individual becomes the opinion of the country at large." And the mere act of litigating a case that centers on harmful speech, he predicted, would draw more attention to that speech: "the very principles which no book would have ventured to avow are blazoned forth in the pleadings, and what was obscurely hinted at in a single composition is then repeated in a multitude of other publications." To de Tocqueville, censorship often is ineffective. "If you establish a censorship of the press, the tongue of the public speaker will still make itself heard, and you have only increased the mischief," he wrote.[1]

De Tocqueville's doubt about censorship's efficacy applies equally to modern debates about misinformation. The prospect of regulatory fines, criminal convictions, or civil liability will discourage people from uttering false words. But such a regime is an imperfect tool, for a few reasons. First, the prospect of liability will chill not only false speech, but also a good deal of speech that is either true or of unknown veracity. A rational speaker will seek to avoid any reasonable chance of facing existential damage awards or loss of liberty. Second, as discussed in chapter 5, truth is not a static concept; it evolves with knowledge. Thus any attempts by courts or regulators to define "truth" may soon become outdated, yet the speaker may have faced liability based on that outdated notion of truth. Third, and perhaps most importantly, there is no guarantee that civil or criminal liability would deter the worst liars. They may not know about the potential legal liability or simply not care about the risks. Or they have hidden their identities via technological or operational security. Or, as with Russian disinformation, they are located abroad and unlikely to face any legal consequences as long as they stay out of the United States or its allied nations.

Courts have recognized the questionable efficacy of regulating falsehoods when striking down restrictions on speech, particularly after the Supreme Court in *United States v. Alvarez* ruled that false speech is not categorically unprotected. One of the most prominent such cases involved Ohio's political false statements law. The statute made it a crime to "[p]ost, publish, circulate, distribute, or otherwise disseminate a false statement concerning a candidate, either knowing the same to be false or with reckless disregard of whether it was false or not, if the statement is designed to promote the election, nomination, or defeat of the candidate." The law separately made it a crime to "[m]ake a false statement concerning the voting record of a candidate or public official," provided that they knew that the statement was false. Violating the law could lead to a misdemeanor conviction and sentence of up to six months in prison and a fine of up to $5,000.[2]

The Susan B. Anthony List, a pro-life organization, in 2010 planned an advertising campaign against local members of Congress, including Steve Driehaus, who had voted for the Affordable Care Act. Among its planned tactics was a billboard that stated "Shame on Steve Driehaus! Driehaus voted FOR taxpayer-funded abortion." Driehaus complained to the Ohio Elections Commission that the billboards violated the false statements law because the health care law did not explicitly direct money to abortions.[3] The Susan B. Anthony List argued that the statement was true because the law could direct public money to abortions.[4] In a 2–1 vote, the elections commission agreed with Driehaus that there was probable cause that the group violated the criminal law (a requirement before the government can prosecute under the statute).[5] The Susan B. Anthony List filed a First Amendment lawsuit to prevent the government from enforcing the law. Driehaus lost reelection that year, leading to a long dispute as to whether the Susan B. Anthony List had standing to continue to challenge the law. In 2014, the US Supreme Court ruled that the group still could challenge the law, and sent it back to Ohio federal district court judge Timothy S. Black.

In a thorough opinion, Black ruled for the Susan B. Anthony List and declared the false statements law unconstitutional, blocking its future enforcement. "Lies have no place in the political arena and serve no purpose other than to undermine the integrity of the democratic process," Black wrote at the start of his opinion. "The problem is that, at times, there is no clear way to determine whether a political statement is a lie or the truth. What is certain, however, is that we do not want the

Government (i.e., the Ohio Elections Commission) deciding what is political truth—for fear that the Government might persecute those who criticize it. Instead, in a democracy, the voters should decide."[6]

Black relied heavily on the marketplace theory, pointing not only to the recent *Alvarez* opinion, but also to a quote from Frank Underwood, the fictional US president in the Netflix series *House of Cards*: "There's no better way to overpower a trickle of doubt than with a flood of naked truth."[7] Guided by the *Alvarez* plurality, Black applied strict scrutiny, examining whether the Ohio law met the high bar of being narrowly tailored to serve a compelling government interest. Key to Black's conclusion that the law was unconstitutional was his skepticism of the Ohio Election Commission's ability to be the arbiter of truth. "In fact, the statute does not even ensure that the hearing process will conclude in time to preserve the integrity of the election, because most false-statement complaints are filed days before an election, preventing the OEC from determining the truth or falsity of the statement before the election takes place," Black wrote.[8]

The factual disputes that the Ohio Election Commission (OEC) must adjudicate, Black wrote, are particularly ill-suited for the government. "Allegedly, Ohio's law is meant to protect voters from being swayed by lies," he wrote. "Accordingly, the state interest is not protecting citizens from personal injuries, but rather paternalistically protecting the citizenry at large from 'untruths' identified by Government appointees. Unlike in *Alvarez*, where the only factual issue, whether you have been awarded medals or not, was easily ascertainable, the factual issues raised before the OEC are far more complicated and require a sophisticated analysis."[9] Black also concluded that the Ohio law was not narrowly tailored, as it could chill truthful speech, in line with the *Alvarez* court's conclusion about the Stolen Valor Act. "Here, in this case, notwithstanding the statutory mens rea requirements, the chilling effect is more powerful, because the falsehoods concern politics, and even the truthful speaker is subject to substantial burdens and costs from the OEC proceedings, even if ultimately acquitted,"

Black wrote. "Moreover, the fact that the speaker's subjective knowledge bears on the liability actually becomes a basis for broad and hugely burdensome discovery into the speaker's political communications and affiliations, such as strategic discussions with political parties, other candidates, or campaign allies."[10]

Black wrote that he doubts that counterspeech in the marketplace of ideas could adequately counteract all lies. But he questioned whether the election commission was able to make factual determinations, particularly in the final days before an election. "Moreover, given the complexity of some political statements, it is entirely possible that a candidate could make a truthful statement, yet the OEC would determine in a probable cause finding a few days before an election that the statement is false, penalizing the candidate for speaking the truth and chilling further truthful speech," Black wrote.[11] Black's reasoning is grounded in the marketplace of ideas, as explained in *Alvarez* and dating to Holmes's *Abrams* dissent. But an equally potent theme that runs throughout his reasoning is that the Ohio Elections Commission is simply not able to make factual judgments about truth. The marketplace of ideas does not merely assume that speakers and listeners are able to sort truth from lies; it also presumes that courts and government agencies are particularly ill-equipped to do so.

The commission appealed Black's ruling to the US Court of Appeals for the Sixth Circuit, arguing that the types of statements covered by the statute do not receive First Amendment protection, and even if they do, the statute satisfies strict scrutiny. "Ohio's compelling interest in protecting the integrity of its elections is well-established," the state wrote in its brief. "As such, Ohio may properly restrict fraudulent false statements designed to affect elections. Thus, Ohio's provisions carefully target intentional lies likely to cause harm and contain numerous limiting features to insulate innocent speech."[12]

In a unanimous opinion issued in 2016, the three-judge panel affirmed Black. Writing for the panel, Judge R. Guy Cole Jr. acknowledged that the state had a compelling interest in maintaining election integrity. But he concluded that the law was not narrowly tailored to meet that goal. And many of his concerns focused on the efficacy of the commission's review process. Cole noted that many complaints could "linger for six months" before receiving a ruling from the commission. "Even when a complaint is expedited, there is no guarantee the administrative or criminal proceedings will conclude before the election or within time for the candidate's campaign to recover from any false information that was disseminated," Cole wrote. "Indeed, candidates filing complaints against their political opponents count on the fact that an ultimate decision on the merits will be deferred until after the relevant election."[13] Cole also criticized the inability of the commission to block "frivolous" complaints from receiving probable cause hearings. "While this permits a panel of the Commission to review and reach a probable cause conclusion on complaints as quickly as possible, it also provides frivolous complainants an audience and requires purported violators to respond to a potentially frivolous complaint," he wrote.[14] Ohio argued that the laws only apply to materially false statements, but Cole noted that the law has no materiality requirement. "Thus, influencing an election by lying about a political candidate's shoe size or vote on whether to continue a congressional debate is just as actionable as lying about a candidate's party affiliation or vote on an important policy issue, such as the Affordable Care Act," Cole explained.[15]

Some of Cole's reasoning focused on the ability of the commission to effectively combat the harms of false speech. An early ruling that finds probable cause may harm a speaker who ultimately is found to not have violated the false statements law, Cole wrote. "At the same time, the law may not timely penalize those who violate it, nor does it provide for campaigns that are the victim of potentially damaging false statements," he reasoned.[16] This dichotomy, according to Cole, means that "the law is both over-inclusive and underinclusive."[17]

The dispute that sparked the Susan B. Anthony List's lawsuit shows why the concerns raised by Judges Black and Cole are not misplaced.

Deciding whether Driehaus's vote for the Affordable Care Act was a vote for "taxpayer-funded abortion" requires subjective judgment from the commission. Driehaus had a viable argument that the claim was false, yet Susan B. Anthony List reasonably defended its statement by linking the Affordable Care Act to potential abortion funding. The Ohio Election Commission is not specially equipped to be the final arbiter of truth in such a case. Allowing a group of election commissioners—all of whom may have their own political biases for or against a candidate—to determine whether there is probable cause that a statement is false seems to be a highly subjective, unfair, and inefficient way to combat falsehoods.

Not all factual disputes are as difficult to adjudicate. Imagine instead that the Susan B. Anthony List ran an advertisement that falsely stated, "Shame on Driehaus for missing 95 percent of his votes in Congress last year!" Such a claim would be easy to adjudicate as false, as his congressional voting record is publicly accessible. But much of the damage to Driehaus's campaign would have already been suffered after the initial claim, no matter how quickly the commission adjudicated the dispute or the speaker was prosecuted. The most effective way to combat such false claims would be for Driehaus to produce information that rebuts the claims—an avenue that is available in the marketplace of ideas and does not depend on the existence of Ohio's criminal statute against false speech. A criminal charge or conviction—which may occur months or years after the election—is unlikely to be terribly effective at countering the falsehood.

A likely justification for the Ohio law is that the mere prospect of criminal penalties would deter such verifiably false statements as a claim that a politician committed multiple murders. Yet it is unclear whether such a law would have a significant deterrent effect on such obviously outlandish false statements. Those who make the most outrageously false claims might disregard any legal risks. They might be untraceably anonymous, using technology such as Tor to mask their identifying information. Or they might be located in another country, far out of reach of the jurisdiction of US criminal laws. A criminal law such as Ohio's might deter *some* false speech from ever being uttered, but it is a blunt object that is not terribly efficient in meeting its goals.

And therein lies one of the primary challenges to effectively regulating false speech. Although the Supreme Court in *Alvarez* held that false speech is not categorically exempt from the First Amendment, few judges or legal scholars would argue that First Amendment protections for false speech are absolute. But one reason that a wider swath of false speech does not fall within an exception to the First Amendment is because regulation is simply not terribly effective at achieving the government's goals.

The Sixth Circuit is not alone in its skepticism of the efficacy of regulating false speech. In a 2014 opinion, *281 Care Committee v. Arneson*, the US Court of Appeals for the Eighth Circuit agreed with grassroots groups that challenged the constitutionality of a provision in the Minnesota Fair Campaign Practices Act that was intended to promote truthful advertisements about ballot measures. The law stated: "A person is guilty of a gross misdemeanor who intentionally participates in the preparation, dissemination, or broadcast of paid political advertising or campaign material ... with respect to the effect of a ballot question, that is designed or tends to ... promote or defeat a ballot question, that is false, and that the person knows is false or communicates to others with reckless disregard of whether it is false."[18]

If a complaint is filed by any member of the public, it goes through a multistep process adjudicated by administrative law judges, who can issue fines of up to $5,000. After the administrative law process is complete, a county attorney could prosecute further under the law.[19]

Because the regulation targeted political speech, the Eighth Circuit, like the Sixth Circuit, applied strict scrutiny. The court was ambivalent as to whether Minnesota had shown that the law served a compelling interest in ensuring fair elections and preventing fraud.

"We concede that regulating falsity in the political realm definitely exemplifies a stronger state interest than, say, regulating the dissemination and content of information generally, given the importance of the electoral process in the United States," Judge C. Arlen Beam wrote for the court. "Even in that context, however, the state does not have carte blanche to regulate the dissemination of false statements during political campaigns and the Supreme Court has yet to specifically weigh in on the balancing of interests when it does."[20]

But the Eighth Circuit did not need to determine whether Minnesota had a compelling interest because it concluded that the law was not narrowly tailored—the other requirement of strict scrutiny. And key to this finding was the inefficacy of the law. The statute is unconstitutional, Beam wrote, "because it tends to perpetuate the very fraud it is allegedly designed to prohibit."[21] Anyone can file an administrative complaint alleging a violation of the law, Beam noted. "There is no promise or requirement that the power to file a complaint will be used prudently," he wrote, noting the likelihood of political opponents using this process to file complaints. "Complaints can be filed at a tactically calculated time so as to divert the attention of an entire campaign from the meritorious task at hand of supporting or defeating a ballot question, possibly diffusing public sentiment and requiring the speaker to defend a claim before the [state Office of Administrative Hearings, or OAH], thus inflicting political damage," Beam continued.

Beam also faulted the prosecutors who were defending the Minnesota law for failing to show why counterspeech, rather than regulations, would not promote fair elections and prevent fraud. "Especially as to political speech, counterspeech is the tried and true buffer and elixir," Beam wrote. "Putting in place potential criminal sanctions and/or the possibility of being tied up in litigation before the OAH, or both, at the mere whim and mention from anyone who might oppose your view on a ballot question is wholly overbroad and overburdensome and chills otherwise protected speech."[22] The statute "actually opens a Pandora's box to disingenuous politicking itself," creating more potential for the kind of election fraud that it is intended to combat. "The citizenry, not the government, should be the monitor of falseness in the political arena," Beam wrote. "Citizens can digest and question writings or broadcasts in favor or against ballot initiatives just as they are equally poised to weigh counterpoints."[23]

Similar reasoning was partly behind the Massachusetts Supreme Judicial Court's 2015 ruling that struck down a state law that imposed criminal penalties for some types of false statements about political candidates and ballot measures. Writing for a unanimous panel, Justice Robert Cordy reasoned that "even in cases involving seemingly obvious statements of political fact, distinguishing between truth and falsity may prove exceedingly difficult. Assertions regarding a candidate's voting record on a particular issue may very well require an in-depth analysis of legislative history that will often be ill-suited to the compressed time frame of an election."[24] Cody's concerns about efficacy were compounded because the Massachusetts law allows anyone to request a criminal complaint for false statements. This means that a private citizen who is "unconstrained by the ethical obligations imposed on government officials" could lodge an "unmeritorious application."[25]

The courts' First Amendment–based rejections of the Ohio, Minnesota, and Massachusetts laws stemmed from many concerns, including the chilling effect that the laws would have on campaign speech and the potential for abuse. But one thread that underlies all three opinions is that speech regulations and liability often are not effective ways of addressing falsehoods. Government speech restrictions could increase public mistrust of the government and lend more credibility to blatant lies. And even if the penalties could discourage at least some false speech, states have understandably had a difficult time justifying that their censorious laws are any more effective than other solutions, such as counterspeech.

PART II
Regulating Falsehoods?

Part I explained the various rationales for protecting false speech and argued why these protections have been a net benefit for society. These reasons help us understand why US law protects false speech. This part briefly synthesizes these reasons and then examines what can and cannot be regulated while maintaining these core values. The marketplace of ideas that Holmes articulated in 1919 has guided much of the American approach to free speech over the past century, but it has shortcomings and does not tell the full story of why the law protects some false speech.

Courts have recognized that false speech often is best combatted with truthful speech, and they depend on the truth to prevail in the marketplace of ideas. This helped shape the outcome in *United States v. Alvarez*, as the justices debated whether less intrusive means, such as a public database of Medal of Honor recipients, could accomplish the goal of the Stolen Valor Act without regulating speech.

A marketplace approach to speech envisions not only truth prevailing over falsehoods, but also listeners being more confident in that truth when the government is not overseeing speech. If the United States were to take a more authoritarian approach and strictly regulate "misinformation," the recipients of the government-sanctioned "truth" have far more reason to doubt its veracity.

And the marketplace of ideas implicitly recognizes the value of some false speech. This is best illustrated in Judge Kozinski's concurrence in the rehearing denial in *Alvarez*, in which he highlighted the many benefits of lies, such as avoiding offensive statements, preventing embarrassment, building a public persona, and protecting privacy.

But the marketplace of ideas is far from perfect, with some speakers—often those with more power and wealth—having greater access to the marketplace. So, it is not surprising that the marketplace theory does not account for all the protections that courts and legislators have provided for false speech. Preventing regulation, lawsuits, and indictments based on false speech also helps to rebalance the power dynamic and enable people with limited clout and financial resources to openly criticize politicians without fear of existential defamation verdicts or jail time. This reflects the Meiklejohnian approach to viewing free speech as a mechanism for self-government. Although courts never achieved Meiklejohn's vision of absolute protection for public speech, *New York Times v. Sullivan* and its progeny have provided robust protections for journalists and others who investigate and criticize those in power. And the fair report privilege and precedent of *Philadelphia Newspapers v. Hepps* have provided further protections for reporting about public agencies, court cases, and other high-profile actors and events. By shielding speakers from defamation lawsuits— even when the reporting might be false—these protections give the speakers the necessary breathing room to criticize those who have far more power and ability to retaliate through litigation. Thus examining US free speech protections solely through the lens of the marketplace is incomplete. The protections *empower* speakers, particularly those whose speech brings light to high-profile people and events.

"Truth" is difficult to achieve. Errors may happen, as reflected in the broad acceptance of the substantial truth doctrine. Many statements may be viewed as opinion rather than fact, and not the basis of defamation lawsuits, even if they likely lead the listener to a factually incorrect conclusion. Courts also provide strong protection for allegedly false speech such as scientific conclusions because they recognize that our concept of truth evolves as we obtain more knowledge. Rather than declare one enduring truth, the courts are willing to allow a great deal of speech, even that which seems outlandish at the time.

The law empowers both speakers and recipients of their speech. The law empowers speakers by ensuring that they have adequate access to speech that is not censored by government powers. And of equal importance, the law empowers speech recipients by largely holding them responsible for how they react to false speech. As seen in *Jaillet v. Cashman* and its related cases, the law does not view speech recipients as passive and easily swayed by misinformation. Rather, it expects that speech recipients will be discerning in how they respond to false speech. For instance, the law expects you to verify the outcome of a Supreme Court case before making an important stock trade based on the news, and to look both ways before crossing a busy highway, even if Google Maps lists it as a walking route.

Regulation and liability are not terribly effective ways to address the harms of false information. Such a regime is overinclusive in that it will chill a good deal of true (or at least arguably true) speech from well-intentioned people who fear even the prospect of civil or criminal liability. But it also is underinclusive in that it will fail to prevent at least some of the most damaging and dangerous falsehoods, either because the liars disregard the legal risks, are untraceably anonymous, or are located outside of the United States and able to avoid legal consequences here.

Part II explores the scope of the threat of misinformation, disinformation, and other falsehoods, and when the government can impose liability for that speech. The First Amendment allows civil actions and criminal prosecutions for fraud and some civil liability for defamation. But the bar for such government regulation is high. Contrary to the "fire in a crowded theater" position, the government should not and cannot easily avoid the First Amendment merely by claiming that false speech is harmful.

Chapter 9

The Scope of the Problem

Before exploring the options to address false speech, we must better identify the problem. There is no shortage of modern commentary about misinformation and disinformation and other falsehoods, but we do not have a widespread consensus as to the scope or magnitude of the problem, nor do we have a particularly coherent taxonomy.

I take the rare position of admitting that we do not know precisely the scope of the harms that falsehoods have caused in the United States. That is largely because we have a limited—but growing—body of research on false speech. Without minimizing the problems that falsehoods have caused, I readily admit that there is much that we do not know. And that includes even basic definitions.

Misinformation is "false or misleading information that is unwittingly shared," according to Steven Vosloo of UNICEF. In contrast, Vosloo writes, disinformation "is deliberately created and distributed with an intent to deceive or harm."[1] But the definitional boundaries are not clear-cut, and the terms are sometimes used interchangeably. And as Michael J. O'Brien and Izzat Alsmadi observed, disinformation "can turn into misinformation when spread by unwitting readers who believe the material."[2] Some harmful statements might not be demonstrably false but can be devastatingly misleading, by omitting key facts or making statements with no context.[3] Many of these utterances may be misleading opinions that imply factual claims ("I can't imagine why anyone would get the COVID vaccine" or "There is no way that he won the election without cheating"). Renée DiResta has noted that "persuasive communication with an agenda" has long been known as propaganda.[4] The *Cambridge Dictionary* defines propaganda as "information, ideas, opinions, or images, often only giving one part of an argument, that are broadcast, published, or in some other way spread with the intention of influencing people's opinions."[5] DiResta coined a new term, "ampliganda," for using online amplification to deliver propaganda and shape public perception. While there are narrow avenues—such as defamation lawsuits—in which verifiably false statements might result in penalties, a good deal of propaganda and ampliganda cannot result in legal consequences for the speakers, even if it is harmful. In recent years, two topics have become of particular concern as targets for misinformation, disinformation, and propaganda: politics and health.

In the political realm, beginning with the 2016 presidential election and extending to the current day, US government officials are concerned that domestic and foreign actors have spread false information to influence US elections. For instance, in 2018, Special Counsel Robert Mueller indicted Russians who worked for the country's Internet Research Agency for their attempts to influence the 2016 presidential election. "Defendants, posing as U.S. persons and creating false U.S. personas, operated social media pages and groups designed to attract U.S. audiences," Mueller wrote in the indictment. "These groups and pages, which addressed divisive U.S. political and social issues, falsely claimed to be controlled by U.S. activists when, in fact, they were controlled by Defendants."[6] To measure the effect of misinformation on the 2016 election, Ohio State University researchers surveyed 585 voters who voted for Barack Obama in 2012. Among the questions were summaries of three "fake news" stories: that Hillary Clinton was seriously ill, that Clinton had sold weapons to the Islamic State while secretary of state, and that Pope Francis endorsed Donald Trump. "Belief in these fake news stories is very strongly linked to defection from the Democratic ticket by 2012 Obama voters," the researchers wrote. "Among respondents who didn't believe any of the fake news stories, 89 percent cast ballots for Hillary Clinton in 2016. Sixty-one percent of those who believed one fake news item voted for Clinton. But only 17 percent of those who believed two or all three of these false assertions voted for Clinton."[7]

The concerns about falsehoods persisted throughout and after the 2020 election cycle, particularly as President Trump and his supporters challenged the pending electoral college win for Joe Biden. Many of the challenges involved the increased use of early voting and absentee ballots, which occurred in response to public health concerns during the COVID-19 pandemic. In the days after the election, Trump put forward theories of voter fraud that were either unsupported or highly misleading. In a review of Trump's tweets on November 16, 2020, 13 days after the election, the *New York Times* found that Trump "has posted over 300 tweets attacking the integrity of the 2020 election since election night, unleashing a cascade of false and misleading claims." Trump tweeted about cases in which his electoral lead disappeared, or that "ballot dumps" suddenly appeared. "What he was describing was simply vote counting. Election officials warned for months that counting ballots might take days or even weeks to complete, given the prevalence of absentee ballots this year," the *Times* wrote.[8]

Indeed, reporters could not find evidence of any election fraud that would have altered the ultimate outcome of the 2020 presidential election. In the days after the election, the *New York Times* called election officials in every state and asked if they had any evidence or suspicion of illegal votes being cast. The newspaper found none. "Election officials in dozens of states representing both political parties said that there was no evidence that fraud or other irregularities played a role in the outcome of the presidential race, amounting to a forceful rebuke of President Trump's portrait of a fraudulent election," the *Times* reported on November 10, 2020.[9] In a more comprehensive review in 2021, the Associated Press found that there were no more than 475 possible voter fraud cases in the six disputed battleground states. "The cases could not throw the outcome into question even if all the potentially fraudulent votes were for Biden, which they were not, and even if those ballots were actually counted, which in most cases they were not," the Associated Press wrote. "The review also showed no collusion intended to rig the voting. Virtually every case was based on an individual acting alone to cast additional ballots."[10] Nonetheless, Trump's claims about a "rigged election" continued throughout the transition, particularly after the electors of each state met in mid-December, leading to a 306–232 Electoral College victory for Biden. Between the election and Congress's January 6 certification of the electoral college results, Trump or his allies filed 62 lawsuits challenging various aspects of the election. They lost 61 of the lawsuits, with the one minor victory, in Pennsylvania, being irrelevant to the outcome of the state's presidential election.[11]

These falsehoods about election rigging harmed not only public confidence in elections, but they were also what prompted many people who stormed the Capitol on January 6, as Congress was trying to certify the electoral vote count. Among the highest profile of Trump's election tweets came on December 19, 2020: "Statistically impossible to have lost the 2020 Election. Big protest in DC on January 6th. Be there, will be wild!"[12] Prosecutors and members of Congress who investigated the January 6 riots often point to that tweet as inciting extremist groups to plan to storm the Capitol. In March 2022, the *New York Times* reported that investigations had "shown how Mr. Trump's post was a powerful catalyst, particularly for far-right militants who believed he was facing his final chance to reverse defeat and whose role in fomenting the violence has come under intense scrutiny."[13] Politi-

Fact, part of the nonprofit Poynter Institute, reviewed the case files for more than 400 people who were arrested for their participation in the January 6 insurrection. It found that the belief that Biden was not the legitimate victor of the 2020 election was a "key driver" of the day's events. "These people don't think they're spreading lies," Kate Starbird, a University of Washington professor, told PolitiFact. "They sincerely believed that they were going to be cheated. They experienced the election as if they were cheated."[14]

Political falsehoods are not the only concern. Health experts have worried that online commentary about the coronavirus pandemic has discouraged public health measures like masking and vaccinations. Pew Research surveys in 2020 found that nearly half of Americans believed that they saw some data about COVID-19 that appeared to be fabricated, and that about 25 percent of American adults believed the coronavirus had been planned by those in power.[15] A November 2021 Kaiser Family Foundation report examined belief in many prevalent COVID-19 falsehoods. "Among other common myths, one-third believe or are unsure whether deaths due to the COVID-19 vaccine are being intentionally hidden by the government (35%), and about three in ten each believe or are unsure whether COVID-19 vaccines have been shown to cause infertility (31%) or whether Ivermectin is a safe and effective treatment for COVID-19 (28%)," the foundation wrote. "In addition, between a fifth and a quarter of the public believe or are unsure whether the vaccines can give you COVID-19 (25%), contain a microchip (24%), or can change your DNA (21%)."[16]

Some experts argue that the Internet, particularly social media, allows misinformation and disinformation to cause more damage than it would have in earlier times. For instance, a prominent 2018 study published in *Science* by Massachusetts Institute of Technology researchers examined about 126,000 true and false news stories (as classified by multiple fact-checking organizations) that were shared on Twitter. "Falsehood diffused significantly farther, faster, deeper, and more broadly than the truth in all categories of information, and the effects were more pronounced for false political news than for false news about terrorism, natural disasters, science, urban legends, or financial information," the researchers wrote. "We found that false news was more novel than true news, which suggests that people were more likely to share novel information."[17]

New technology drives not only the reach of false information, but also how it is created. Of particular concern are "deepfakes." The term originated in 2017, when a poster on Reddit operating under the pseudonym "deepfakes" shared digitally altered pornographic video clips. In the videos, the faces of celebrities were grafted onto the bodies of the actors via artificial intelligence (AI). The term soon became more widely associated with photos and videos that people manipulate with machine learning.[18] Although there is not one widely accepted definition of deepfakes, James Vincent wrote in *The Verge* that "one baseline characteristic is that some part of the editing process is automated using AI techniques, usually deep learning," which is noteworthy "not only because it reflects the fact that deepfakes are *new*, but that they're also *easy*."[19] In a 2019 law review article that provided one of the first thorough reviews of the national security and democracy challenges posed by deepfakes, law professors Bobby Chesney and Danielle Citron began with the story of Emma Gonzalez, a survivor of the 2018 Parkland, Florida, high school shooting who became a nationally known gun control advocate. Chesney and Citron told the story of a viral social media image that appeared to show Gonzalez ripping up the US Constitution. The image was a deepfake, a manipulation of a real photograph of Gonzalez tearing up a bullseye target.[20] The Gonzalez story illustrates the broader potential for problems caused by deepfakes, they wrote. "Imagine a deep fake video, released the day before an election, making it appear that a candidate for office has made an inflammatory statement," Chesney and Citron wrote. "Or what if, in the wake of the Trump-Putin tête-à-tête at Helsinki in 2018, someone circulated a deep fake audio recording that seemed to portray President Trump as promising not to take any action should Russia interfere with certain NATO allies."[21]

Some falsehoods are pervasive and have metastasized over the years. Among the most prominent such examples is QAnon, a conspiracy theory that began in 2017. QAnon has many characteristics of the previous year's PizzaGate conspiracy, which drove an armed man named Edgar Maddison Welch to visit a restaurant in Washington, DC, called Comet Ping Pong. QAnon began with posts on the message board 4chan by a user named "Q," who claimed to have a high-level security clearance. Q alleged that Donald Trump was recruited by the military to overthrow powerful members of the deep state who are pedophiles running a sex-trafficking ring. QAnon adherents believe in The Storm, an event in which the heads of this sex-trafficking ring will be arrested.[22] QAnon spread not only on 4chan, but also on more mainstream platforms like Reddit and Facebook. Two people who had once expressed some support for QAnon theories were elected to Congress in 2020. And dozens of the people who were arrested at the January 6 Capitol riots had QAnon ties.[23] But even before the January 6 riots, QAnon had posed other real-world safety problems. In 2018, a QAnon adherent who was angry that The Storm had not yet occurred blockaded a bridge located near the Hoover Dam in a vehicle laden with handguns and rifles. Later that year, a California resident had planned to detonate a bomb in the Illinois state capitol to raise awareness of PizzaGate and related conspiracies. In 2019, a QAnon supporter vandalized a Sedona, Arizona, church.[24]

Some communications are not as blatantly false as QAnon misinformation but are still misleading, and can be broadly classified as propaganda. For instance, the QAnon focus on child sexual exploitation has opened the door to statements that are technically true but misleading. This was seen in the March 2022 confirmation hearings of Supreme Court Justice Ketanji Brown Jackson, who had served as a federal district judge in the District of Columbia. In the days before her hearing, Senator Josh Hawley tweeted a long thread about "an alarming pattern when it comes to Judge Jackson's treatment of sex offenders, especially those preying on children." While also criticizing a law review article that she wrote as a law student about sex offender registries and statements that she had made as a member of the US Sentencing Commission about mandatory minimum sentences for defendants in child sex abuse material cases, Hawley described a "pattern of letting child porn offenders off the hook for their appalling crimes, both as a judge and as a policymaker." As a district court judge, Hawley wrote, in "every single child porn case for which we can find records, Judge Jackson deviated from the federal sentencing guidelines in favor of child porn offenders." He then described the seven child pornography cases, noting the guidelines ranges and the sentences that Jackson imposed. "Protecting the most vulnerable shouldn't be up for debate," Hawley tweeted. "Sending child predators to jail shouldn't be controversial."[25]

Hawley's tweets were factually accurate, but they omitted vital context. Jackson is not among a small group of judges who deviate from the sentencing guidelines in child pornography cases. A 2021 US Sentencing Commission report found that 59 percent of nonproduction child sex abuse material cases resulted in sentences below the guidelines, reflecting widespread criticism that the guidelines often are too high. "Indeed, guidelines sentences *are* so harsh that even many prosecutors advise judges not to follow them," Ian Millhiser wrote for Vox.[26] Writing for the conservative *National Review*, former federal prosecutor Andrew McCarthy wrote that "there just isn't anything that unusual" about the seven sentences about which Hawley had tweeted.[27] Yet a member of the public confronting Hawley's tweets, or the coverage of them, or the expansion upon the theme by many senators during Jackson's confirmation hearings, might believe that Jackson is extraordinarily soft on child predators. In fact, after Hawley's tweets, a prominent QAnon supporter declared Jackson to be an "apologist for child molesters" and claimed that Democrats were "elevating pedophiles and people who can change the laws surrounding punishment" for such crimes.[28]

Hawley's tweets were technically true, so it would be unfair to classify them in the same misinformation category as many of the QAnon claims. But they missed crucial context. A more fitting category for them might be the broader umbrella of accurate speech with material omissions. This speculation about Jackson's supposed lenience toward child predators spread across both social media and institutional media, including popular conservative news sites. For instance, *The Federalist* ran a March 28, 2022, opinion piece titled "It Shouldn't Be Hard to Condemn Ketanji Brown Jackson's Leniency for Child Predators." Some senators raised the issue during her confirmation hearing. And on April 4, 2022, after Republican Senators Lisa Murkowski, Susan Collins, and Mitt Romney announced their support of Jackson's confirmation, Congresswoman Marjorie Taylor Greene tweeted: "Murkowski, Collins, and Romney are pro-pedophile. They just voted for #KBJ."[29] Hawley's tweets would not give rise to a successful defamation claim, not merely because Jackson is a public figure but because he stated facts, albeit in a way that some would argue is misleading. Even Greene's tweets, branding three senators as "pro-pedophile," likely would receive legal protections as opinion. Yet the misleading nature of the speech skewed the public debate. When examining the harms of misinformation, disinformation, and propaganda, we must look at both the outright lies and the true statements that lack sufficient context and might mislead and influence public opinion.

Another example of misleading—or at least incomplete—information coming from politicians can be seen in the discussions of the various investigations into Russia's interference in the 2016 US presidential election. Although some claims arose from Russia's dissemination of misinformation into the United States, some of the speculation about what the investigations would conclude also could be seen as misleading. For instance, as the House Intelligence Committee was investigating

Russia's interference throughout 2017, Representative Adam Schiff, the panel's top Democrat, said this on CNN about Trump's campaign and Russia: "The Russians offered help, the campaign accepted help. The Russians gave help and the President made full use of that help. That is pretty damning, whether it is proof beyond a reasonable doubt of conspiracy or not."[30] Yet transcripts of 57 interviews that the committee conducted, released more than two years after Schiff's statements, did not support such a certain conclusion. For instance, former director of national intelligence James Clapper had told the committee in July 2017: "I never saw any direct empirical evidence that the Trump campaign or someone in it was plotting/conspiring with the Russians to meddle with the election."[31]

That Clapper and other officials told the committee that they did not see any definitive evidence of collusion does not mean that we can say with certainty that collusion had not occurred. And Schiff is entitled to make his own assessment of the evidence. But Schiff's overly confident statements to the media could at the very least be seen as misleading and not fully representative of the facts that the committee had gathered. "President Trump often spreads falsehoods and invents facts, but at least he's paid a price for it in media criticism and public mistrust," the *Wall Street Journal* wrote in an editorial. "An industry of media fact checkers is dedicated to parsing his every word. As for Mr. Schiff, no one should ever believe another word he says."[32] Moreover, to the extent that Schiff has legitimate concerns about Trump's ties with Russia, overstating his case reduces the likelihood that the public will believe him. Former congressman Will Hurd, a moderate Republican, wrote in his 2022 book that Schiff was the "biggest contributor to Russian disinformation campaigns" because he repeatedly claimed that the evidence of collusion between the Trump campaign and Russia was not just circumstantial. "Everyone—many House colleagues, the media, the public—was operating under the assumption that Schiff had access to intelligence that other people didn't possess and that he knew something we did not know," Hurd wrote. "But he didn't."[33]

While there are reasonable arguments that both Hawley and Schiff were doing what politicians often do—spinning facts for political purposes—their portrayals of those facts, at the very least, left listeners and readers with skewed impressions of what was known then. But courts rightly hesitate to impose legal liability for such skewed presentations of facts, in part because they recognize that "truth" and "falsity" evolve with more knowledge, whether or not a claim is properly viewed as "misinformation." Among the most controversial recent examples of evolving perceptions of truth was an October 14, 2020, story in the *New York Post* headlined "Smoking-Gun Email Reveals How Hunter Biden Introduced Ukrainian Businessman to VP Dad." The story's lede claimed that Hunter Biden had introduced his father, then the vice president, "to a top executive at a Ukrainian energy firm less than a year before the elder Biden pressured government officials in Ukraine into firing a prosecutor who was investigating the company." The newspaper based this reporting on emails that it had obtained. The *Post* wrote that the emails came from a water-damaged laptop that was left at a Delaware repair shop in 2019 and not picked up by the person who had dropped it off.[34]

Such a story could have huge implications, coming just weeks before the presidential election. Indeed, James Comey, then director of the Federal Bureau of Investigation, announcing in late October 2016 that agents were examining a newly discovered laptop that contained Hillary Clinton's emails certainly did not help her in the final stretch of the campaign. Would this be the second laptop story to upend a presidential election? Not surprisingly, Donald Trump seized on the news. At a campaign rally the same day that the *Post* published the story, he called Biden "a corrupt politician who shouldn't even be allowed to run for the presidency." Biden's campaign dismissed the story as potential Russian disinformation, noting that Trump lawyer Rudy Giuliani was involved

and his "discredited conspiracy theories and alliance with figures connected to Russian intelligence have been widely reported."[35]

Many of the mainstream media outlets that covered the story did
so by questioning the newspaper's credibility. For instance, two days
after the story ran, Wolf Blitzer discussed the story with Congressman Schiff on *The Situation Room*.

"Does it surprise you at all that this information Rudy Giuliani is
peddling very well could be connected to some sort of Russian government disinformation campaign?" Blitzer asked.

"Well, we know that this whole smear on Joe Biden comes from
the Kremlin," Schiff responded. "That's been clear for well over a year
now that they've been pushing this false narrative about the vice president and his son."[36]

Also questioning the story were some of the largest technology
companies. Within hours of the story's publication, Facebook's policy
communications director, Andy Stone, tweeted that Facebook's third-
party fact-checkers would review the *Post* story. "In the meantime, we
are reducing its distribution on our platform," he tweeted.[37] Twitter
also quickly took action, preventing users from sharing the story on
its platform. If users tried to share it, they received a message that read,
"We can't complete this request because this link has been identified
by Twitter or our partners as being potentially harmful." The company at least partly justified the decision out of concern not about misinformation, but its policies against allowing content that results from
hacking and content containing private information. That evening,
Twitter CEO Jack Dorsey said that the company's communication
about the action "was not great."[38] That is not to say that the social
media companies' efforts were necessarily successful. Their decisions
to block the *Post* story drew more attention to it, particularly in conservative media. The day after the story ran, Fox News media reporter
Brian Flood wrote an article with the headline "Twitter's Double Standard Emerges after NY Post Hunter Biden Story Blocked, Other
Media Get Pass, Critics Say." The article described the "unrelenting

backlash" that Twitter was facing. Although Flood cautioned that Fox had not yet fully verified the newspaper's reporting, he recounted the general gist of the article.[39]

At the time of this book's publication, there were a lot of open questions and not enough concrete information to fully answer them. In March 2022—more than a year into Joe Biden's presidency—some of those questions were answered when the *New York Times*, reporting on a grand jury investigation into Hunter Biden's international business affairs, mentioned that the *Times* and prosecutors had examined emails "from a cache of files that appears to have come from a laptop abandoned by Mr. Biden in a Delaware repair shop," and that people familiar with the investigation had authenticated the files.[40] Conservative media pounced on the news, arguing that supporters of the social media platforms' initial restrictions were wrong to call the *Post*'s report misinformation. Though, as Andrew Prokop wrote in Vox soon after the *Times* article, even if the emails are authentic, it is unclear whether they show the vast corruption that Biden critics claim.[41]

Was it fair for social media outlets to take such quick action to suppress the *Post* story? I hesitate to give a definitive answer as I write this in 2022, as it is impossible to know what more information will emerge between now and this book's publication. And that is the danger of reflexively tagging speech as "misinformation." Our knowledge of the veracity of a claim is only as good as the facts available when we make the assessment. We can control certain aspects, such as fairly analyzing all data available, trying to gather more information if possible, and recognizing the limits of the data on which we are drawing our conclusion. Claiming in October 2020 that the Hunter Biden laptop story *might* be incomplete or inaccurate may be a reasonable conclusion. But confidently branding it as a Russian misinformation operation, without evidence to support the claim, is unwise and could lead to future mistrust of the brander.

Indeed, not everyone is sold on the degree of the misinformation problem. Among the more cautionary voices was that of journalist

Joseph Bernstein, in a September 2021 cover story for *Harper's Maga-zine*. Bernstein cited research that questioned the impact that disin-formation and misinformation has had in recent years, and pointed out that the research is nascent, with experts failing to even agree on what constitutes misinformation and disinformation. "'Misinformation' and 'disinformation' are used casually and interchangeably to refer to an enormous range of content, ranging from well-worn scams to viral news aggregation; from foreign-intelligence operations to trolling; from opposition research to harassment," Bernstein wrote. "In their crudest use, the terms are simply jargon for 'things I disagree with.'"[42]

Bernstein observed that those who comment the most about dis-information are powerful pre-digital institutions such as television networks, large newspapers, universities, and think tanks, a collective that he dubbed "Big Disinfo." And he noted that Big Disinfo had suc-cessfully urged some large social media companies to remove claims that COVID-19 was man-made, until new reporting made such claims more plausible. "Whatever the brilliance of the individual disinforma-tion researchers and reporters, the nature of the project inevitably places them in a regrettably defensive position in the contemporary debate about media representation, objectivity, image-making, and public knowledge," Bernstein wrote. "However well-intentioned these pro-fessionals are, they don't have special access to the fabric of reality."[43]

Skeptics of Big Disinfo do not argue that we simply should ignore the problems that are caused by misinformation and disinformation. Rather, they generally question the magnitude of the harms given the limited evidence, and whether at least some harms can be attributed not only to the false information but also to the underlying social prob-lems that drive people to so readily believe and act on the false infor-mation. Any examination of misinformation and disinformation should consider whether it is a symptom of a larger problem rather than a standalone challenge divorced from any broader societal issues such as economic inequality, lack of adequate mental health services, and insufficient media literacy and civics education.[44]

I largely agree with the cautious skepticism of taking drastic actions. We should not discount the harms and challenges created by misinformation and disinformation, particularly as it can spread rapidly on social media. Nor do I rule out all liability for false speech; indeed, our legal system has always left the door open for defamation civil claims and criminal charges such as fraud and lying to government agents. But the bar for such liability has been and should be extraordinarily high. Rather than reflexively banning speech that we believe is false, we should look at other options to mitigate the underlying causes of false speech.

Any debate about the harms of modern falsehoods must consider the long-standing dissemination of alleged falsehoods and propaganda. Consider how Octavian, Julius Caesar's adopted son, approached his succession fight with Mark Antony, Caesar's general, after Caesar's assassination in 44 BC. Among the propaganda that Octavian used were coins containing brief phrases that questioned Antony's ability to succeed Caesar, including claims that his romance with Cleopatra would cause him to be loyal to Egypt, and that Antony was a drunkard.[45] "Public opinion had to be won, and every sort of intrigue was to be used if there was any chance of its success," historian Kenneth Scott wrote of the propaganda battle between the two men.[46]

Politicians have long dismissed unfriendly news coverage as lies. For instance, from 1768 to 1769, the *New York Journal* printed the "Boston Journal of Occurrences," written by Samuel Adams and others and depicting in great detail the mistreatment of people in Boston by English soldiers. "Nine tenths of what you read in the Journal of Occurrences in Boston is either absolutely false or grossly misrepresented," said Thomas Hutchinson, a British loyalist who would become Massachusetts governor before the American Revolution.[47]

After independence, politicians continued to bemoan fake news. "It is a melancholy truth, that a suppression of the press could not more compleatly deprive the nation of its benefits, than is done by its abandoned prostitution to falsehood," President Thomas Jefferson wrote in 1807. "Nothing can now be believed which is seen in a newspaper. Truth itself becomes suspicious by being put into that polluted vehicle."[48] The Sedition Act, which Jefferson opposed, was only one of the attempts to address fake news through the law. For instance, Virginia officials sought to keep the public from learning of the 1791 slave revolt on the French colony of St. Domingue (now Haiti). In response, the Virginia General Assembly passed "An act against divulgers of False News."[49] After finding that "many idle and busy headed people do forge and divulge false rumors and reports," lawmakers created a criminal offense applying to those who "forge or divulge false reports, tending to the trouble of the country."[50] Virginia's legislature used the possibility of false speech as a vehicle to suppress information that might have threatened the institution of slavery.

America has long worried about the effect of new technology in distributing false information. A *New York Times* article from 1858 warned of the dangers of the new transatlantic telegraph. "Superficial, sudden, unsifted, too fast for the truth, must be all telegraphic intelligence," the *Times* wrote. "Does it not render the popular mind too fast for the truth? Ten days bring us the mails from Europe. What need is there for the scraps of news in ten minutes? How trivial and paltry is the telegraphic column?"[51] Adrienne LaFrance of *The Atlantic* in 2014 aptly compared nineteenth-century concerns about the telegraph with modern worries about social media and online news. "Anti-tech criticism isn't wrong—there are plenty of legitimate warnings about how the ease with which anyone can publish something today can exacerbate problems in accuracy and ethics," she wrote. "But that also doesn't mean previous technologies were inherently better, or that they'll ever reclaim their standing."[52]

False speech originating in foreign countries did not begin with the Internet. For instance, in the 1980s, Soviet agencies including the KGB spread a conspiracy theory that US Army medical researchers had created the human immunodeficiency virus (HIV).[53] As Douglas Selvage and Christopher Nehring of the Wilson Center recounted in an extensive review of primary documents, the "smoking gun" that started the disinformation campaign was a cable from the KGB to Bulgarian State Security, describing "a new type of biological weapon by the secret services of the USA and the Pentagon that spun out of control." The KGB based its claims on an anonymous letter published in an Indian newspaper that the KGB had previously used for disinformation.[54] The East German Stasi security service distributed a "study" by East German scientist Jakob Segal that was published in a brochure titled *AIDS: USA Home-Made Evil, NOT Out of AFRICA.*[55] The disinformation campaign, which eventually became known as Operation INFEKTION, soon spread the false claims to appear in publications in more than 80 nations.[56] The campaign evolved to claim that the Pentagon created HIV to kill gay people and African Americans, and even received coverage on the CBS Evening News, with anchor Dan Rather attributing it to a Soviet newspaper.[57]

The US government responded via its Active Measures Working Group, an interdepartmental group that it had formed in 1981 to deal with disinformation. As Thomas Boghardt documented in his authoritative 2009 history of Operation INFEKTION, this effort had some glitches. A US State Department spokesman, relying on an incomplete news archives search, denied that the anonymous letter had ever appeared in the Indian newspaper. A Soviet publication responded with an article titled "It Existed, It Existed, Boy" and referred to the working group as a bureau that conducts "disinformation, analysis, and retaliatory measures."[58] Still, as Boghardt documents, the group "spent time and effort dissecting Segal's theses and highlighting their inconsistencies and contradictions to lawmakers and the public."[59] Despite the US government's efforts, Operation INFEKTION had an impact for years. A 1992 survey in the United States found that 15 percent of respondents thought it was probably or definitely true that "the AIDS virus was created deliberately in a government laboratory."[60]

While many concerns about false speech are warranted, and the Internet makes problems seem all the more ubiquitous, it also is important to keep in mind the potential to use the label of "false news" to suppress dissent. As I argue in chapter 10, we should resist the urge to automatically regulate away the problems of falsehoods, as such censorship is inconsistent with the approach that courts and legislatures have taken for the past century.

Chapter 10

When Regulation or Liability Is Not the Answer

Payton S. Gendron murdered ten people and injured three in a Buffalo, New York, supermarket on May 14, 2022. His victims were mostly Black, and the media soon reported a screed that Gendron had written, citing racist conspiracy theories that have long circulated both online and in conservative media. Two days later, US Senator Kirsten Gillibrand of New York appeared on MSNBC to discuss the shooting and potential responses to prevent future tragedies.

"Can you regulate speech on the Internet without violating free speech?" reporter Katy Tur asked.

"You don't have to regulate speech," Gillibrand said. "You can regulate misinformation. You could say you can't yell fire in a theater. You can . . . there's many ways you can abrogate speech rights that are consistent with the Constitution."[1]

While Gillibrand is correct that it is possible to regulate some speech without raising First Amendment problems, the rest of her statement is wrong. Misinformation *is* speech. While some speech undisputedly can be regulated, the Supreme Court has explicitly rejected a broad exception for false speech. Invoking the crowded theater will not magically create an avenue for unchecked censorship.

The concerns about false speech have driven many commentators and politicians to propose new laws that would penalize at least some types of false statements that have long received legal protection. While many of these proposals are well intentioned, they generally diverge from the free speech principles outlined in part I of this book. For many of the same reasons that courts and legislatures have protected falsehoods for centuries, imposing broad new "misinformation" laws would be stifling, ripe for abuse, inefficient, and largely inconsistent with the US legal system's approach to false speech.

Among the most notable of such recent proposals came from Washington Governor Jay Inslee, on the first anniversary of the January 6, 2021, storming of the US Capitol. He issued a press release that touted his support for "legislation currently being written that would outlaw attempts by candidates and elected officials to spread lies about free and fair elections when it has the likelihood to stoke violence." State lawmakers, he said in the statement, were drafting a bill that would create a gross misdemeanor for elected officials or political candidates in Washington State who tell knowing lies about elections. "The proposed law is narrowly tailored to capture only those false statements that are made for the purpose of undermining the election process or results and is further limited to lies that are likely to incite or cause lawlessness," Inslee said.[2] Inslee appeared to rely on *Brandenburg v. Ohio*, the 1969 case that refined the *Schenck v. United States* "clear and present danger" test that Holmes articulated in 1919. "The U.S. Supreme Court has made it clear that speech can be limited where it is likely to incite lawlessness," Inslee's press release stated. But the statement did not capture the narrowness of the *Brandenburg* opinion. In that ruling, the court wrote that the First Amendment prohibits state regulation of advocacy unless that advocacy "is directed to inciting or producing imminent lawless action and is likely to incite or produce such action."[3] Inslee's press release omitted any mention of an imminence requirement. As First Amendment scholar Eugene Volokh told *Reason* in an article about Inslee's proposal, imminence is a high bar. An example of imminent lawless action, Volokh said, is "standing outside a police station and yelling 'burn it down.'" But claiming fraudulent election results, Volokh said, is not incitement.[4]

And therein was the problem with Inslee's initial proposal. While it was well intentioned and arose from a legitimate desire to prevent a repeat of the unrest at the Capitol, Inslee could not easily explain how a politician's lie about election administration rose to the level of imminent incitement of lawless action.

Throughout January 2022, Inslee tried to justify the proposal as constitutional and urgently necessary. At an event on the day of his announcement, which took place as Trump continued to contest the election results, Inslee resorted to a comfortable and censorious metaphor. "The defeated president as recently as an hour ago is yelling fire in the crowded theater of democracy," Inslee said.[5] But no amount of references to fires or crowds or theaters could justify jailing politicians just because their speech was found to be untrue.

Perhaps in response to the criticism that Inslee's announcement received, lawmakers over the next few weeks consulted legal scholars and released a revised version of the bill.[6] The proposal begins with legislative findings that contain bold statements about Washington State's election integrity. The bill would create a gross misdemeanor, punishable by up to 364 days in jail, for any elected official or candidate who "knowingly, recklessly, or maliciously makes false statements or claims related to any pending or completed and certified election conducted in the state, regarding the legitimacy or integrity of the election process or election results," provided that the false speech is: (1) "intended to incite or produce imminent lawless action and do incite or produce such action resulting in harm to a person or to property"; (2) "made for the purpose of undermining the election process or the election results"; or (3) "falsely claim entitlement to an office that an elected official or candidate did not win after any lawful challenge made pursuant to this title is completed and the election results are certified."[7] To the credit of those who drafted the revised bill, they at least tried to hew more closely to the language of *Brandenburg* than Inslee did in his press release. But even the narrower language—tying the false statements to imminent lawless action—was not guaranteed to survive constitutional scrutiny. And the revised bill covered two other types of false speech that were unrelated to the *Brandenburg* standard.

At a January 28, 2022, state senate hearing on the bill, state senator David Frockt, the bill's primary sponsor, discussed the delicate balancing act that was required to address election lies while adhering to *Alvarez, Brandenburg,* and other First Amendment precedents. "It's kind of like trying to drive a toaster through a car wash," Frockt said. "You have to get it just right. And so we do not take the First Amendment for granted. I don't. We don't treat it cavalierly."[8] Others who testified were more skeptical both about the bill's constitutionality and its potential impacts. Paul Guppy, vice president for research of the conservative Washington Policy Center think tank, pointed to the state's close 2004 gubernatorial election, which required a recount that lasted more than a month. "That was exactly a time period when we needed the maximum open and transparent debate of different opinions about what was happening with that election than ever," Guppy said. "If this bill had been in effect, public officials and candidates would have been restricted or chilled or fearful about what they could say about that election."[9] The bill could undermine its primary goal, Guppy said. "It doesn't increase the confidence in the outcome of the election," he said. "It actually creates more suspicion when people are not allowed to debate the outcome of elections honestly."[10] The opposition was substantial enough to prevent the bill from passing. A few weeks after the hearing, Frockt issued a statement acknowledging that the proposal would not progress in the legislature in 2022.[11]

Had the bill passed, would it have survived a constitutional challenge? It is hard to predict with certainty. The revised bill at least attempted to address First Amendment concerns by mimicking the *Brandenburg* imminent incitement standard. While adding the *Brandenburg* language increases the chances of the law surviving a First Amendment challenge, it also reduces the number of scenarios in which the government could hold a politician accountable for lying about election integrity. In a 1973 opinion, *Hess v. Indiana*, the US Supreme Court highlighted the narrowness of the *Brandenburg* exception that it had articulated four years earlier. The case involved an antiwar protest at Indiana University. After police began clearing the street, the defendant said something like "We'll take the fucking street later," and was arrested for disorderly conduct.[12] The Supreme Court reversed his conviction, finding that the *Brandenburg* exception did not apply. "Since the uncontroverted evidence showed that [the defendant's] statement was not directed to any person or group of persons, it cannot be said that he was advocating, in the normal sense, any action," the court wrote. "And since there was no evidence, or rational inference from the import of the language, that his words were intended to produce, and likely to produce, imminent disorder, those words could not be punished by the State on the ground that they had a tendency to lead to violence."[13]

And even with the *Brandenburg* language, the law still might face First Amendment problems. A politician challenging the law might argue that the uncertainty about what constitutes imminent incitement would chill a wider swath of constitutionally protected speech. A politician who has legitimate concerns about how an election was administered may understandably refrain from saying anything to avoid even the prospect of being prosecuted and sentenced to up to a year in prison. Even though the prosecution would face a high burden of proving all elements of the crime beyond a reasonable doubt, it is not inconceivable that a politically biased judge could sway a guilty verdict. And even if they were not ultimately convicted, they would need to spend substantial time and money defending the case. So perhaps it is more attractive to not say anything about their concerns.

Nor does the bill's limitation to knowing, malicious, or reckless false-hoods directed toward particular goals eliminate concerns of a chill-ing effect, as illustrated in the Eighth Circuit's opinion in *281 Care Committee v. Arneson* (see chap. 8). In striking down the Minnesota law that criminalized intentional falsehoods about ballot questions, the court rejected the argument that limiting the misdemeanor to inten-tional falsehoods avoided constitutional problems. "The risk of chill-ing otherwise protected speech is not eliminated or lessened by the mens rea requirement because, as we have already noted, a speaker might still be concerned that someone will file a complaint with the [Office of Administrative Hearings], or that they might even ul-timately be prosecuted, for a careless false statement or possibly a truthful statement someone deems false, no matter the speaker's ve-racity," the court wrote. "Or, most cynically, many might legitimately fear that no matter what they say, an opponent will utilize [the law] to simply tie them up in litigation and smear their name or position on a particular matter, even if the speaker never had the intent required to render him liable."[14]

Even if this bill were somehow found to comport with the First Amendment, I question whether it would meet its goals of instilling further confidence in elections and preventing repeats of the January 6 violence. The mere presence of the law on Washington State's books might make some segments of the public *more* skeptical of the state's elections procedures, perhaps fueling speculation that politicians might be aware of problems but stay quiet out of fear of jail time. This would not be an unreasonable worry; after all, they might think, why would Washington State need to threaten politicians with jail time if its elec-tions actually were secure? And it is far from certain that such a law would substantially reduce the most harmful false speech about elec-tions. Of course, President Trump and some other elected officials spread false claims about the 2020 elections, but they were not the only ones. Washington State's law does not (and could not) regulate false speech spread by talk radio hosts, social media trolls, foreign governments, and others.

The opposition to and failure of Washington State's proposal reveals the many difficulties of addressing falsehoods through legal penalties. First Amendment precedent guides the legal analysis, but even if it survived a constitutional challenge, the law would reveal many practical problems in effectively regulating false speech. All the reasons for allowing falsehoods, as outlined in part I of this book, apply to arguments against new misinformation regulations. Censorious new laws threaten to chill the ability of people to express criticism of those in power. They also reduce the ability of speakers to shine light on public functions such as the elections system. And it's unclear whether they are effective.

While Inslee's bill is among the highest-profile attempts to regulate away the problems of falsehoods, he was not alone in recent years. Efforts to regulate other sorts of false speech, even indirectly, are likely to suffer from similar shortcomings. One such effort is the Health Misinformation Act, which Senators Amy Klobuchar and Ben Ray Luján introduced in July 2021. The senators proposed the bill after more than a year of false speech about COVID-19 that discouraged many people from taking reasonable steps to protect the health of themselves and others. In a news release announcing the bill, the senators focused on the failure of large social media platforms to take action on health misinformation.[15]

The senators' particular concern is Section 230 of the Communications Decency Act. The 1996 law, which is analyzed in depth in chapter 13, broadly protects online platforms from legal claims arising from content that was provided by users and other third parties. Section 230 contains a few exceptions, including for federal criminal law enforcement and intellectual property law. In an October 2021 interview with the *Wall Street Journal*, Klobuchar described her frustration with both the platforms and Section 230 by using a familiarly heated hypothetical.

"As you know, what that means is they can't be sued," Klobuchar said of Section 230. "And the way I describe this to people is, if you yell fire in a crowded theater, that's not protected speech. If there's a stampede, the theater probably won't be sued. . . . If the theater decides to use speakers and have it broadcast what the person is saying or whatever misinformation they're putting out there . . . they'd be sued."[16] Klobuchar and Luján's bill attempts to pressure platforms to be more responsive to complaints about false health claims by creating an exception to Section 230 for "health misinformation" that the platform algorithmically promotes via a non-neutral mechanism during a public health emergency.

It is hard to imagine a platform that does not use algorithms for user content, so it is reasonably likely that any information that these platforms display could seem to have been "promoted" in a non-neutral manner. This exception would only apply to "health misinformation," but the bill does not define precisely what health misinformation is. Instead, it states that within 30 days of the bill's enactment, "the Secretary of Health and Human Services, in consultation with the heads of other relevant Federal agencies and outside experts determined appropriate by the Secretary, shall issue guidance regarding what constitutes health misinformation."

The bill allows one political appointee to unilaterally define health misinformation, with no statutory limits or oversight, and the consequences of that definition would be to strongly influence what health-related speech people are more likely to see on the Internet. Imagine a secretary of Health and Human Services who bristles at criticism. The secretary could define health misinformation as any commentary at odds with the government's approach to public health. Even if the Health and Human Services secretary was not acting with a nefarious motive, the official's job of defining health misinformation would be difficult, if not impossible. For the same reasons that courts refused to adjudicate the factual accuracy of books such as *The Last Chance Diet* and *The Encyclopedia of Mushrooms*, the secretary would face a great challenge in deciding what qualifies as health misinformation. Our understanding of truth evolves with more knowledge and debate. Defining health misinformation in one static guidance document would stifle further discussion and knowledge.

The Section 230 exception in this bill likely would cause platforms to more aggressively block speech that potentially qualifies as health misinformation. When Congress in 2018 added a Section 230 exception for certain civil and state criminal actions related to sex trafficking and prostitution, platforms responded quickly. For instance, Craigslist removed its personals advertisements section because of the increased legal risks, and other platforms similarly restricted content that had even a remote possibility of falling under the exception.[17] If public health commentary or claims even potentially fell within the secretary's definition of health misinformation, a platform likely would either delete it or stop algorithmically "promoting" it, which could have an impact similar to deletion.

That is not to say that the exception would help the victims of false health claims. The bill only creates an exception to Section 230; it does not create a new cause of action under which people could sue platforms for health misinformation. Plaintiffs would need to sue platforms under an existing legal cause of action, and it is hard to conceive of one easily working for health misinformation. As seen in part I, courts are reluctant to allow people to bring lawsuits based on their *reactions* to alleged misinformation.

Another attempt to regulate coronavirus-related false speech came not from a new legislative proposal, but from a creative attempt to apply the existing, narrow avenues for speech regulation. The Supreme Court has long allowed the Federal Communications Commission to impose some regulations on broadcasters that use the public spectrum in ways that the government could never regulate other forms of media such as newspapers or websites.[18] The FCC issues broadcast licenses based in part on finding that they are in the "public interest."[19] Under that authority, the FCC adopted "broadcast hoax" regulations, which allow the FCC to fine a radio or television station that broadcasts false information about crimes or catastrophes if the broadcaster knows that it is false, it is "foreseeable that the broadcast of the information will cause substantial public harm," and broadcasting the information "does in fact directly cause substantial public harm." The regulations state that programming that contains a disclaimer is presumed not to pose such foreseeable harm "if the disclaimer clearly characterizes the program as a fiction and is presented in a way that is reasonable under the circumstances."[20]

Until it passed its current rule in 1992, the FCC only had the authority to warn stations that broadcasted hoaxes. But a series of high-profile lies in the late 1980s and early 1990s, such as a false report of a station being taken hostage and another about a volcanic eruption in the area, caused the commission to add teeth to its regulatory authority. "Recently, serious broadcast hoaxes have occurred where the stations involved fabricated stories concerning a crime or catastrophe that alarmed the public and resulted in the needless diversion of public safety or law enforcement resources," the FCC wrote as it adopted the 1992 regulation.[21]

Some media organizations objected to the FCC's proposal on First Amendment grounds, worried about the chilling effect on other speech. The FCC wrote that it addressed these concerns by limiting the application of the rule to certain types of hoaxes, and that the rule is not intended to prevent "harmless pranks" or broadcasts that merely upset some listeners. "We instead focus on a narrow category of cases—those involving the false report of a crime or catastrophe— which present the greatest potential for substantial public harm," the

FCC wrote. "Moreover, within this narrow category of cases, we restrict the reach of the rule even further by holding licensees liable only when they know the report to be false and can foresee that the report will, and does in fact, result in substantial public harm."[22] Not surprisingly, the commission cited Holmes's line about shouting fire in a crowded theater as a "bedrock principle of First Amendment doctrine."[23] The commission's representation of the rule as applying to a narrow set of circumstances has proven to be correct. In a 2019 article, communications professor Joel Timmer found only a few complaints and no FCC findings of violations under the rule since the FCC passed it nearly three decades earlier.[24]

The most prominent complaint to date under the broadcast hoax rule came in March 2020, as the nation was locking down in response to the COVID-19 pandemic. Free Press, an advocacy group, was particularly concerned about broadcasters carrying statements of President Donald Trump regarding the pandemic that it believed to be misleading and harmful. Among the statements to which the group objected were his promotion of hydroxychloroquine as a treatment, his minimization of the virus's harms, and his claims that testing was widely available.[25] Free Press also objected to radio host Rush Limbaugh's characterization of coronavirus as a "common cold," and talk host Mark Levin claiming that opponents of Trump were "using this as another opportunity to hype and dramatize their agenda."[26] Free Press pointed to polling that found that 49 percent of people who listened to the radio said that they were "worried" about COVID-19, compared to 72 percent of people who read national newspapers.[27] "When the president tells dangerous lies about a public health emergency, broadcasters have a choice: don't air them, or put those lies in context with disclaimers noting that they may be untrue and are unverified. And certainly the FCC has a duty to rein in radio broadcasters that seed confusion with lies and disinformation," Free Press wrote in a March 26, 2020, petition to the FCC, asking it to investigate whether radio broadcasters violated the commission's hoax rule, and to provide guidance that recommends broadcast stations "prominently disclose when information they air is false or scientifically suspect."[28]

About two weeks later, the FCC emphatically denied Free Press's request, concluding that it "seeks remedies that would dangerously curtail the freedom of the press embodied in the First Amendment."[29] FCC Media Bureau Chief Michelle M. Carey and General Counsel Thomas M. Johnson Jr. wrote that the commission "does not—and cannot and will not—act as a self-appointed, free-roving arbiter of truth in journalism."[30] The FCC officials recognized both the urgency for broadcasters to report on public statements by the president and other officials about the pandemic and the changing understanding of truth about a novel coronavirus as more facts emerged. "At this moment, broadcasters face the challenge of covering a rapidly-evolving, national, and international health crisis, in which new information—much of it medical or technical in nature and therefore difficult to corroborate or refute in real time—is continually revealed, vetted, and verified or dismissed," the FCC officials wrote.[31] The FCC also recognized that many of Free Press's complaints involved opinions about COVID-19. The commission wrote that it would leave to broadcasters "the editorial decisions about airing political commentary and trusting the American public's ability to differentiate between medical advice and political opinion."[32]

The FCC was correct to swiftly and unambiguously deny Free Press's request. Although the commission's 1992 rule has yet to be tested in court, it likely complies with the First Amendment because it is narrowly applied to a small category of false broadcast statements, such as reporting that a volcano had erupted. Free Press was seeking to dramatically expand this regulation to all commentary about the biggest news story of 2020. Regulating such a wide range of allegedly false information conflicts with many values outlined in the cases in part I of this book. Most importantly, in the earliest stages of the pandemic, little was known about COVID-19 with anything close to certainty. Even if one were to agree that the FCC *should* regulate false information about COVID-19, it is hard to conceive how it could confidently determine which speech to allow and which to suppress. And the regulation would likely not be effective; the hoax regulations only extend to broadcasters, so any half-truths or lies would continue to proliferate on cable television and the Internet.

Government officials have sometimes taken anti-misinformation crusades into their own hands, even when they have no legal authority to do so. Consider the story of Amyiah Cohoon. In March 2020, the 16-year-old high school sophomore in Oxford, Wisconsin, went on a trip to Disney World with her band class.[33] As the nation began to lock down in response to the COVID-19 pandemic, Cohoon and her bandmates returned to Wisconsin earlier than scheduled.[34] Within days of her return home, she had COVID-19 symptoms, including a dry cough and a fever, and she eventually had enough trouble breathing that her mother took her to the emergency room.[35] After evaluating her, the doctors said Cohoon's symptoms were consistent with COVID-19, but they could not arrange a test for her. So, they sent her home and told her to quarantine.[36] On a work release form dated March 22, 2020, a doctor wrote that "Amyiah Cohoon has symptoms consistent with COVID-19."[37] After returning home, Cohoon's mother left a message for the band teacher to inform her that her daughter might have COVID-19.[38]

Cohoon took to Instagram, posting a picture of herself sitting in front of a window. The caption read: "Hey guys . . . sorry I've been on a long break . . . i wont be back for a while longer due to me noe [*sic*] having the COVID-19 virus . . . I don't want the attention its [*sic*] just the truth . . . I am now in self quarantine and am not allowrd [*sic*] to leave my room and have an inhaler since they said to go home . . . best of wishes love you guys."[39] After three days of quarantine, Cohoon had more difficulty breathing, so she went back to the emergency room and from there was taken by ambulance to the University of Wisconsin Children's Hospital.[40]

Cohoon's mother, while waiting at the children's hospital, told the high school principal that her daughter was in the hospital and that the principal should consider informing the parents of the other teenagers who went on the Disney trip. The principal said he would touch base with the band teacher.[41] From the hospital, Cohoon posted to Instagram that she was "in the ER might need to stay."[42] A COVID test administered to Cohoon at the children's hospital came back negative. The doctors told her family that she likely had the virus but had missed the testing window.[43] Cohoon went home the next day and posted to Instagram a selfie taken in the hospital, with an oxygen mask on her face. She wrote: "I am finally home after being hospitalized for a day and a half. I am still on breathing treatment but have beaten the coronavirus. Stay home and be safe."[44]

The next evening, Cohoon answered the front door to find a Marquette County Sheriff's patrol sergeant, who asked to talk with her father. The sergeant told her father that Marquette County Sheriff Joseph Konrath received a complaint from the school superintendent about his daughter's Instagram posts and showed a copy of one of her posts, according to the Cohoon family's account of the conversation.[45] In their retelling, the sergeant told them that because no cases of COVID-19 had yet been confirmed in Marquette County, Konrath ordered him to demand that Cohoon delete the post, and that failure to do so could lead to a disorderly conduct citation for her or her parents and that he should "start taking people to jail."[46]

The sergeant's incident report confirms that he told Cohoon's father "that if they were not willing to take the post down, that there would be the possibility of a County Ordinance Disorderly Conduct or being arrested for Disorderly Conduct."[47] The Cohoons say that the sergeant declined their offer to review her medical records,[48] though the sergeant says that he did in fact view the records, and that the sergeant never mentioned the possibility of a disorderly conduct citation or arrest while Amyiah Cohoon was present.[49] Afraid that the sergeant would arrest her or her parents, Cohoon deleted the Instagram post and showed her Instagram account to the sergeant, who then departed, according to the Cohoons' account of the visit.[50]

Later, the Cohoons learned of an email that the school district administrator had sent to families earlier that day. Although he did not mention Cohoon by name, the administrator addressed her Instagram posts. "It was brought to my attention today that there was a rumor floating out there that one of our students contracted Covid-19 while on the band trip to Florida two weeks ago," he wrote. "Let me assure you there is NO truth to this. This was a foolish means to get attention and the source of the rumor has been addressed." He then included a statement from the county health department that they had "zero confirmed cases of COVID-19."[51]

At this point, the Cohoons received legal representation from the Wisconsin Institute for Law and Liberty, a conservative nonprofit law firm in Milwaukee. A week after the sergeant's visit, a lawyer at the institute, Luke Berg, wrote to Konrath informing him that the altercation violated Cohoon's First Amendment rights and requested a public apology and a confirmation that Cohoon could repost the deleted material. "Even setting aside the First Amendment issue, your order to cite the Cohoons for disorderly conduct is clearly an abuse of that ordinance, as neither Amyiah's posts nor her refusing to take them down could lawfully be prosecuted as 'disorderly conduct' under Marquette County's ordinance or the corresponding state statute," Berg wrote. "Your actions are particularly troubling in light of the fact that they were taken against a high school student who simply wished to communicate with her friends about a serious medical issue she was facing."[52]

Samuel Hall, a lawyer for the sheriff's office, emailed Berg to state that although the Cohoons probably would not receive an apology, Hall thought he "could likely get some sort of a written correspondence to your clients from the sheriff indicating that any investigation of the matter is closed and that he is not recommending or referring any charges—or something to that effect." Berg replied that the Cohoons needed more than just confirmation that the investigation of the posts was finished. They also sought reassurance that they would not face citations or threats for other similar First Amendment–protected posts in the future.[53]

Hall replied that the sheriff would not apologize, and wrote that any litigation involving the issue would be meritless. Not surprisingly, the assessment involved a crowded theater. "There was no arrest, no prosecution and frankly this seems an awful lot like the 2020 version of screaming fire in a crowded movie theater, which as you know, could be subject to criminal prosecution under existing precedent," Hall wrote.[54]

The next week, the institute filed a lawsuit in Wisconsin federal court against Konrath and the sergeant on behalf of the Cohoons, asking the court to declare that the First Amendment protected the posts, the threats to jail the Cohoons violated the First Amendment, and that the sheriff cannot cite the Cohoons for First Amendment–protected speech. The sheriff's office moved for summary judgment, arguing that the defendants were entitled to qualified immunity because it was not "clearly established" that the First Amendment protected the posts. The lawyers wrote that the "unprecedented" circumstances of the pandemic warranted efforts to calm "panic" caused by the post, particularly given the county health department's request for law enforcement assistance. Predictably, the government once again directed attention to Justice Holmes's metaphorical theater. "Under these circumstances, it was entirely reasonable for Defendants to believe that they were within their authority to carry out the request of the Health Department in order to ensure that potentially dangerous misinformation about the pandemic would not spread," the government's lawyers wrote. "It was also entirely reasonable for Defendants to believe, even if ultimately incorrectly, that falsely claiming to have

COVID-19 is the modern-day equivalent to shouting fire in a crowded theater 100 years ago and therefore does not constitute protected speech."[55]

The case went to Judge Brett Ludwig, a former bankruptcy court judge whom President Trump had recently appointed to the Milwaukee federal court.[56] In an order dated September 24, 2021, Ludwig ruled for the Cohoons, reasoning that they stated a viable First Amendment retaliation claim because they showed that her post was protected by the First Amendment, and the sheriff's department took an adverse action against her that was at least partly motivated by that protected speech.[57]

The First Amendment even protects "short and often grammatically scurrilous" social media posts, Ludwig wrote. The sheriff's claims that the panic caused by her posts rendered it unprotected because it was like "screaming fire in a crowded movie theater" did not change Ludwig's mind. "Even setting aside that the popular movie theater analogy actually referred to *'falsely* shouting fire in a theater and causing a panic,'" Ludwig wrote, citing *Schenck*, "Defendants' argument still fails. While content-based speech restrictions are permissible in limited circumstances (incitement, obscenity, defamation, fighting words, child pornography, etc.), the Supreme Court 'has rejected as startling and dangerous a free-floating test for First Amendment coverage ... based on an ad hoc balancing of relative social costs and benefits.'"[58] The government cannot censor speech just because it determines that censorship might benefit society, Ludwig reasoned. "Defendants may have preferred to keep Marquette County residents ignorant to the possibility of COVID-19 in their community for a while longer, so they could avoid having to field calls from concerned citizens, but that preference did not give them authority to hunt down and eradicate inconvenient Instagram posts," he wrote.[59]

The sheriff argued that Cohoon's posts were lies because she tested negative yet had declared her victory over COVID-19. Ludwig rejected this argument, and his reasoning showed why courts are particularly ill-suited to declare a single undisputed truth. He noted that although Cohoon tested negative, her doctors said she still might have had the virus. "Her Instagram posts were, therefore, at worst, incomplete," Ludwig wrote. "The notion that the long arm of the government—redaction pen in hand—can extend to this sort of incomplete speech is plainly wrong. The Marquette County Sheriff had no more ability to silence Amyiah's posts than it would to silence the many talking heads on cable news, who routinely pronounce one-sided hot takes on the issues of the day, purposefully ignoring any inconvenient facts that might disrupt their preferred narratives." Rather than seeking to censor a teenager's social media posts, Ludwig wrote, it should attempt to persuade the public in the marketplace of ideas. "The government here had every opportunity to counter Amyiah's speech, but it opted instead to engage in the objectionable practice of censorship," Ludwig wrote.[60]

Ludwig's opinion demonstrates why uncertainty about the truth should weigh against government regulation of allegedly false speech. We can't know with absolute certainty that Cohoon *never had* COVID-19 in March 2020. We can't know with absolute certainty that Cohoon *did have* COVID-19 in March 2020. At best, we know two facts: Cohoon tested negative after days of experiencing symptoms, and her doctors said she still might have had COVID-19 despite testing negative. "Fire in a crowded theater" cannot salvage the fundamental First Amendment problems with law enforcement's actions in this case.

Some proponents of more stringent false speech regulations urge the courts to rethink the breadth of their First Amendment protections. One such argument came from legal scholar Cass Sunstein in his 2021 book *Liars: Falsehoods and Free Speech in an Age of Deception.* After providing a thorough review both of the scope of the problem of misinformation and the legal protections for false speech, Sunstein concluded with a proposed principle: "False statements are constitutionally protected unless the government can show that they threaten to cause serious harm that cannot be avoided through a more speech-protective route."[61] He also proposes a lower standard of review for lies than for "unintentional falsehoods." Sunstein recognized that the Supreme Court in *Alvarez* provided stronger protection for false speech, but he criticized that specific holding as "difficult to defend" under the facts of that case. While recognizing that absolute bans on false speech could have a chilling effect, he questioned whether false speech deserves such strong safeguards. His analysis, he wrote, suggests "that in the United States, current constitutional law fails to strike the right balance."[62] Sunstein is particularly concerned about the ability of both high-profile people and private citizens to respond to falsehoods, not necessarily through censorship but through other avenues such as warnings.

Sunstein makes compelling arguments about the harms of falsehoods, particularly intentional ones. But if courts were to eschew *Alvarez* and other First Amendment protections for falsehoods for Sunstein's lower standard, legislatures, the executive branch, and courts would have far more flexibility to abusively use censorship powers. In the name of "misinformation," they could impose content-based restrictions that harm dissenting voices and benefit those in power. Imagine, for instance, that a president and his party, which controls both houses of Congress, believes that "fake news" about health—which also just happens to criticize the administration's handling of a public health crisis—is causing people to make dangerous health decisions. If Congress were to pass a law that allows the Department of Health and Human Services to define "fake health news" and fine those who disseminate it, current First Amendment doctrine would almost certainly lead to the conclusion that such a law was unconstitutional. Under a lower standard, such as that proposed by Sunstein, a court might at least be more likely to conclude that fake health news causes a "serious harm" that cannot be addressed through a "more speech-protective route." Perhaps such a law would not withstand even this lower First Amendment standard, but at the very least the weaker First Amendment scrutiny would increase the chances of survival.

Sunstein attempts to avoid such concerns by suggesting that an "independent tribunal" such as a "court, free from political pressures and not subject to the control of any president or prime minister, should be the institution to resolve the question of truth or falsity."[63] This tribunal, Sunstein writes, would need to determine "that there is no reasonable doubt about the matter." While such a suggestion is well intentioned, it minimizes both the potential for even a life-tenured judge to have political bias and the difficulty of resolving with certainty whether a statement is false. Such a proposal also chills the ability to enhance our understanding of whether a statement is true with more debate. "The history of what judges have concluded is beyond reasonable doubt does not inspire complete confidence in this proposal," commentator Jamie Whyte wrote in response to Sunstein. "But the more compelling objection is Sunstein's remarkable political naiveté. The independence of a tribunal with such astonishing political influence would soon be subverted."[64]

Another call to consider reining in First Amendment protections for falsehoods comes not only from academics, but also from politicians and judges who want to consider abandoning the "actual malice" requirement of *New York Times v. Sullivan*. The modern-day push to overturn *Sullivan* began in February 2016, when presidential candidate Donald Trump said at a Texas rally that, if victorious, he would "open up our libel laws," though he did not specify how he would do so. "So when the *New York Times* writes a hit piece which is a total disgrace or when the *Washington Post*, which is there for other reasons, writes a hit piece, we can sue them and win money instead of having no chance of winning because they're totally protected," Trump said.[65]

Although he did not explain how the president (or Congress) could "open up" state libel laws, it was generally presumed that he meant removing *Sullivan*'s actual malice requirement, something that only the

Supreme Court could do. But a year into his presidency, Trump reiterated his call. "We are going to take a strong look at our country's libel laws, so that when somebody says something that is false and defamatory about someone, that person will have meaningful recourse in our courts," Trump said.[66]

About a year after that statement, Trump's goal appeared to move a bit closer to reality. This movement arose from a 2014 lawsuit that Kathrine McKee brought against actor Bill Cosby, who she alleged had raped her 40 years earlier and defamed her via his attorney's response to her allegations. The district court concluded that she was a limited purpose public figure who was required to show actual malice and dismissed her case for failure to meet that high bar. The appellate court affirmed this dismissal, and the Supreme Court denied McKee's petition for certiorari.[67]

In a concurrence accompanying the denial of certiorari, Justice Clarence Thomas wrote that he agreed that the Supreme Court should not review the factual determination on whether McKee was a limited purpose public figure, but that he believed the court should "reconsider" *Sullivan* and its progeny.[68] Thomas, an originalist, wrote that "there appears to be little historical evidence suggesting that the *New York Times* actual-malice rule flows from the original understanding of the First or Fourteenth Amendment."[69]

Some scholars disagree with Thomas's assessment. Matthew Schafer reviewed libel disputes that occurred right around the nation's founding and argued that, at the very least, Thomas's originalist assessment is not as clear-cut as he portrays. "Far from being out of step with history, *Sullivan* is the obvious next step in what was then more than 150 years of tussling between libel and freedom of the press," Schafer wrote. "Republicanism, freedom of the press, actual malice, the role of public officials and public figures—it is all in these dusty pages. It was all there long before L.B. Sullivan sued the *New York Times*."[70]

Two years after Thomas's questioning of *Sullivan*, another jurist launched even more pointed criticism of the precedent. Judge Laurence

Silberman, appointed to the US Court of Appeals for the DC Circuit by President Ronald Reagan in 1985, wrote a partial dissent in a March 2021 defamation opinion in which he primarily argued that the majority misapplied the actual malice rule in affirming the dismissal of the case. But he concluded his partial dissent by urging the Supreme Court to overrule *Sullivan*.

Silberman echoed Thomas's concerns about *Sullivan* creating a requirement for defamation plaintiffs that is unrelated to the history or text of the First Amendment. But he also used the opportunity to criticize what he viewed as the long-standing liberal agenda of the mainstream media. "Two of the three most influential papers (at least historically), *The New York Times* and *The Washington Post*, are virtually Democratic Party broadsheets," Silberman wrote. "And the news section of *The Wall Street Journal* leans in the same direction. The orientation of these three papers is followed by The Associated Press and most large papers across the country (such as the *Los Angeles Times*, *Miami Herald*, and *Boston Globe*). Nearly all television—network and cable—is a Democratic Party trumpet. Even the government-supported National Public Radio follows along."[71] This biased approach to news reporting, Silberman wrote, disproportionately helps Democratic candidates. "It should be borne in mind that the first step taken by any potential authoritarian or dictatorial regime is to gain control of communications, particularly the delivery of news," he wrote. "It is fair to conclude, therefore, that one-party control of the press and media is a threat to a viable democracy. It may even give rise to countervailing extremism."[72]

Silberman's screed appears more like a talk radio rant than it does a judicial opinion, as it mainly focuses on what he views as a biased press. Although Silberman discusses why he believes that an originalist reading of the First Amendment does not include the actual malice requirement, his opinion does not credibly link that legal analysis with his rant about the liberal media. A less charitable reading of his opinion is that he appears to have an axe to grind with the media, and he believes that they no longer deserve the protections of *Sullivan*. But isn't that the same sort of policy-making function that Silberman believes judges should not engage in?

Silberman's polemic was not the last high-profile criticism of *Sullivan*. Less than four months later, the Supreme Court declined to review the summary judgment dismissal of a defamation lawsuit filed against a book author and publisher by the son of Albania's former prime minister. The plaintiff asked the Supreme Court to reconsider the requirement that public figures must prove actual malice. The Supreme Court declined to take the case, and Justice Clarence Thomas dissented from the denial of certiorari. This time, he was joined by a colleague, Justice Neil Gorsuch.[73]

Thomas's criticism of *Sullivan* was sharper than in his concurrence two years earlier. He questioned the Supreme Court's rationale that public officials and figures should prove actual malice because they invited public attention: "it is unclear why exposing oneself to an increased risk of becoming a victim necessarily means forfeiting the remedies legislatures put in place for such victims."[74]

Thomas asserted that the court has provided "scant explanation" for the actual malice rule, but that understates the reasoning of Justice William Brennan and the jurists who came before and after him. Those who have entered the political arena—or public life in general—are not merely assuming an increased risk of being the subject of falsehoods. They are seeking positions of power, and the media and public at large should carefully scrutinize their backgrounds, record, and character. The core of *Sullivan* is not merely that public officials deserve scrutiny, but that the public benefits from that scrutiny.

Thomas also pointed to modern harms of misinformation, such as Edgar Maddison Welch's shooting at Comet Ping Pong. "Our reconsideration is all the more needed because of the doctrine's real-world effects," Thomas wrote. "Public figure or private, lies impose real harm."[75]

But it is unclear how the actual malice requirement fosters that sort of false speech. Granted, the Democratic Party officials would need to establish actual malice, but the owner of an independent pizza shop might not. And even if he had that burden, actual malice would be far from his biggest barrier in being made whole. The countless anonymous trolls who spread the pizza shop rumor did so not because the *Sullivan* rule would protect them in a libel lawsuit; they probably would never be tracked down to be sued in the first place, even if they could be identified. Those posters might be impossible to identify, and even if unmasking were possible, a plaintiff would face great expense and uncertainty in attempting to do so. If the posters were not wealthy, an expensive defamation lawsuit simply would not be financially feasible for many plaintiffs. Gorsuch called for the court to reconsider *Sullivan*, though he did not necessarily think that it needs to be reversed. The media landscape in 2021, Gorsuch wrote, differs dramatically from that in 1964, with the decline of newspapers and the dominance of cable and Internet news, and when so many more people have avenues to speak. "In 1964, the Court may have seen the actual malice standard as necessary to ensure that dissenting or critical voices are not crowded out of public debate," Gorsuch wrote. "But if that justification had force in a world with comparatively few platforms for speech, it's less obvious what force it has in a world in which everyone carries a soapbox in their hands."[76]

Gorsuch is correct that the media landscape has changed drastically since 1964, and sources of information are far less concentrated. But that makes the *Sullivan* standard *more* necessary than ever. While a libel judgment is costly to even the largest news organizations, it could drive a blogger or citizen journalist into bankruptcy. I think about the hyperlocal website that is an essential source of news for my community in Arlington, Virginia, particularly since the *Washington Post* has all but abandoned substantive local government coverage. Without the protections of *Sullivan*, this small website could be forced out of business by a single frivolous lawsuit brought by a politician who is angry about receiving public scrutiny.

Gorsuch suggested that the *Sullivan* rule has created many incentives for the media to avoid fact-checking and rigorous reporting. "If ensuring an informed democratic debate is the goal, how well do we serve that interest with rules that no longer merely tolerate but encourage falsehoods in quantities no one could have envisioned almost 60 years ago?" Gorsuch wrote.[77]

Gorsuch pointed to the decline in defamation trials and the increased likelihood that verdicts in favor of plaintiffs will be reversed. But that does not necessarily mean that news reporting is generally less rigorous than it was before 1964. News organizations, while far from perfect, continue to invest in hard-hitting journalism. Granted, some commenters on social media will hurl unfounded accusations, though their claims are less likely to be taken seriously than those from a large newspaper or television station. Moreover, anyone familiar with the heyday of yellow journalism or the colonial political pamphlets is accustomed to thinly sourced accusations about public officials and figures.

The ability of private citizens to "become 'public figures' on social media overnight," Gorsuch wrote, also might counsel against *Sullivan*'s requirement that public figures show actual malice.[78] Yet that possibility also supports retaining the requirement; those private citizens now can respond to falsehoods in ways that they never could before. Such "self-help" is among the Supreme Court's primary justifications for requiring public figures but not private figures to establish actual malice.[79]

While Justices Thomas and Gorsuch are correct that much has changed since 1964, the *Sullivan* precedent serves an important role in American democracy, by limiting the ability of the powerful to threaten to silence journalists and other critics. *Sullivan* might leave the door open for more falsehoods than would otherwise be published. But by providing the media with breathing space, it also enables the publication of accurate reporting and criticism that would otherwise be too risky. The fundamental reasons for the actual malice rule have not changed since 1964. And overturning *Sullivan* still would have a chilling effect on speech critical for self-governance.

The calls to overturn *Sullivan* also ignore the very real possibility of such a change *increasing* the amount of false speech in the United States. Imagine a well-resourced and litigious politician who routinely lies to the public. *Sullivan* provides the media, online commentators, and others with enough protection to call the politician out for lying without fearing existential defamation damages. If the Supreme Court were to overturn *Sullivan*, not only could that politician continue to lie with impunity, but others would face much greater risk in pointing out those lies.

The proposals to increase criminal or civil liability for false information conflict with the First Amendment values set forth in part I of this book. But values can evolve in light of new threats. Does the modern climate for falsehoods warrant expanding the government's ability to regulate purportedly false speech?

It does not. The potential for authoritarian misuse and chilling effects is as great today as it was when the Supreme Court issued *Sullivan* in 1964. We can see that in the countries that have passed "fake news" laws in recent years.

Some of the most comprehensive efforts to regulate false speech are in China. A 2017 law[80] includes a requirement that social media providers only link to articles from registered media outlets, not independent media.[81] The government also has investigated large social media platforms for allowing rumors and other harmful content to proliferate.[82] An assessment of China's efforts in a 2018 *Foreign Policy* article concluded that these regulations were unsuccessful in addressing the problem. "Misinformation spreads not simply because there are technologies to circulate it," political scientist Maria Repnikova wrote. "Rather, in China, a deep sense of societal insecurity, the increasing politicization and commercialization of information, and a craving for self-expression propel it."[83]

Despite its inefficacy, China has used its authorities to suppress dissent. Freedom House, in its 2022 report, ranks China as among the "most restrictive media environments" in the world, in part because of its tight censorship of online speech. "Numerous new rules and regulations governing the media and internet usage came into effect during 2021, including measures that restricted news dissemination and contributed to the banning of mobile apps focused on minority languages, Bible content, and foreign-language learning, among other topics," Freedom House wrote. "Censors also removed large numbers of social media groups, accounts, or posts that dealt with LGBT+ issues, financial advice, critical views of CCP history, and celebrities."[84]

Among the worst recent abuses of "fake news" censorship came in Russia, in the weeks after its 2022 invasion of Ukraine. To prevent Russian citizens from learning of Russia's actions, the government blocked them from accessing foreign news and social media providers such as Facebook. It also enacted a law that created a crime, punishable with up to 15 years in prison, for publishing "false information" about the war. Among the possible ways to violate it was characterizing the situation as a "war" rather than a "special military operation."[85]

Russia's fake news law had an immediate chilling effect, causing dozens of reporters to flee the country. "When it comes to a potential threat to somebody, that far and away outweighs everything else in the consideration," Michael Bass, CNN's executive vice president of programming, told the *New York Times* after its reporters left Russia in the days following the law's passage. "It would be better for our reporting and our coverage of the story to continue reporting every single day and multiple times a day from Russia, but an assessment had to be made of what can be done for your people."[86]

In recent years, some countries have seized on the concept of fake news to justify their censorious new laws. For instance, in 2018, Bangladesh's parliament passed the Digital Security Act (DSA), which allows people to be imprisoned for up to 10 years for disseminating "propaganda or campaign against liberation war, spirit of liberation war, father of the nation, national anthem, or national flag."[87] The new law also strengthened the criminal defamation laws that already had long been enforced.[88] Additionally, in the run-up to the January 2019 national elections, government security agencies and paramilitary forces increased surveillance of social media. "There is a blanket of fear spreading over this country, and I don't know when we are going to be freed," a journalist told Human Rights Watch soon after the law's passage.[89]

That fear was justified. Amnesty International reported that from the law's passage in October 2018 through July 2021, authorities arrested almost 1,000 people under the law, and more than 100 journalists faced lawsuits. "The DSA, a vague and overly broad law, has been increasingly used to stifle dissent on social media, websites, and other digital platforms with punishments that go up to life imprisonment," Amnesty International wrote in a report. "The authorities have targeted critical voices under the pretext of containing false, offensive, derogatory or defamatory information, and it is being deployed as a tool for repression."[90]

Likewise, in 2019, the parliament of the small west African country Burkina Faso passed an amendment to its penal code to make it a crime to "intentionally communicate, divulge, publish, or relay, by any means, false information of a kind to suggest that a destruction of property or an attack against persons has been committed or will be committed." Another portion of the new law criminalized publishing information about the nation's security forces or images about the scene of an act of terrorism. The crime carries prison time of up to five years.[91] The Committee to Protect Journalists sharply criticized the law, pointing out that it creates criminal penalties for a wide range of press functions, including reporting about terrorist attacks. "Under no circumstances should journalists face imprisonment or crippling financial penalties for their work," Angela Quintal, the group's Africa coordinator, said at the time.[92]

A 2021 study examined the fake news laws passed in Burkina Faso and 10 other sub-Saharan nations from 2016 through 2020. The authors found that most of these laws sought not "to correct the false information or facilitate improved access to accurate information," but to "punish publication." Most of those whom the governments punished under the fake news laws, the researchers found, were journalists or members of opposition parties.[93]

But were the laws effective in combatting falsehoods? The researchers concluded that they were not. They found only 12 fake news–related criminal actions in those 11 countries over a three-month period in 2020, and they found an "objectively legitimate aim" in only three of them. "This pales in comparison to the hundreds of cases of misinformation tackled by the growing number of fact-checking organisations in Africa, and the millions of content moderation decisions made worldwide by tech platforms daily, many of which [are] made to counter misinformation," the researchers wrote.[94]

And laws against fake news are not only features of authoritarian countries. In recent years, some Western democracies have proposed or passed laws that give the government greater authority to regulate or penalize the dissemination of falsehoods. For instance, in 2018, the French Parliament passed a law that allows for quick judicial review, during campaign season, of alleged falsehoods about political campaigns. The law allows judges to act "with any means," but "proportionally" to impede distribution if falsehoods are spread on the Internet "massively, deliberately, artificially or automatically."[95] French President Emmanuel Macron, whose campaign had been the subject of online falsehoods, supported the legislation, but it received a good deal of pushback from many in France. French newspaper *Le Monde* argued that a future authoritarian government could misuse the law, and that the more immediate problem was the willingness of the public to accept fake news, "a major crisis in our democracies, people's grow-ing mistrust towards their institutions."[96]

The experiences of other countries that have imposed regulations on false speech validate the US legal system's aversion to such laws. The foreign misinformation laws are harmful for many of the same reasons that US courts and legislatures have chosen to protect purport-edly false speech. The fake news laws are ripe for abuse, and they threaten to disenfranchise dissenting voices in favor of the powerful. The laws also are incredibly difficult to enforce fairly, requiring courts or regulators to determine "truth" often in times of uncertainty. And as seen in Africa, fake news laws are not terribly effective at combat-ting pervasive falsehoods.

This is not to say that US law should foreclose all avenues to im-pose penalties for false speech. As the next chapter shows, despite the high bars set by the First Amendment and other free speech protec-tions, legal consequences are available in even worse circumstances, and can help deter the most damaging and malicious lies.

Chapter 11

When Regulation or Liability Might Be an Answer

Until this point in the book, I have mainly discussed legal claims that have failed in the face of strong legal protections for false speech. Indeed, the protections for false speech in the United States are far greater than they are in most other parts of the world. But US law does not protect all false speech.

As Justice Anthony Kennedy wrote in the *United States v. Alvarez* plurality opinion, in which he rejected a categorical rule that false speech is unprotected, "[s]ome false speech may be prohibited even if analogous true speech could not be."[1] Examples of permissible regulations of false speech, Kennedy wrote, include defamation lawsuits, prohibiting false statements to federal officials, perjury laws, and impersonating government officers. "This opinion does not imply that any of these targeted prohibitions are somehow vulnerable," Kennedy wrote. "But it also rejects the notion that false speech should be in a general category that is presumptively unprotected."[2] This chapter examines the cases in which speakers can be held legally accountable for their false statements, both through existing laws such as defamation and new avenues that reflect the First Amendment principles outlined in this book.

Defamation law allows subjects of some particularly harmful and targeted misinformation campaigns to attempt to hold the speakers accountable, despite the high bar set by the actual malice requirement of *New York Times v. Sullivan*, the burden shifting of *Philadelphia Newspapers v. Hepps*, the fair report privilege, and other protections. Among the most prominent uses of defamation lawsuits to address modern falsehoods arose from commentary and media coverage of claims by President Donald Trump and his allies that Smartmatic and Dominion Voting—two companies that provide many jurisdictions nationwide with voting technology—were part of broader election fraud that threw the election to Joe Biden. As of March 2022, the two companies had filed 12 lawsuits against Trump-friendly media outlets and allies of Trump who allegedly spread lies about the companies' actions in the 2020 elections.[3] And at least in some cases in which judges had issued early rulings, the many First Amendment, common-law, and statutory protections did not appear to be a substantial barrier.

One such high-profile example is the lawsuit that Dominion filed against Fox News Network in March 2021, in Delaware state court. A frequent guest on Fox in the weeks after the election was lawyer Sidney Powell, who had filed lawsuits challenging the election results. On November 8, 2020—a day after Fox projected that Biden had defeated Trump—Powell told Fox host Maria Bartiromo that there was "a massive and coordinated effort to steal this election from We the People of the United States of America, to delegitimize and destroy votes for Donald Trump, to manufacture votes for Joe Biden."

"Sidney, we talked about the Dominion software," Bartiromo said. "I know that there were voting irregularities. Tell me about that."

"That's putting it mildly," Powell responded. "That is where the fraud took place, where they were flipping votes in the computer system or adding votes that did not exist. . . . That's when they had to stop the vote count and go in and replace votes for Biden and take away Trump votes."

"I've never seen voting machines stop in the middle of an election, stop down and assess the situation," Bartiromo replied.[4]

Powell and Trump's lawyer, Rudy Giuliani, claimed in Fox News appearances that Hugo Chavez had rigged elections in Venezuela using Dominion machines, though that apparently was based on the false assumption that Smartmatic owned Dominion.[5]

Dominion emailed Fox producers and reporters correcting the false information, yet the channel continued to broadcast the conspiracy theories on many of its shows. For instance, Powell appeared on Lou Dobbs's Fox Business show to repeat the Venezuela claim and say that "Smartmatic owns Dominion."[6] The claims on Fox continued, even after officials in Arizona and Georgia completed audits verifying their initial results in favor of Biden. Dobbs said on the air that he was having Powell back on his show to "provide more details on how Dominion voting machines and Smartmatic software were used to help Joe Biden."[7]

About three weeks after the election, Dominion sent another email to Fox News employees, this time correcting specific factual errors, but that did not stop the claims. On a November 30, 2020, appearance on Sean Hannity's show, Powell repeated the claims about Dominion machines awarding Trump votes to Biden, allegations that Dominion had addressed in its email to Fox. Also that day, Dobbs said, "We have, across almost every state, whether it's Dominion, whatever the company—voting machine company is, no one knows their ownership, has no idea what's going on in those servers, has no understanding of the software, because it's 'proprietary.' It is the most ludicrous, irresponsible, and rancid system imaginable in the world's only superpower."[8] The claims continued into December, with Dobbs asking Powell on the air how Dominion had participated in a "coordinated effort to actually bring down this President," while claiming that he had evidence that backed up Powell's allegations.[9]

Despite this apparent confidence, just a few weeks later, on January 4, 2021, Dobbs said that "we still don't have verifiable tangible support for the crimes that everyone knows were committed. That is, defrauding other citizens who voted with fraudulent votes ... we have had a devil of a time finding actual proof."[10] Although some Fox hosts—such as Hannity, Dobbs, and Bartiromo—provided frequent platforms for the false claims about Dominion, other Fox employees refrained from the conspiracy theories. For instance, on November 6, 2020, Fox News anchor Bret Baier said, "We are not seeing any evidence of widespread fraud. We are not seeing anything that can change, right now at least, the split in these different States." And Fox News anchor Eric Shawn said on November 12, 2020, that the claims about Dominion were "disinformation."[11] The barrage of accusations took a toll on Dominion, leading to threats that caused it to spend more than $600,000 for private security. Constituents emailed election officials, urging them to not use Dominion's voting machines, and Dominion lost some contracts. The company spent more than $700,000 countering the false claims about its machines.[12]

On March 26, 2021, Dominion sued Fox for defamation in Delaware state court. Its complaint—which is more than 400 pages, including exhibits—details the precise false statements and argues why they meet the high bar required to succeed in a defamation lawsuit. "The truth matters," Dominion wrote in the complaint. "Lies have consequences. Fox sold a false story of election fraud in order to serve its own commercial purposes, severely injuring Dominion in the process. If this case does not rise to the level of defamation by a broadcaster, then nothing does."[13] About two months later, Fox moved to dismiss the lawsuit, arguing that the free press has the obligation to report on controversies with stakes as significant as a presidential election. "When a sitting President of the United States and his legal team challenge a presidential election in litigation throughout the nation, the media can truthfully report and comment on those allegations under the First Amendment without fear of liability," Fox's lawyers wrote in a brief to the court.[14] In addition to arguing that Dominion failed to establish actual malice, Fox based its motion on three free speech defenses: the neutral reportage privilege that the Second Circuit had recognized in *Edwards v. National Audubon Society*; the fair report privilege that protects fair and accurate reports of public proceedings; and the opinion defense, which Rachel Maddow had successfully claimed in the lawsuit brought by OAN.

In a 52-page opinion on December 16, 2021, Judge Eric M. Davis rejected all three defenses and denied Fox's motion to dismiss. Davis questioned whether modern First Amendment doctrine, as explained by the Supreme Court, still would support the neutral reportage privilege that the Second Circuit developed in 1977.[15] But even if the court still were to recognize it, the privilege would not protect Fox, Davis reasoned, because Fox would need to show that it provided neutral coverage and not a "personal attack." And Dominion's complaint, he wrote, supports "the reasonable inference that Fox's reporting was not accurate or dispassionate."[16] Davis pointed to Fox's continued reporting about the election fraud claims after receiving Dominion's correction emails as sufficient evidence that the reporting was inaccurate. And the allegations that Fox failed to report evidence that weighed against election fraud claims, Davis wrote, supported his conclusion that the reporting was not dispassionate.[17]

Davis also found that the fair report privilege did not shield Fox from Dominion's claims. The privilege requires a "fair and true report" of an "official proceeding," and it must be "substantially accurate." Most of the statements that formed the basis of the lawsuit, Davis wrote, were made before any election fraud lawsuits containing the allegations were filed. Davis also questioned whether the statements transmitted by Fox were substantially accurate. "At various times, Fox published statements made by guests who stated their allegations were supported by evidence," Davis wrote. "The Complaint, however, alleges that none of these sources adduced any evidence for these allegations."[18]

The opinion defense also failed to save Fox from the lawsuit. Fox had argued that its hosts' on-air statements were opinion and not factual allegations, and therefore could not support a defamation lawsuit. Davis rejected this framing, reasoning that the complaint supported a reasonable inference that Fox had presented its reporting as facts. "Fox's news personnel repeatedly framed the issue as one of truth-seeking and purported to ground interview questions in judicial proceedings and evidence," Davis wrote.[19]

In addition to denying Fox's three free speech defenses, Davis rejected Fox's argument that Dominion's complaint failed to meet the high bar of pleading actual malice. The allegations, Davis said, reasonably support the inference that Fox either knew that the statements were false or had a "high degree of awareness" of the falsity. "For example, Fox possessed countervailing evidence of election fraud from the Department of Justice, election experts, and Dominion at the time it had been making its statements," Davis wrote. "The fact that, despite this evidence, Fox continued to publish its allegations against Dominion, suggests Fox knew the allegations were probably false."[20] Davis also noted that the complaint alleged that some Fox employees had publicly stated that the claims about Dominion were false. "Yet, certain Fox personnel (e.g., Mr. Dobbs) continued to push the fraud claims," Davis wrote.[21] The Delaware Supreme Court denied Fox's request for an early appeal of the denial of its motion to dismiss, finding that the company had not shown the "exceptional circumstances" necessary for such review.

In 2023, Davis ruled the on-air statements were false, leaving the jury to determine whether Fox acted with actual malice. But on the day trial was scheduled to start, the case settled for $787 million. The massive settlement shows that many of the robust free speech protections described in part I are not impenetrable barriers for defamation plaintiffs. These defenses set an exceedingly high bar in their quest to protect free speech. But they leave room for egregious cases in which a plaintiff—such as Dominion—can establish that the speaker's reckless falsehoods caused harm.

Successful defamation lawsuits are nothing close to a panacea for false speech. Many harmful online falsehoods—such as lies about COVID-19—are not viable launching pads for defamation claims because they are not false statements concerning a particular person or company, nor do they damage an individual's reputation. Even if false speech might be defamatory, a plaintiff may not want to take on the costs of suing, particularly if winning is far from certain. The resolution of issues such as actual malice and substantial truth often is difficult to predict with certainty. While a company like Dominion might have the resources and resolve to bring a defamation case, other potential plaintiffs who have strong cases might understandably be unwilling to assume the costs and uncertainty of filing a defamation lawsuit. And even if the plaintiffs could afford to sue, the time required and emotional toll of litigating defamation are substantial, particularly for individual plaintiffs.

Relatedly, attempts to censor speech through litigation could result in *more* attention to that speech. This is known as the "Streisand effect," a term coined by Techdirt's Mike Masnick in 2005, referring to Barbra Streisand's lawsuit against a photographer who had taken an aerial photo of her home. The lawsuit resulted in far more online views of the photo than it had received before she sued.[22] Because of the Streisand effect, filing a defamation lawsuit could bring even more attention to the speech that the plaintiff claims is defamatory. The Streisand effect is less of a concern for a case such as Dominion's than for a suit involving less publicized false speech. Trump allies had been making these claims for months both in mainstream media such as Fox and on social media. While Dominion's lawsuits received media coverage, it is hard to imagine that many people first learned of the claims about its voting machines from the coverage of the lawsuit. So, at least in some cases, defamation lawsuits can be viable avenues to address falsehoods. And the prospect of such claims might discourage others from spreading those falsehoods in the future. The safeguards described in part I, such as the actual malice requirement, substantial truth doctrine, and fair report privilege, at least reduce the likelihood that such claims would chill non-defamatory speech, though it certainly is a risk as more such defamation cases are successfully litigated.

Defamation is not the only type of lawsuit that people can bring to seek justice for specific and concrete damages caused by some types of dissemination of false, misleading, or harmful speech. A prominent recent example, also involving Fox News, arose from the July 10, 2016, shooting and murder of Seth Rich, a 27-year-old staffer of the Democratic National Committee. Washington, DC, police did not solve the murder, which they believed resulted from a robbery attempt.[23] The tragedy soon led to fringe conspiracy theories that Rich was murdered because he had leaked Democratic National Committee (DNC) emails to WikiLeaks, prompting Rich's parents to issue a public statement requesting the end to such baseless speculation. In late 2016 and early 2017, Fox News guest commentator Ed Butowsky allegedly befriended Rich's parents and asked them about their son and WikiLeaks. Fox News reporter Malia Zimmerman also spoke with Rich's family.[24]

The Riches would later allege in court filings that Butowsky and Zimmerman asked former detective Rod Wheeler, a Fox News contributor who also worked as a private investigator, to help them build the WikiLeaks story. Butowsky introduced Wheeler to the Riches, who initially declined Wheeler's services, the filings allege, but they eventually agreed after receiving a contractual guarantee that Wheeler would not speak with the media about the investigation unless the Riches consented. Yet Wheeler kept working with Zimmerman and Butowsky, and shared information about the investigation not only with them but also with the White House, the Riches alleged.[25]

In May 2017, according to the Riches' court filings, Butowsky and Zimmerman pressured Wheeler to speak with Fox News on the record, including by claiming that an FBI source had told them that

Seth Rich had been in touch with WikiLeaks. Fox published two Zimmerman-authored articles on May 16. The first, titled "Slain DNC Staffer Had Contact with WikiLeaks Say Multiple Sources," quoted an anonymous federal investigator who claimed to have seen emails between WikiLeaks and Seth Rich. "The revelation is consistent with the findings of Rod Wheeler, former DC homicide detective and Fox News contributor and whose private investigation firm was *hired by Rich's family* to probe the case," Zimmerman wrote. The second, titled "Family of Slain DNC Staffer Seth Rich Blasts Detective over Report of WikiLeaks Link," reported that Wheeler "made the WikiLeaks claim, which was corroborated by a federal investigator who spoke to Fox News."[26] The next day, *Newsweek* reported that Wheeler told the publication that he did not have "firsthand" information and he had not spoken with a "federal investigator." Two days after the articles' publication, the Riches demanded a retraction from Fox, and Zimmerman responded that "much of our information came from a private investigator, Rod Wheeler." Fox retracted the article five days later, writing that it "was not initially subjected to [a] high degree of editorial scrutiny." Despite the retraction, guests on Fox News still discussed the article for months afterward.[27]

In the United States, defamation suits typically cannot be filed on behalf of dead people, so Seth Rich's parents could not bring a defamation claim. But Rich's parents said that the experience with Fox News caused them to experience social anxiety disorder and posttraumatic stress disorder. Rather than suing for defamation, they brought a complaint in New York federal court against Fox News, Butowsky, and Zimmerman for intentional infliction of emotional distress and tortious interference with contract. They also sued Fox News for negligent supervision and/or retention.[28] The district court judge granted the defendants' motion to dismiss the lawsuit, concluding that the allegations in the complaint failed to state viable claims. The Riches appealed, and on September 13, 2019, the US Court of Appeals for the Second Circuit reversed the dismissal.

Intentional infliction of emotional distress is a common-law tort that imposes liability on those whose "extreme and outrageous conduct intentionally or recklessly causes severe emotional distress to another."[29] For the unanimous three-judge panel, Judge Guido Calabresi wrote that he agreed with the Riches' argument that their complaint alleges "a series of acts that, taken together, constitute extreme and outrageous conduct." Even if the alleged individual acts, standing alone, might not meet such a high bar, Calabresi agreed with the Riches' argument that "taken together, these acts might amount to a deliberate and malicious campaign of harassment." Separately, he wrote, he agreed with the Riches that because the defendants were aware that the Riches were susceptible to emotional distress, "their conduct became extreme and outrageous when the [defendants] chose to proceed with their plan in spite of that knowledge."[30] Zimmerman and Fox had argued that the Riches' emotional distress claim was merely a way to sue for the alleged defamation of their son, and that plaintiffs cannot bring defamation lawsuits on behalf of the deceased. But Calabresi rejected that argument and concluded that emotional distress claims are distinct from defamation.[31]

Nor did Calabresi agree with the district judge's dismissal of the tortious interference of contract claim, which allows a plaintiff to sue if the defendant knew of a contract between the plaintiff and another party, and intentionally and without justification caused the other party to breach the contract, causing damages to the plaintiff. The Riches argued that the defendants caused Wheeler to breach the confidentiality agreement with them. Calabresi reasoned that even though the complaint alleged that the defendants' communications with Wheeler allegedly began before the contract was even signed, the complaint sufficiently alleged that their behavior was a cause of the breach.[32] The district court had dismissed the claim against Fox News that alleged that the station negligently supervised or retained Zimmerman and Wheeler in part because the complaint did not adequately allege that Zimmerman and Wheeler acted within the scope of their Fox employment. Calabresi agreed that the complaint "is not lucid on this point," but gave the Riches an opportunity to amend the complaint to clarify.[33]

We will never know whether the Riches would have ultimately prevailed in their claims at trial. In November 2020, the Riches and Fox announced that they had settled on undisclosed terms. Yahoo News reported that the settlement included "a lucrative seven figure payment to the Rich family consistent with the size of payouts Fox News and related corporate entities have made in other cases that have brought them negative publicity."[34]

Like Dominion's lawsuit, the Riches' defeat of the motion to dismiss is an example of the potential use of tort law to remedy the harms of especially bad false speech. Yet both cases involved unique circumstances in which the alleged harms targeted and fell specifically on the named plaintiffs. Could tort law be used effectively by members of the general public to hold the disseminators of misinformation accountable as long as the members of the public suffered harm from the misinformation?[35] I have serious doubts, particularly because of many of the court opinions discussed in part I of this book. Under reasoning that is informed by both the First Amendment and common law, courts have rejected a wide range of tort claims from plaintiffs who claim to have suffered from the allegedly false information published or distributed by the defendants. And their harms were substantial: investment losses, liver transplants, and even death. Both implicitly and explicitly, courts often avoid imposing responsibility on the speaker because the plaintiff relied on that speech.

Imagine what liability for false public health information would have on discussions about issues like the coronavirus. In the earliest days of the COVID-19 pandemic, so little was known about how the virus was transmitted, the harms that it caused, and how its spread could be prevented. It is unclear precisely what would have been considered false information at the time, as public health officials did not know very much (and they backed away from many of their initial statements, including about whether the virus was airborne). Even with limitations such as actual malice and the application to purposeful dissemination, such liability for editorial commentary could create a chilling effect. Of course, even defamation claims brought by public figures could succeed upon a showing of actual malice, but a generalized cause of action available to all listeners applies to so much more speech than defamation, which is limited to speech about the plaintiff. Such general misinformation torts would cause media outlets and other speakers to be far more likely to avoid analysis of current public health issues due to the mere possibility of defending against claims down the road. While such liability might prevent some fringe and dangerous health misinformation, it also would likely reduce any criticism or questioning of the government's health positions. Taken to an extreme position, a media outlet might even face liability for repeating the government's public health advice if that advice is later found to be dangerous.

It is hard to predict with certainty how the courts would react to a request for a new First Amendment carveout. There always is a chance that the courts will determine that they should expand the existing fraud exception to include these substantial public harms. But we should be completely aware that such liability would require a substantial broadening of the conception of tort principles and an abrogation of First Amendment protections, and Chief Justice John Roberts has already firmly rejected a proposal to create First Amendment exceptions based on "a categorical balancing of the value of the speech against its societal costs."[36] At the very least, it is possible for the subjects of alleged falsehoods—such as Dominion—to use tort law to hold misinformation disseminators liable so long as they meet the high bars of the First Amendment and common law. Courts are unlikely to allow more generalized misinformation-based claims from the public at large, both because that diverges from the standard elements of information torts and because the chilling effects would raise substantial First Amendment problems.

Tort law is not the only mechanism to hold speakers accountable for particularly harmful falsehoods. The First Amendment provides the government with greater leeway to regulate businesses' claims about the products and services that they offer. The US Supreme Court concluded decades ago that the First Amendment does in fact apply to commercial speech, reasoning that "speech does not lose its First Amendment protection because money is spent to project it, as in a paid advertisement of one form or another," nor does speech lose First Amendment protections "even though it is carried in a form that is 'sold' for profit" or if it involves "a solicitation to purchase or otherwise pay or contribute money."[37] In a 1980 case, *Central Hudson Gas & Electric Corp. v. Public Service Commission of New York*, the Supreme Court applied a First Amendment test for restrictions of commercial speech that is less burdensome than the scrutiny applied to political speech limits. But the protections apply only if the commercial speech is "neither misleading nor related to unlawful activity."[38] This provides regulators and litigants with the flexibility to hold companies accountable for misleading statements about their products or services.

The Federal Trade Commission, for instance, has long had the power under Section 5 of the FTC Act to bring enforcement actions and lawsuits against companies for "deceptive acts or practices in or affecting commerce."[39] The FTC, in a 1983 policy statement, said that it considers bringing deception actions in cases involving a material "representation, omission, or practice that is likely to mislead the consumer," and it evaluates those practices "from the perspective of a consumer acting reasonably in the circumstances."[40]

In late 2020, Congress bolstered the FTC's authority to police deceptive practices by passing the COVID-19 Consumer Protection Act. The law makes it illegal, during the COVID-19 public health emergency, to engage in a deceptive act that is associated with "the treatment, cure, prevention, mitigation, or diagnosis of COVID-19" or "a government benefit related to COVID-19."[41] By allowing the FTC to seek monetary penalties, the law supplements Section 5 of the FTC Act, which typically precludes the agency from fining first-time violators. Within months of the law's passage, the FTC brought a case against a chiropractor and his company that the agency alleges engaged in deceptive practices by selling Vitamin D and zinc products as a prevention or treatment for COVID-19. "In short, Defendants are selling their products by disseminating misinformation, exploiting fears in the midst of a pandemic, and posing a significant risk to public health and safety," the federal government wrote in an April 2021 complaint filed in Missouri federal court.[42] As this book was being written in 2022, the case was still ongoing.

Regulating deceptive commercial speech can address some concerns that arose during the COVID-19 pandemic, particularly from companies that tried to peddle bogus cures. Commercial speech regulation would not address many types of false speech, such as a high-profile commentator on social media who urges followers to avoid vaccines or engage in risky behavior. But at the very least, it could address, in a targeted manner, some of the worst exploitations of misinformation distribution.

Can the government more easily regulate the false speech of licensed professionals? A 2018 US Supreme Court opinion suggests that might be a tricky question. In a 5–4 opinion, the court struck down the California Reproductive Freedom, Accountability, Comprehensive Care, and Transparency Act, which required pro-life crisis pregnancy centers to provide women with notice about the availability of other reproductive health services, including abortion.[43] Writing for the majority, Justice Clarence Thomas refused to conclude that "professional speech" is a separate, unprotected category of speech. He acknowledged that the court has provided professional speech with less protection in two situations: first, where professionals are required "to disclose factual, noncontroversial information in their 'commercial speech,'" and second, if states are regulating "professional conduct, even though that conduct incidentally involves speech."[44] Thomas concluded that the California law fell into neither category. The law, he wrote, "requires these clinics to disclose information about *state*-sponsored services— including abortion, anything but an 'uncontroversial' topic."[45] Likewise, he wrote, the law is not an incidental speech regulation, as it "applies to all interactions between a covered facility and its clients, regardless of whether a medical procedure is ever sought, offered, or performed."[46] The state's interest in "providing low-income women with information about state-sponsored services," he wrote, does not satisfy First Amendment scrutiny, as alternative mechanisms exist, such as state-run public information campaigns.[47] The California law involved a notice requirement and not a government prohibition of false speech, so it is difficult to draw any definitive conclusions about how courts would apply it to regulations of false speech by doctors, lawyers, and other licensed professionals. But it shows that governments do not have open-ended power to regulate the speech of professionals.

Still, some professions, such as lawyers, might face greater restrictions than the general public. "Lawyers' freedom of speech is constrained in many ways that no one would challenge seriously under the First Amendment," Kathleen Sullivan wrote in 1998. "Rules of evidence and procedures, bans on revealing grand jury testimony, page limits in briefs, and sanctions for frivolous pleadings, to name a few, are examples of speech limitations that are widely accepted as functional necessities in the administration of justice, much like rules of order in a town meeting."[48] Among the acceptable limits on lawyers' speech are penalties for certain falsehoods. For instance, the New York Rules of Professional Conduct prohibit attorneys from knowingly making "a false statement of fact or law" to a tribunal or other person or engaging in "conduct involving dishonesty, fraud, deceit or misrepresentation" or "any other conduct that adversely reflects on the lawyer's fitness as a lawyer."[49] Under these rules, the New York Supreme Court

Appellate Division in 2021 granted the state Attorney Grievance Committee's request for an interim suspension from the practice of law of former New York mayor Rudolph Giuliani based on "demonstrably false and misleading statements" that Giuliani made to the public, lawmakers, and courts while representing Trump in his postelection challenges in 2020.[50] The court rejected Giuliani's claim that the application of the professional conduct rules to his statements violated the First Amendment. "This disciplinary proceeding concerns the professional restrictions imposed on respondent as an attorney to not knowingly misrepresent facts and make false statements in connection with his representation of a client," the court wrote.[51] Such restrictions, according to the court, help to promote the integrity of the profession. "While there are limits on the extent to which a lawyer's right of free speech may be circumscribed, these limits are not implicated by the circumstances of the knowing misconduct that this Court relies upon in granting interim suspension in this case."[52]

The Giuliani case shows that although the First Amendment protects the speech of licensed professionals, courts in some cases are more willing to provide the government and licensing boards with the ability to penalize them for allegedly disseminating falsehoods.

As with commercial and professional speech, the government has more leeway to impose penalties for false statements to courts or government agents. In his *Alvarez* plurality opinion, Justice Kennedy affirmed the "unquestioned constitutionality" of laws that criminalize committing perjury. "Unlike speech in other contexts, testimony under oath has the formality and gravity necessary to remind the witness that his or her statements will be the basis for official governmental action, action that often affects the rights and liberties of others," Kennedy wrote. "Sworn testimony is quite distinct from lies not spoken under oath and simply intended to puff up oneself."[53] Likewise, Section 1001 of the federal criminal code imposes penalties on someone who "in any matter within the jurisdiction of the executive, legislative, or judicial branch of the Government . . . makes any materially false, fictitious, or fraudulent statement or representation."[54] Kennedy also endorsed the constitutionality of this statute, while taking care to recognize that it applies only in particular circumstances. "Section 1001's prohibition on false statements made to Government officials, in communications concerning official matters, does not lead to the broader proposition that false statements are unprotected when made to any person, at any time, in any context," he wrote.[55]

How far does the exception that Kennedy had recognized extend? One answer came out of the prosecution in Illinois of Michelle C. Leader, for allegedly falsely telling a police officer that she had been kidnapped. She was convicted by a jury of violating an Illinois law that prohibits the knowing transmission "in any manner to any peace officer, public officer or public employee a report to the effect that an offense . . . has been committed, knowing at the time of the transmission that there is no reasonable ground for believing that the offense . . . has been committed."[56] On appeal, Leader relied on *Alvarez* in challenging the Illinois law's constitutionality, but the Illinois appellate court affirmed her conviction. "The trouble with her argument is that *her* false speech—the false report that she had been kidnapped—is not like the speech found to be constitutionally protected in *Alvarez*," Justice Mary S. Schostok wrote in an unpublished opinion for the unanimous panel.[57]

Statutes such as the Illinois law, Section 1001, and perjury laws are limited to false statements to courts and government officials and cannot, for instance, be used to impose liability on people who lie on social media. But the laws are a potential tool to combat certain types of false speech.

Some of the most contentious debates about false speech involve claims about elections. As discussed in chapter 10, courts likely would not allow laws such as the one that Inslee supported, penalizing politicians for false speech about election integrity. But the Supreme Court has suggested that it might allow bans on false speech that is narrowly targeted at interfering with the actual mechanics of voting.

For instance, in 2018, the US Supreme Court struck down a Minnesota law that prohibited wearing political buttons and badges in polling places. In a footnote, the court stated that it does "not doubt that the State may prohibit messages intended to mislead voters about voting requirements and procedures."[58] In his 2022 book *Cheap Speech*, election law expert Rick Hasen builds on the Supreme Court's statement and suggests a narrow ban on verifiably false speech about elections, which he defines as "false speech about the mechanics of voting." As Hasen explains:

> One should face appropriate punishment for lying about when, where, and how people may vote. Saying, "You can now vote by text," or "You need a photo ID to vote" in a state that does not require it, is demonstrably false speech that interferes with the franchise. So is speech that contains demonstrably false statements about an upcoming election's being rigged, such as a false claim that election officials do not count ballots submitted by mail. Government officials acting under a false election speech law could punish someone who spreads such information with actual malice (that is, knowing that it is false or acting in reckless disregard to its truth or falsity). They also could order social media platforms and websites to remove such false speech when detected.[59]

Hasen correctly notes that the court would be more likely to strike down a broader law that bans generally misleading speech about a campaign. Given the Supreme Court's statement in the 2018 case, it is likely—though not certain—that his proposal would survive a constitutional challenge. The combination of the narrowness of his proposal—applying only to false speech about the mechanics of voting rather than a broader array of political speech—and the actual malice requirement would make it rather unlikely for the regulation to have a broader chilling effect.

Other proposals focus on addressing harmful lies told by the president of the United States, inspired by concerns over lies that Donald Trump told while he was president. The most thoroughly developed proposal came from Professor Catherine J. Ross in her 2021 book *A Right to Lie: Presidents, Other Liars, and the First Amendment*. Ross argues that "presidents should be held to a higher standard of truthfulness than can be imposed on the population at large or on mere candidates for public office." Her reasoning is twofold. First, presidential lies can cause far more harm than those spouted by others. And second, First Amendment doctrine provides greater latitude for regulating the speech of public employees. While no court has definitively ruled whether the public speech doctrine applies to the president, Ross makes a compelling case for its application. Ross proposes that "presidents should be subject to extreme penalties for a continuing pattern of material verifiable falsehoods that harm the body politic or the well-being of the American people." What might these penalties include? Ross suggested that Congress could hold oversight hearings, and perhaps consider consequences such as censure or impeachment. Although the Constitution limits impeachment to "high crimes and misdemeanors," Ross makes a strong case about why Congress has a great deal of flexibility in deciding what meets this threshold. The president is not a member of the general public, and there is good reason to expect the president to be truthful.

Existing First Amendment doctrine sets a high bar for imposing legal consequences for falsehoods, but that bar is not insurmountable. There are extraordinary cases in which lying can lead to fines, damages, and other penalties. But as part III of this book shows, regulation often is not the best way to address false speech.

PART III
Empowering
Rationality

Free speech protections have both explicit and implicit assumptions not only about speech, but also about the audience that reads and listens to that speech. As free speech scholar Lyrissa Barnett Lidsky thoroughly documented in a 2010 article, First Amendment protections assume that a "rational audience" is receiving the speech. "Only rational consumers can sort through undifferentiated masses of information to discern what is valuable, to pluck the wheat from the chaff," Lidsky wrote. "Indeed, the marketplace metaphor even contains a model of the reasoning process of these consumers."[1]

Of course, not all audiences are rational. They may lack the education or background to understand the torrent of information bombarding them on cable television and the Internet. They may not have access to diverse speech venues. They may lack the proper incentives to react to speech rationally.

Part III provides a road map for encouraging and empowering rationality among audience members. Chapter 12 evaluates mechanisms of counterspeech and "self-help" for subjects of misinformation to correct the record, and other extralegal ways to hold liars accountable, such as publicizing the truth. Chapter 13 considers the role of platforms in the dissemination of falsehoods, and ultimately concludes that both platforms *and* their users should be empowered to combat false speech, but that empowerment should be separate from any government pressure. Chapter 14 argues that people should be accountable for how they respond to falsehoods. Chapter 15 examines proposals to better educate, empower, and equip the recipients of speech to operate in the marketplace of ideas.

Chapter 12

Counterspeech and Self-Help

Although litigation and regulation are available to penalize particularly harmful forms of false speech, they are extraordinary remedies that are not often available in the United States. But those who are harmed by false speech have extralegal recourse. And one of the primary tools is known as "self-help," which includes counterspeech. While counterspeech and self-help alone never will be anything close to a panacea for modern falsehoods, they are an important component of any strategy to combat the problems.

Broadly conceived, self-help includes the freedom of individuals to assess, ignore, or respond to speech. "It is an insufficiently noticed aspect of the First Amendment that it contemplates the vigorous use of self-help by the opponents of given doctrines, ideas, and political positions," First Amendment scholar Harry Kalven wrote in 1973. "It is not the theory that all ideas and positions are entitled to flourish under freedom of discussion. It is rather then that they must survive and endure against hostile criticism."[1] Pointing to Kalven's words, media law professor David Kohler argued that self-help is a key underpinning of the marketplace of ideas that Oliver Wendell Holmes Jr. and Louis Brandeis developed a century ago. "At the core of the First Amendment is the ideal of a citizen who makes up her own mind as to how to inform herself, what to believe, and how—and even whether—to express that belief," he wrote. "And, however one chooses to respond to ideas or expression, there is the question of the individual's obligation to avoid exposure to that which is deemed offensive instead of seeking state protection."[2] Self-help, Kohler wrote, includes "resistance through counter-speech to expression that the individual finds noxious, harmful or otherwise lacking merit."[3]

The ability to respond via self-help was succinctly described in a 1974 US Supreme Court opinion, *Gertz v. Robert Welch*, in which the court declined to extend the actual malice requirement of *New York Times v. Sullivan* to defamation lawsuits brought by private figures. Writing for the majority, Justice Lewis Powell concluded that it was reasonable to set a somewhat lower barrier to defamation lawsuits for private figures who did not have a chance to easily respond to lies about their reputations. "The first remedy of any victim of defamation is self-help—using available opportunities to contradict the lie or correct the error and thereby to minimize its adverse impact on reputation," Powell wrote. "Public officials and public figures usually enjoy significantly greater access to the channels of effective communication and hence have a more realistic opportunity to counteract false statements than private individuals normally enjoy."[4]

A recent example of self-help by a prominent public official came from Judge Ketanji Brown Jackson during her US Supreme Court confirmation hearing in March 2022 and the controversy described in chapter 9. After days of media coverage of the charges from Senator Josh Hawley and others that Jackson's sentences for child sex abuse material defendants were too light, Jackson had the opportunity for self-help at the hearing. After a day of opening statements from herself and senators, Jackson faced two days of questions. The first senator to question her was a supporter of her nomination, Senate Judiciary

Committee Chairman Dick Durbin. He began by asking Jackson to describe what she was thinking when she heard the charges that she was soft on child sex abuse material defendants. She paused, and thanked Durbin for the question.

"As a mother and a judge who has had to deal with these cases, I was thinking that nothing could be further from the truth," Jackson said. "These are some of the most difficult cases that a judge has to deal with because we're talking about pictures of sex abuse of children. We're talking about graphic descriptions that judges have to read and consider when they decide how to sentence in these cases and there's a statute that tells judges what they're supposed to do."

Jackson went into great detail about how she approaches these cases, and said that at many sentencings for child sex abuse material cases, she tells the story of a victim who wrote to her to say that she developed agoraphobia, fearful that anyone who saw her in public might have seen the pictures online. "At the most vulnerable time of her life, and so she's paralyzed," Jackson said. "I tell that story to every child porn defendant as a part of my sentencings so that they understand what they have done. I say to them that there's only a market for this kind of material because there are lookers, that you're contributing to child sex abuse, and then I impose a significant sentence and all of the additional restraints that are available in the law."

Jackson also explained why her sentences in child sex abuse materials that did not involve production of the content were lower than the ranges suggested in the nonbinding sentencing guidelines. The guidelines, she explained, were developed before the crime of child pornography was largely committed via the Internet, so the sentences were based on the volume of images received through the mail, she said. "The way that the Guideline is now structured based on that set of circumstances is leading to extreme disparities in this system because it's so easy for people to get volumes of this kind of material now by computers," she said. "So it's not doing the work of differentiating who is a more serious offender in the way that it used to."

In addition, Durbin noted that from 2015 to 2020 in the Washington, DC, federal court where Jackson sat, as well as in the federal courts of Hawley's home state of Missouri, approximately 80 percent of non-production child sex abuse material sentences were below the range recommended in the sentencing guidelines.

Although Jackson also fielded more aggressive commentary and questions from Hawley and other senators, she had a chance to add context to their narrative about her sentencing practices. Jackson's self-help likely did not change the minds of everyone who heard Hawley's claims about how she handled child sex abuse material cases, but she used her large platform to provide an explanation, and that explanation was widely reported in media coverage.

It is hard to measure precisely what impact her statements at the hearing had, but in a Quinnipiac University poll of 1,462 Americans taken in the days after the hearings, 51 percent said that she should be confirmed, 30 percent opposed her confirmation, and 19 percent had no opinion. And 52 percent of Americans said they did not like how Republicans handled her confirmation.[5] Nor did the criticism ultimately block Jackson from the Supreme Court, with the Senate confirming her in a 53–47 vote.

Most people do not have access to the same large platforms as Jackson, who spoke for hours at a nationally televised confirmation hearing that received substantial media coverage. And that is one of the main reasons that the Supreme Court in *Gertz* made it easier for private figures to bring defamation lawsuits. But the avenues for self-help are different than when the Supreme Court issued its decision in 1974. As early as 1997, the Supreme Court recognized the potential of the Internet to provide a voice to the masses, as it struck down a law regulating online indecency as unconstitutional. Justice John Paul Stevens hailed the Internet as "a unique and wholly new medium of worldwide human communication."[6]

In 1974, publicly distributing a response to misinformation often required a newspaper editor or broadcast reporter to choose to allow that distribution. Those in power were more likely to have the ability to at least attempt to correct the record—a reality that was reflected in the *Gertz* opinion. In 2000, media law professors Robert D. Richards and Clay Calvert correctly observed after reviewing case studies that "counterspeech is most effective when its proponents are able to call journalistic attention to their message, place it on the media's agenda, and thereby exponentially increase the audience to whom the message is disseminated."[7]

Even in the early days of the Internet, the multilateral nature of the new medium presented new opportunities for counterspeech and self-help. In 2006, technology law professor Susan Crawford recognized that people should be able to protect their reputations from bloggers' malicious lies. Yet she noted the new avenues for self-help created by the Internet. "In an era in which anyone can be a publisher, libel law seems much less relevant—rather than sue, you can just write back," Crawford wrote. "And if you sue, you're likely to bring the libel to the attention of many more people than would ever have heard about it in the first place. You'll be ruining your reputation just by going to court. And many bloggers don't have a dime, so if you're looking for damages you won't be satisfied by suing."[8] Since then, the opportunities for any American to express views on the Internet have flourished, both with the growth of broadband availability and the emergence of large social media platforms. As of 2021, 93 percent of Americans reported using the Internet, and 72 percent used social media.[9] While there still are gatekeepers—for instance, most online platforms have developed and enforce user content guidelines—it is easier to distribute counterspeech in 2023 than it was in 1974.

Even with the monumental communications developments over the past half century, not everyone has the same access to *effective* self-help. Kim Kardashian, for instance, had 300 million Instagram followers and 72 million Twitter followers as of mid-2022. She has a far greater ability to create effective counterspeech than the average American (or even the average celebrity or politician). It is possible for people who lead more private lives than Kim Kardashian to exercise self-help, though they face an uphill battle and usually will be unable to undo all the harms from the falsehoods. Although counterspeech is not the magic solution to all harms arising from falsehoods, it is at least one tool that we should consider in the battle against harmful falsehoods. Ultimately, counterspeech is an extralegal remedy. Counterspeech opportunities cannot easily be mandated by law. But there are a few ways that the law can at least increase the availability of counterspeech.

First, Section 230 of the Communications Decency Act protects online services from liability for content posted by third parties. The increasingly controversial law, discussed in more depth in chapter 13, is often criticized (both rightly and wrongly) for allowing falsehoods to flourish online. While a great deal of false speech is protected by the First Amendment, Section 230 also protects platforms from defamation lawsuits, even if they receive a complaint about the user speech and decide against taking it down. Without Section 230's protections, some platforms might be more likely to take down user content after receiving complaints, or simply would not allow users to post, out of fear of the legal risks. But there is a flipside to Section 230's broad protections: It increases the chances that someone seeking to distribute counterspeech—either to lies that originated online or offline—will do so. Of course, counterspeech is never guaranteed, as the platforms have a First Amendment right to exclude people from their services, just as a newspaper has the right to decline to publish a letter to the editor that responds to an opposing viewpoint.

A second way that law enables counterspeech and self-help is through noncompulsory retraction statutes. Most states have laws that require defamation plaintiffs to demand a retraction before seeking some remedies (such as punitive damages) in a defamation lawsuit, and if the defendant properly publishes the retraction, their damages might be limited in subsequent litigation.[10] These statutes generally avoid being struck down on First Amendment grounds because they do not mandate retractions but do allow potential defamation defendants to limit damages in a later lawsuit.[11] Retraction statutes foster self-help by encouraging the person or company that published the falsehoods to prominently publish a retraction. This can be even more effective than a mere statement by the person who was the subject of the false speech.

Unfortunately, most retraction statutes were drafted and passed before the modern Internet, and many do not explicitly mention it. Many such statutes only apply to media defendants, often excluding newer forms of media such as online publications. For instance, Arizona's retraction statute applies to lawsuits "for the publication of a libel in a newspaper or magazine, or of a slander by radio or television broadcast." Unless the plaintiff shows that the statement was made with actual malice, the plaintiff must demand a retraction within 20 days of learning of the publication or broadcast to recover many types of damages. And those damages are unavailable if the defendant publishes the correction.[12] In 2008, a federal district judge ruled that the statute did not apply to an allegedly defamatory posting in an online forum. "On its face, that section applies only to libel actions based on newspaper or magazine articles," Judge James A. Teilborg wrote.[13] Although there is a reasonable argument that Teilborg's reading aligns with the plain text of the retraction statute, this construction glosses over the developments of modern communications and deprives plaintiffs of the ability to seek self-help.

The Georgia Supreme Court recognized these realities in the early days of the commercial Internet. In 2002, it considered a defamation claim brought by the president of a waste management company against a man who criticized him on a Yahoo bulletin board. The defendant argued that because the plaintiff had not demanded a retraction, he could not receive punitive damages. Georgia's retraction statute stated that punitive damages were unavailable in defamation actions in which "the defendant, in a regular issue of the newspaper or other publication in question, within seven days after receiving written demand, or in the next regular issue of the newspaper or other publication following receipt of the demand if the next regular issue was not published within seven days after receiving the demand, corrected and retracted the allegedly libelous statement in as conspicuous and public a manner as that in which the alleged libelous statement was published."[14]

Another part of the law imposed a similar requirement for broadcasts. Georgia's intermediate Court of Appeals, applying a print media–focused interpretation of the law that it had first adopted in 1984, ruled that under the plain language of the statute, it "would not appear to be applicable to Internet postings."[15] Why would the Yahoo boards not be considered "other publications"? Internet bulletin boards and chat rooms, the appellate court reasoned, have audiences that are not as static as traditional media, but "in a constant state of flux."[16]

The Georgia Supreme Court disagreed with this narrow reading, construing "publication" as "a communication made to any person other than the party libeled."[17] Writing for the majority, Justice Norman S. Fletcher wrote that the Court of Appeals' 1984 interpretation as limiting it to "print media" was inconsistent with both the statute's legislative history and evolutions in modern communications. "For example, under its view the retraction statute would not apply to a story that appears only on the on-line version of a newspaper or an advocacy group's monthly electronic newsletter to its members reporting on congressional voting," Fletcher wrote.[18] The static nature of traditional media, Fletcher reasoned, does not make it more likely for the initial audience to view a retraction posted there than on an online medium. Fletcher also pointed to the broader interpretation as encouraging counterspeech, and he quoted *Gertz* in support of his reasoning. "It encourages defamation victims to seek self-help, their first remedy, by 'using available opportunities to contradict the lie or correct the error and thereby to minimize its adverse impact on reputation,'" he wrote.[19]

Justice Carol Hunstein, joined by two other justices, dissented. The brunt of her disagreement was not with the self-help reasoning, but with the interpretation of the statute's text. Requiring a retraction "in a regular issue of the newspaper or other publication in question," she wrote, does not apply to someone who posted on Internet bulletin boards. "That is not to say that the retraction statute is entirely inapplicable to Internet publications of defamatory statements," Hunstein continued. "To the contrary, there may well be circumstances where an individual or media defendant who regularly publishes an Internet newspaper, magazine or other publication will be subject to the mandatory provisions of the retraction statute, but that is not the case here."[20]

While Hunstein and Fletcher each had reasonable interpretations of an arguably ambiguous statute, Fletcher's reasoning about the "self-help" nature of retraction statutes supports his conclusion. Corrections and retractions can be prominently displayed on the Internet. While it is true that not everyone who saw the initial inaccurate post by an individual on the Internet will see a subsequent retraction that is posted on the same forum, the same is true of traditional media such as newspapers and television stations. The goal of a retraction statute should be encouraging the original speaker to mitigate as much harm as possible.

And that is where the Internet may be particularly well suited for self-help through retraction statutes. Because many retraction statutes do not even have the ambiguity of Georgia's law and are more explicitly limited to traditional media, this would require states to pass more modern retraction statutes. Like their predecessors, they would limit some damages, such as punitive damages, unless the plaintiff had made a retraction demand and the defendant did not retract. A modern retraction statute would explicitly include online speech and specify methods for an effective online retraction. Because of the many ways in which people can disseminate speech online, the statute might have different retraction methods. For example, a post on an online forum that allows users to edit their initial posts might require a retraction to be appended to the top of the post. If it is impossible to edit the initial speech, an effective retraction might include posting the retraction on the same platform from the same account.

As with traditional retraction statutes, a potential defendant's decision to post an online retraction would be voluntary. Failing to post a retraction would not lead to new liability; rather, posting a retraction and the counterspeech associated with it would reduce the amount of damages that a defendant would face in a defamation lawsuit. Rather than imposing new regulations for false speech, effective retraction statutes encourage the distribution of counterspeech. As Justice Fletcher correctly wrote, this regime advances the "self-help" that the US Supreme Court recognized in *Gertz*.

Counterspeech and self-help are not limited to potential defamation cases. People who have been harmed by false speech—but not necessarily defamed—can mitigate some of the worst effects by sharing their own stories. One such example of effective counterspeech came in the criminal case of Silver Spring, Maryland, personal trainer and bartender Joshua Pruitt, who was among those arrested for storming the Capitol on January 6, 2021, with the far-right Proud Boys group.[21] Pruitt pleaded guilty to one count of obstruction of an official proceeding. Before sentencing in August 2022, federal prosecutors filed a 61-page brief, asking the judge to sentence Pruitt to five years in prison. Among the attachments to the government's brief was a victim impact statement written by someone identifying himself only as C.T., a US Capitol police sergeant. C.T. wrote that he encountered Pruitt on January 6, describing Pruitt as an "agitator" who entered the law enforcement officer's personal space and attempted to incite a reaction and justify the violent behavior of those who stormed the Capitol. C.T. said that Pruitt told C.T., "You better stop eyeballing me."[22]

In a three-page, single-spaced statement, C.T. wrote of the negative personal impact of January 6, including making it more difficult to sleep and causing C.T. to be more withdrawn from friends and family members. Perhaps the most effective parts of his statement were the sections in which C.T. urged the courts to punish those involved with the riot and the attempts to overturn the election results. "The United States legal system must not tolerate any form of insurrection or coup due to a lie," C.T. wrote. "To not hold these individuals accountable for their actions will only encourage the horrific behavior again and again when they do not get their way." C.T., who is a parent, compared this to a toddler's tantrum. "If it isn't addressed immediately the tantrums become worse and worse," C.T. wrote. C.T. criticized political candidates who refused to accept their electoral losses. "Their tactics include but are not limited to slogans such as, 'fraudulent election,' 'fake news,' and disinformation campaigns against subject matter experts who go against the grain of their ideology," C.T. wrote.[23]

The judge sentenced Pruitt to 55 months in prison—just five months short of the prosecutors' request. But C.T.'s blunt criticism of misinformation and the leaders who spread it was heard outside of the courtroom where Pruitt was being sentenced. The day after the government filed the document, NBC News posted an online story about it, titled "Capitol Sergeant Who Survived Jan. 6 Fears Another Attack over Trump's Election Lies." By explaining the harmful personal impact of misinformation, C.T. sent a warning call that was heard across the country. This sort of counterspeech helps to push back on misinformation by demonstrating its harms.

Another example of effective self-help—on a larger scale—is a Reddit community called QAnonCasualties, which was founded in July 2019 as a refuge for family and friends of QAnon followers. As of April 2022, the community had 235,000 members. "Have a friend or loved one taken in by QAnon?" the group's description begins. "Look here for support, resources and a place to vent. Peruse old posts, settle in and relax. Learn to heal, deal and deprogram." The forum is filled with pseudonymous posters seeking strategies for helping to save their loved ones from the harmful falsehoods that propagate generally under the QAnon umbrella, such as how to block far-right news sites from parents' computers. But many posts are simply cries for moral support, which often are met in abundance.

For instance, in April 2022, in a post titled "Hired Divorce Lawyer—Finding It Hard to File," a woman described her "q adjacent" husband's many troubling signs, including being unvaccinated and buying a generator and deep freezer that he wants to stock with meat. She wrote of his attempts to stifle his political views, but they still often come through. "Why oh why am I finding it so hard to file?" she wrote. "The writing is on the wall. In red. Bolded. Help me get the strength." More than 200 people responded, mostly urging her to follow through with the divorce. More importantly, many shared their stories of dealing with QAnon-following spouses. One responder described getting a divorce during the COVID-19 pandemic. "Filing was *hard*, what came after was on[e] of the most freeing thing[s] I have ever done," the poster wrote. "You and your little girl deserve that freedom too. You got this." Another person was in a similar situation as the poster, about ready to end her marriage but also constantly second-guessing the decision. "It's hard because we know the immediate destruction that happens once we end the marriage + hand over divorce papers," the poster wrote. "From one mom ending her toxic marriage to another, sending you a big hug! We can do this! For our kids, for ourselves + so we can find real peace again."

Other posters simply look for some light at the end of the tunnel. Another post that month, titled "Is it hopeless," came from a woman whose husband was increasingly focused on QAnon and cults involving space aliens. "I feel like I've been slowly dying for the last couple of years not literally but emotionally with all this," she wrote. Many of those replying took an optimistic tone. "I believe there is hope ... I have to," a man wrote, describing how his wife of two decades had fallen into the QAnon conspiracies, leading to huge arguments and divorce threats. But in recent months, he wrote, the arguments became less intense, and she had more trouble denying realities like COVID. "My goal has been to keep my wife off social media, we've been watching re runs of Madmen, the whole family watch and enjoy Star Trek episodes together," he wrote. "I know she still has her views but they have moderated. . . . the household vibe is good, so I'm hoping :-)." Another poster warned of the difficulties of debunking and arguing. "Remind them of shared experiences/old times and get them to laugh," the poster wrote. "Exercise/activity, sleep/diet, old/new hobbies, old/new surroundings (fav restaurant/day trip) help. Psychoactive drugs should be stopped. Avoid whatever makes them tense or angry. Pick something that's not volatile and ask them to tell you the details."

The lies and conspiracy theories that permeate QAnon forums have had disastrous impacts not only on the lives of the movement's followers but also on the lives of their friends and families. The Reddit forum provides a way to at least reduce some harms of QAnon, by allowing loved ones to seek support, share their stories, and receive advice from others who have gone through similar struggles. While the Reddit community is unlikely to provide tools that will restore their lives to how they were before QAnon shook their lives, it provides them with at least some ways to cope.

Just as self-help does not mitigate all the harms of defamatory speech, it does not eliminate all troubles brought into families and friendships by QAnon misinformation. But it is a tool that can *help*, and should be considered when evaluating how to address online misinformation.

The Reddit page for QAnon casualties is only one example of an effective self-help mechanism created without government intervention. Among the most successful examples of online counterspeech is PolitiFact, which the *St. Petersburg Times* launched in 2007 to evaluate the accuracy of factual claims by politicians. PolitiFact, now owned by the nonprofit Poynter Institute, has expanded by partnering with regional news organizations and opening more than a dozen state-specific sites. Each evaluation includes a rating on the "Truth-O-Meter," which is either True, Mostly True, Half True, Mostly False, False, or Pants on Fire.[24] Despite the blunt Truth-O-Meter names, PolitiFact tries to be a by-the-books evaluation of the factual support for politicians' and commentators' claims. Consider Congresswoman Marjorie Taylor Greene's 2022 claim that the three Republican senators who voted to confirm Judge Ketanji Brown Jackson to the Supreme Court "are pro-pedophile." In an article totaling more than 500 words,

PolitiFact correspondent Jon Greenberg documented the three sena-tors' proposals to combat child exploitation, and also examined the weak evidence that Jackson was "soft" in sentencing child sex abuse material defendants. Greenberg concluded that Greene's claim merits a "Pants on Fire" rating. "All three lawmakers have clear track records of moving against child exploitation, whether online or in person," he wrote. The article was followed by citations to 11 sources on which Greenberg relied in evaluating Greene's claim.[25] To be sure, many, if not most, people who view an inaccurate claim are unlikely to see a subsequent fact-check. And even if they see the fact-check, there is no guarantee that they will believe it. But fact-checking, like other forms of counterspeech and self-help, is one of many tools in the arsenal against falsehoods.

Counterspeech such as PolitiFact—and other sites such as the ur-ban legend–debunking Snopes—are precisely the form of counter-speech that helps to rebut online misinformation. While such coun-terspeech helps, online intermediaries also play an important role in combatting online falsehoods.

Chapter 13

Intermediaries

This book has focused on when the government can—and cannot—regulate the flow of alleged falsehoods. But in recent years, much of this discretion also has been in the hands of social media companies and other online services. These intermediaries have wide latitude to moderate harmful content such as misinformation. This is an imperfect and incomplete solution, as platforms are destined to make some mistakes in determining whether the vast amount of speech that they distribute constitutes misinformation. Indeed, such adjudication often is impossible when facts are few and opinions are heated. And critics understandably worry about a few massive companies playing the role of speech police and allowing their political biases and economic interests to shape their decisions. Platforms should continue to have discretion to remove false speech, as long as the government does not coerce those decisions. But platforms should be transparent about their moderation. And users—rather than a few centralized companies—ultimately should control the information that they receive.

Platforms have been increasingly aggressive in removing misinformation and other content that they deem harmful. In its early years, for instance, Twitter took a relatively hands-off approach on moderation. In 2011, the company's chief executive officer, Dick Costolo, famously said that Twitter is in "the free speech wing of the free speech party."[1] But in recent years, this corporate philosophy has changed. For example, soon after the start of the COVID-19 pandemic, Twitter developed a detailed COVID-19 misinformation policy. From January 2020 to July 2021, it suspended more than 6,700 accounts and removed more than 78,000 pieces of content for violating its policies.[2] Such moderation has received both praise from people who believe that platforms should aggressively block harmful falsehoods, and criticism from those who argue that large companies are ill-positioned to be arbiters of truth. And the companies receive criticism from those who argue that platforms still are not aggressive enough in blocking dangerous falsehoods. (As this book was in the final editing stages in late 2022, new Twitter owner Elon Musk expressed a desire to avoid moderation of constitutionally protected speech, and the company said that it stopped enforcing its COVID-19 misinformation policy.)

Critics on all sides of the argument are engaged in a spirited debate about whether platforms *should* play arbiters of truth. But before addressing whether platforms should preside over disputes about online falsehoods, we first must look at whether they have the legal authority to do so. From a legal standpoint, platforms have great latitude to restrict—or not restrict—the spread of what they believe is false or misleading information for three interrelated reasons. First, the platforms' users do not have a First Amendment right to force the platform to carry their speech. Second, the platforms *do* have a First Amendment right to decide whether and how to distribute user-generated content. Third, Section 230 of the Communications Decency Act provides platforms with additional breathing space to moderate.

A concept known as the state action doctrine is the underpinning for the first legal rationale for platform intervention. As Supreme Court Justice Brett Kavanaugh summarized in 2019, the First Amendment's speech protection "constrains governmental actors and protects private actors."[3] Kavanaugh made that observation in *Manhattan Community Access Corp. v. Halleck*, a case in which critics of a nonprofit that ran a cable access channel were banned from airing their film. Their lawsuit alleged that the nonprofit violated their First Amendment rights. Although the cable station was operated by a private nonprofit, the plaintiffs argued that state action occurred because state law required cable systems to carry public access stations, and New York City had designated this nonprofit as a public access provider.

Kavanaugh, joined by four other justices, rejected this argument. Private companies can be deemed state actors for First Amendment purposes only under a "few limited circumstances—including, for example, (i) when the private entity performs a traditional, exclusive public function; (ii) when the government compels the private entity to take a particular action; or (iii) when the government acts jointly with the private entity."[4]

The plaintiffs argued that the nonprofit performs a traditional and exclusive public function. The Supreme Court has found that only a narrow set of activities—such as running a company town—fall into that category. And Kavanaugh concluded that cable access stations were not traditionally and exclusively provided by the government. He made clear that the court has good reason to hesitate before taking an expansive view of the state action doctrine. "It is sometimes said that the bigger the government, the smaller the individual," Kavanaugh wrote. "Consistent with the text of the Constitution, the state-action doctrine enforces a critical boundary between the government and the individual, and thereby protects a robust sphere of individual liberty."[5]

What does this mean for lawsuits asserting that social media platforms are state actors bound by the First Amendment? It makes such claims practically impossible, unless the government is coercing a platform to take down user content. Less than a year after Kavanaugh's opinion, the US Court of Appeals for the Ninth Circuit considered a claim that YouTube is a First Amendment state actor. PragerU, a conservative media and education nonprofit, sued YouTube for First

Amendment violations after the video-hosting platform had designated dozens of the nonprofit's videos to be inaccessible to computers operating under the site's "Restricted Mode" and prohibited advertising on certain PragerU videos.[6]

The three-judge panel unanimously held that YouTube is not a state actor. "Despite YouTube's ubiquity and its role as a public-facing platform, it remains a private forum, not a public forum subject to judicial scrutiny under the First Amendment," the court wrote.[7] YouTube, the court reasoned, is not like a company town, as it "merely operates a platform for user-generated video content," rather than performing the functions of a municipality.[8]

The Ninth Circuit's opinion is a straightforward application of *Halleck*. If a nonprofit that operates a public cable station is not a state actor, it is hard to conceive of any logical way to conclude that a private social media company is. That is not to say that there are no situations in which social media companies' moderation practices raise First Amendment concerns. Both online and offline, government officials have long tried to pressure companies to restrict the distribution of speech that the officials view as harmful. The practice, known as "jawboning," is aptly described by Genevieve Lakier as "the tendency of government officials to use informal means, rather than democratically elected laws, to pressure the social media companies to take down what they consider to be harmful or offensive speech."[9] In 1963, the Supreme Court ruled that the Rhode Island Commission to Encourage Morality in Youth had violated the First Amendment when it sent an official letter to wholesale book distributors, informing them "that certain designated books or magazines distributed by him had been reviewed by the Commission and had been declared by a majority of its members to be objectionable for sale, distribution or display to youths under 18 years of age."[10] The Supreme Court concluded that although the commission lacked the authority to impose "formal legal sanctions," the First Amendment still applied because "the record amply demonstrates that the Commission deliberately set about to achieve the suppression of publications deemed 'objectionable' and succeeded in its aim."[11] But in 1982, the Supreme Court adopted a narrower view of state coercion in a different context.[12]

As Lakier aptly summarized in a review of more recent lower court cases, the jawboning case law is "messy," and "what conclusion courts reach about the merits of First Amendment jawboning arguments will depend, to a significant extent, on which line of precedents they rely on."[13] So it is hard to predict, for instance, how a court would rule on allegations of jawboning arising from Surgeon General Vivek Murthy's July 2021 bulletin titled "Confronting Health Misinformation." The document includes eight suggestions for technology platforms, including "[p]rioritize early detection of misinformation 'super-spreaders' and 'repeat offenders,'" and "[a]mplify communications from trusted messengers and subject matter experts."[14] Likewise, jawboning concerns may have arisen after Senators Amy Klobuchar and Ben Ray Luján in April 2021 sent a letter to the chief executives of Facebook and Twitter to highlight a Center for Countering Digital Hate report about the "Disinformation Dozen," 12 people who the nonprofit claimed spread most disinformation about coronavirus vaccines. "We must urgently work to ensure Americans receive accurate and reliable information about coronavirus vaccines," the senators wrote. "A crucial step to increase vaccine confidence is to address primary spreaders of this vaccine disinformation, including the twelve accounts—referred to as the 'Disinformation Dozen' and are responsible for a majority of disinformation—in a swift and decisive manner."

Although the courts have not clearly defined the contours of jawboning in the social media context, they likely will have opportunities in the future. For instance, if someone had been kicked off Facebook for violating its health misinformation policies, that person might claim that their First Amendment rights were violated because Murthy had jawboned Facebook. And although Klobuchar and Luján are only two of a hundred US senators, a few months after their letter, they introduced the Health Misinformation Act, described in chapter 10, to increase the potential liability of platforms for health misinformation. The jawboning argument is by no means certain to succeed. But the more informal pressure that a government exerts on a platform to remove content, the more likely a court will be to accept a jawboning argument. Although it is vital to clearly define impermissible jawboning, the legal system also must allow the government to participate in the marketplace of ideas. This includes giving government officials the ability to criticize what they view as inaccurate information. The government should be free to respond to misinformation, but that is different from using the threat of government action to coerce a private company to suppress speech. Close questions will arise. For instance, imagine a government official encouraging a platform to take down a harmful and inaccurate post without explicitly threatening punishment for failure to remove it. If that official has the power to regulate or impose other penalties on the company, does such a request constitute implicit coercion?

At the very least, the jawboning case law suggests that government officials should avoid exerting pressure on platforms to remove constitutionally protected content, and focus instead on effectively responding to misinformation and building public trust. This caution not only avoids First Amendment problems, but it also prevents the government from using its heavy hand and threats of regulation or other liability to silence speakers. And Congress should consider passing a law that clearly defines the sort of jawboning in which government officials are prohibited from engaging. But if the platforms voluntarily and independently remove harmful content without government pressure, it is hard to conceive of a First Amendment challenge succeeding.

The second reason that platforms can voluntarily moderate harmful but constitutionally protected user content is that the platforms have a First Amendment right to do so. This right was best articulated after

Pat L. Tornillo, a 1972 candidate for the Florida House of Representatives, insisted that the *Miami Herald* publish his letter to the editor that responded to the paper's criticism of him in editorials. His demand had a legal basis: Florida had a "right of reply" statute that stated:

> If any newspaper in its columns assails the personal character of any candidate for nomination or for election in any election, or charges said candidate with malfeasance or misfeasance in office, or otherwise attacks his official record, or gives to another free space for such purpose, such newspaper shall upon request of such candidate immediately publish free of cost any reply he may make thereto in as conspicuous a place and in the same kind of type as the matter that calls for such reply, provided such reply does not take up more space than the matter replied to.[15]

A violation of the law was a first-degree misdemeanor. The state trial court declared the law a First Amendment violation, but the Florida Supreme Court reversed, concluding that the statute advanced the "broad societal interest in the free flow of information to the public."[16]

The US Supreme Court granted certiorari and in 1974 unanimously struck down the right of reply statute as unconstitutional. Writing for the court in *Miami Herald Publishing v. Tornillo*, Chief Justice Warren Burger rejected Tornillo's claim that "government has an obligation to ensure that a wide variety of views reach the public."[17] Among the reasons that Tornillo believed that such government-mandated access was important was the increased consolidation of newspapers and broadcasters, giving fewer companies the power to control public opinion. And it simply was not economically practical for people to solve this problem by starting their own newspaper. "However much validity may be found in these arguments, at each point the implementation of a remedy such as an enforceable right of access necessarily calls for some mechanism, either governmental or consensual," Burger wrote. "If it is governmental coercion, this at once brings about a confrontation with the express provisions of the First Amendment and the judicial gloss on that Amendment developed over the years."[18]

Burger disagreed with Tornillo's claim that requiring the publication of a rebuttal letter is not a restriction on the newspaper's speech. "The Florida statute operates as a command in the same sense as a statute or regulation forbidding appellant to publish specified matter," Burger wrote. "Governmental restraint on publishing need not fall into familiar or traditional patterns to be subject to constitutional limitations on governmental powers."[19] A newspaper, Burger continued, is not just a "passive receptacle or conduit for news, comment, and advertising" but has a First Amendment right to determine what content it does—and doesn't—publish. "The choice of material to go into a newspaper, and the decisions made as to limitations on the size and content of the paper, and treatment of public issues and public officials—whether fair or unfair—constitute the exercise of editorial control and judgment," he wrote.[20]

The Supreme Court reiterated these principles in *Pacific Gas & Electric Co. v. Public Utilities Commission of California*,[21] a 1986 opinion in which the court struck down a California law that required a utility company to include a third party's newsletter in its utility bills, and *Hurley v. Irish American Gay, Lesbian, and Bisexual Group of Boston*,[22] a 1995 case in which the Supreme Court struck down a Massachusetts law that would have barred a private parade organizer from excluding a gay rights group from its parade.

The stringent First Amendment review that the Supreme Court applied in *Tornillo* does not necessarily apply to all such requirements. In 1994, the Supreme Court applied a lower constitutional standard in its review of a federal law that requires cable operators to transmit local broadcast stations. Among the reasons that the court differentiated cable operators from newspapers was the physical aspect of cable lines. "When an individual subscribes to cable, the physical connection between the television set and the cable network gives the cable operator bottleneck, or gatekeeper, control over most (if not all) of the television programming that is channeled into the subscriber's home," Justice Anthony Kennedy wrote for the majority in *Turner Broadcasting System v. FCC.* "Hence, simply by virtue of its ownership of the essential pathway for cable speech, a cable operator can prevent its subscribers from obtaining access to programming it chooses to exclude. A cable operator, unlike speakers in other media, can thus silence the voice of competing speakers with a mere flick of the switch."[23] The court also applied the lower scrutiny because it determined that legislators' goal in passing the law was not to favor a particular type of programming or viewpoint, "but rather to preserve access to free television programming for the 40 percent of Americans without cable."[24]

Which precedent should apply to social media: *Tornillo* or *Turner*? While some commentators and lawyers have argued that social media companies should receive the lower scrutiny applied to cable operators,[25] I think that there is a far stronger argument that online platforms are more analogous to newspapers. Although the fit is far from perfect, modern social media platforms share characteristics with 1970s newspapers that inform the First Amendment analysis. Neither newspapers nor social media platforms have the same sort of *physical* bottleneck that cable operators do. Their power comes from their dominance in the field. While social media platforms no doubt wield substantial power over speech, metropolitan newspapers also did in the 1970s. At most, only a handful of local media were effective vehicles for speakers to disseminate their views to the public. The Supreme Court recognized the potential of the Internet as a vehicle for free speech in 1997 when it rejected calls to apply to an Internet indecency law the less rigorous First Amendment scrutiny that broadcasters receive. In distinguishing the new online media, the court wrote of the "dramatic expansion of this new marketplace of ideas" and found that the "record demonstrates that the growth of the Internet has been and continues to be phenomenal."[26]

Newspapers and social media platforms also are similar in that their content curation is part of the product that they sell to customers. A newspaper's editorial decisions define it, just as a social media platform's moderation practices (or lack thereof) define it. There is no doubt that social media has important differences from newspapers, including the multilateral nature of the communications, and the global dominance of a few platforms that is difficult to compare to even national newspapers like the *New York Times* or *Wall Street Journal*. As of late 2022, the Supreme Court had yet to consider what First Amendment protections social media platforms receive for their moderation decisions, though Justice Clarence Thomas, in a 2021 concurrence to a denial of certiorari, suggested that social media platforms might face the same nondiscrimination requirements as common carriers such as phone companies.[27]

Although the entire Supreme Court has not directly addressed the issue as of late 2022, two federal appellate courts did in 2022, and came to very different conclusions about whether the greater protections for newspapers' editorial discretion also applies to social media content moderation.

The first dispute involved Senate Bill 7072, enacted by the Florida legislature in 2021.[28] At the heart of SB 7072 were limits on social media platforms' ability to moderate content. The law stated that social media providers "may not willfully deplatform a candidate for public office," nor may the platforms "apply or use post-prioritization or shadow banning algorithms for content and material posted by or about . . . a candidate."[29] The law also restricted the platforms' content-based censorship of "journalistic enterprises" of a certain size; requires the platforms to "apply censorship, deplatforming, and shadow banning standards in a consistent manner among its users on the platform"; only allows changes to user terms every 30 days; and requires social media providers to give users the option of displaying content in chronological order.[30] The law also required the platforms to disclose information about its moderation rules and practices, and to provide users access to their data if they were deplatformed.[31]

Technology trade groups challenged SB 7072 as both a violation of the First Amendment and as preempted by Section 230 of the Communications Decency Act, and the district court granted a preliminary injunction blocking the entire law from going into effect, finding that the tech groups were likely to succeed.[32] Florida appealed to the US Court of Appeals for the Eleventh Circuit, and the case went to three judges: Trump appointee Kevin C. Newsom, Ford appointee Gerald Tjoflat, and George H. W. Bush appointee Ed Carnes.

The judges unanimously agreed that Florida's restrictions on "censorship" were likely unconstitutional and upheld the district court's preliminary injunction on those provisions, while reversing the injunction for many of the bill's disclosure and user data access provisions. Writing for the three judges, Newsom reasoned that *Tornillo* and the more recent Supreme Court opinions "establish that a private entity's decisions about whether, to what extent, and in what manner to disseminate third-party-created content to the public are editorial judgments protected by the First Amendment."[33] Newsom focused on the expressive nature of content moderation. "When platforms choose to remove users or posts, deprioritize content in viewers' feeds or search results, or sanction breaches of their community standards, they engage in First-Amendment-protected activity," he wrote.[34]

Newsom also rejected the state's attempts to brand social media platforms as common carriers because "social-media platforms have never acted like common carriers," and "Supreme Court precedent strongly suggests that internet companies like social-media platforms aren't common carriers." Nor can a state law convert the platforms into common carriers, he continued. "Neither law nor logic recognizes government authority to strip an entity of its First Amendment rights merely by labeling it a common carrier," Newsom wrote.[35] The law's restrictions on moderation, Newsom concluded, likely do not advance a substantial or compelling government interest needed to overcome a First Amendment challenge. "At the end of the day, preventing 'unfair[ness]' to certain users or points of view isn't a substantial governmental interest; rather, private actors have a First Amendment right to be 'unfair'—which is to say, a right to have and express their own points of view," he wrote.[36] Newsom noted the absurd consequences of the moderation restrictions, such as barring a video-hosting site geared to children from removing pornography posted by a journalistic enterprise, or prohibiting Twitter or Facebook from deleting a journalistic enterprise's video of a killing spree.[37]

Newsom applied a more relaxed standard in reviewing the disclosure requirements, most of which he found were likely constitutional. "The State's interest here is in ensuring that users—consumers who engage in commercial transactions with platforms by providing them with a user and data for advertising in exchange for access to a forum—are fully informed about the terms of that transaction and aren't misled about platforms' content-moderation policies," he wrote. "This interest is likely legitimate."[38] Some commentators quickly criticized Newsom for glossing over the potential chilling effect of disclosure requirements.[39]

But the Eleventh Circuit was not the only federal appellate court to rule on the constitutionality of state restrictions on content moderation. Later in 2022, the Fifth Circuit issued an opinion that upheld a Texas law, House Bill 20, which states that a large social media platform "may not censor a user, a user's expression, or a user's ability to receive the expression of another person" based on viewpoints or the geographic location of the user.[40] The law has some exceptions, including for the prevention of child sexual exploitation and expression that "directly incites criminal activity or consists of specific threats of violence targeted against a person or group because of their race, color, disability, religion, national origin or ancestry, age, sex, or status as a peace officer or judge."[41]

Do these restrictions on content moderation violate the First Amendment? Fifth Circuit Judge Andrew Oldham came to a different conclusion than fellow Trump appointee Newsom. What Oldham dubbed "Platforms' censorship," he reasoned, is fundamentally different from the "editorial discretion" that the Supreme Court provides to newspapers. "We reject the Platforms' attempt to extract a freewheeling censorship right from the Constitution's free speech guarantee," Oldham wrote. "The Platforms are not newspapers. Their censorship is not speech."[42] Oldham emphasized that platforms do not manually review or choose the vast majority of the content that they distribute. "Unlike newspapers, the Platforms exercise virtually no editorial control or judgment," he wrote. "The Platforms use algorithms to screen out certain obscene and spam-related content. And then virtually everything else is just posted to the Platform with zero editorial control or judgment."[43] Unlike Newsom, Oldham reasoned that the common carrier doctrine allows states to impose nondiscrimination requirements on social media platforms, just as they have done for centuries on railroads, telephone carriers, and other companies. "At bottom, the Platforms ask us to hold that in the long technological march from ferries and bakeries, to barges and gristmills, to steamboats and stagecoaches, to railroads and grain elevators, to water and gas lines, to telegraph and telephone lines, to social media platforms—that social media marks the point where the underlying technology is finally so complicated that the government may no longer regulate it to prevent invidious discrimination," Oldham wrote. "But we may not inter this venerable and centuries-old doctrine just because Twitter's censorship tools are more sophisticated than Western Union's."[44]

Oldham's comparison of social media to telephone companies—and his minimization of the social media providers' own First Amendment interests—rests on his willingness to gloss over the role of content moderation in the companies' product offerings. The policies and moderation practices of social media platforms differ, sometimes significantly, which allows users to choose the services that best meet their needs. Such discretion is not nearly as central to the business offerings of gas lines, telephone companies, railroads, and other common carriers.

As this book was being written in late 2022, the Supreme Court was considering whether to review the Fifth and Eleventh Circuit rulings. I believe that such review is likely, as it is difficult to reconcile the two opinions. Affirming Newsom and overturning Oldham would be more consistent with the Supreme Court precedent. And more importantly, Newsom's reading of the First Amendment gives platforms the flexibility to moderate harmful but constitutionally protected content in a way that they believe best serves their users.

Newsom's opinion makes a strong case for platforms to have the legal authority to determine what content to allow on their services. But the legal question is separate from the question about whether such concentrated power is always best for society. Serious criticism may emerge when private companies have the unilateral authority to be the arbiters of the speech of billions of people. The large platforms' restriction on the distribution of the Hunter Biden laptop story, described in chapter 9, is one such example. Another example came in the days after January 6, 2021, when Facebook and Twitter banned President Donald Trump from their services. While the social media companies had detailed justifications for doing so, it is not necessarily in the best interests of society to ban a sitting president (and potential future presidential candidate) from speaking on a widely used platform. I also question the efficacy of such a ban; did it result in reduced distribution of harmful speech about the election? Even after Twitter banned Trump, journalists and other high-profile Twitter users routinely shared Trump's press releases and screenshots of his posts from his own social media platform, Truth Social.

But even if we do not agree with social media platforms' moderation decisions (and we probably won't agree with all of them), society would be worse off if a government agency or court micromanaged these decisions. Even if you assume that large platforms systematically discriminate against particular viewpoints, the alternative regime— allowing a government agency or court to supervise moderation decisions—creates even greater problems. The uncertainty of what it means to "censor" a user based on their "viewpoint" could lead to platforms simply not moderating at all, or being afraid to moderate anything but the most blatantly illegal content. And allowing courts—or legislators or executive branch officials—to oversee content moderation enables public officials to determine what speech must and mustn't be distributed.

Providing platforms with the discretion to moderate harmful but constitutionally protected false speech is far from a panacea, but it is better than either an entirely unmoderated Internet, or an Internet in which the government can determine what content is blocked from users. While some large platforms have substantial power over speech, they are not the government. They cannot issue fines. They cannot send police to your door. They cannot throw you in prison. They are subject to competitive pressures, though it might not seem like it given their size. Facebook was once seen as an upstart competitor to MySpace. And now TikTok is emerging as a serious challenger to the US market dominance of Facebook, Instagram, and Twitter. While it is harder to dethrone massive social media platforms than it was even a decade ago, it is possible, and content moderation practices help differentiate the companies.

The conservative critique of platform moderation partly hinges on an idealized notion of a town square that is open to anyone, no matter how extreme, inaccurate, or harmful their views are. This ignores that during the past century, so much of the public debate in America has occurred not in actual town squares, but in privately owned media—newspapers, radio, television, and only recently the Internet. These media have always been gatekeepers. Even with aggressive moderation, it is far easier to express viewpoints—even extreme ones—on social media than it ever was in newspapers or on television.

The third reason that platforms have wide latitude to moderate content comes not from the Constitution but from a statute: Section 230 of the Communications Decency Act. As I explain in my 2019 book,

The Twenty-Six Words That Created the Internet, Congress passed Section 230 in 1996 partly in response to a New York state trial court opinion, *Stratton Oakmont v. Prodigy*,[45] which concluded that because Prodigy moderated some of the user content on its online service, it was liable as the publisher for *all* user content on the site. A few years earlier, a different court, in *Cubby v. Compuserve*,[46] held that CompuServe, because it did not exercise sufficient "editorial control" over user content, faced the lower "distributor" liability standard and was liable only if it knew or had reason to know of the defamatory or otherwise illegal content. This created an incentive for platforms to avoid any sort of moderation of user content, something that did not sit well with lawmakers who were concerned about pornography and other harmful content proliferating on the rapidly growing Internet.

Section 230 has two primary subsections: (c)(1) and (c)(2). Subsection (c)(1) contains the 26 words that have given US platforms great flexibility to structure their business models around third-party content: "No provider or user of an interactive computer service shall be treated as the publisher or speaker of any information provided by another information content provider."[47] In a 1997 case, *Zeran v. America Online*, the first and most influential federal appellate court opinion to interpret Section 230, the US Court of Appeals for the Fourth Circuit concluded that these 26 words prevent platforms from being held liable not only as publishers but also as distributors, meaning that they avoid liability even if they knew or had reason to know of the defamatory user content. The Fourth Circuit also wrote that subsection (c)(1) extends beyond lawsuits arising from material left on the site, and "lawsuits seeking to hold a service provider liable for its exercise of a publisher's traditional editorial functions—such as deciding whether to publish, withdraw, postpone or alter content— are barred."[48]

To underscore Congress's desire to give platforms the flexibility to moderate, subsection (c)(2) states that online platforms also are not held liable for "any action voluntarily taken in good faith to restrict access to or availability of material that the provider or user considers to be obscene, lewd, lascivious, filthy, excessively violent, harassing, or otherwise objectionable, whether or not such material is constitutionally protected," or for providing "technical means" to block such material.[49] Section (c)(2) has received particular criticism in recent years, with conservatives arguing to restrict the types of content covered or to interpret "otherwise objectionable" narrowly. Yet subsection (c)(2), which has limits such as "good faith," is not as often litigated as the more absolute (c)(1), even in cases challenging content moderation decisions.[50]

Because Newsom decided that the Florida law likely violated the First Amendment, he declined to analyze the tech organization's alternative argument: that the Florida law also violates Section 230. And the Texas district court did not address whether Section 230 blocked the Texas law, so Oldham abstained from definitively ruling on the issue. But he suggested that Section 230 is not a barrier. Oldham read subsection (c)(2) as applying to "the removal of limited categories of content, like obscene, excessively violent, and similarly objectionable expression," and that it "says nothing about viewpoint-based or geography-based censorship."[51] While Oldham is correct that Section 230 does not specifically discuss "censorship" based on viewpoint or geography, he minimizes the scope of its coverage. Subsection (c)(2) uses the phrase "otherwise objectionable," not "similarly objectionable." Although Oldham attempted to justify his narrow reading by applying a rule of statutory interpretation that supports reading general words in the context of the other words in a statute, the plain language of the subsection provides broad discretion to platforms. Had Congress intended to only cover "similarly objectionable" content, it would have written just that. And the subsection applies to voluntary and good faith actions to limit material that the online service "*considers to be* obscene, lewd, lascivious, filthy, excessively violent, harassing, or otherwise objectionable,"[52] further demonstrating an intent to give the online services leeway in moderation.

Although Section 230 applies to any online service that hosts user content, including Wikipedia, community news sites, and online bulletin boards, in popular debate it is often associated with the largest social media companies. So politicians and commentators who are unhappy with "Big Tech" seek to amend or repeal Section 230. For instance, throughout 2020, President Trump urged the repeal of Section 230 owing to his frustration with social media moderation policies that he viewed as overly aggressive and biased against conservatives.[53]

Conservatives are not the only ones who are urging a repeal or significant revision of Section 230. Since 2019, Democrats have introduced dozens of bills to scale back Section 230, frustrated that platforms have not been aggressive enough in their moderation of harmful but constitutionally protected content such as misinformation. During the 2020 presidential campaign, Joe Biden said that Section 230 "immediately should be revoked."[54]

If critics are concerned with user-generated content that is not constitutionally protected—such as false speech that reaches the high common-law and First Amendment standards to qualify as defamation—then a repeal of Section 230 might allow plaintiffs to recover damages from platforms for that speech. But as this book has shown, a great deal of speech considered to be misinformation is constitutionally protected. With or without Section 230, Congress or state legislatures cannot merely ban all misinformation. Such censorship would run directly into a successful First Amendment challenge. Likewise, it is doubtful that Congress could condition a benefit such as Section 230 on the moderation of constitutionally protected speech, as that would face pushback as an unconstitutional condition.[55]

Repealing Section 230 could have the perverse effect of increasing the amount of misinformation on the Internet. In the worst-case scenario of a Section 230–free world, courts would widely adopt the *Strat-*

ton Oakmont precedent. That would mean that *any* moderation would cause the platforms to be just as liable as the authors for everything that they fail to remove from their sites. This could quickly give platforms the incentive to avoid moderating user-generated content— exactly the outcome that Congress sought to prevent when it passed Section 230 in 1996. Such a reaction could vastly increase the amount of misinformation and other harmful but protected user content. *Stratton Oakmont* is a nonbinding opinion that was not well reasoned, so there is a good chance that courts would not follow its precedent in a world without Section 230. But even under the more balanced *Cubby* standard, platforms would be seen as distributors and become liable for defamation or other tortious user content once they knew or had reason to know of the defamatory or tortious content. Such a liability standard probably would allow people to get content removed by notifying the platform; for instance, a business that is the subject of a negative review might have an easier time convincing Yelp to delete the review, lest it be forced to face a defamation lawsuit on the merits. But a *Cubby*-like distributor liability standard also might discourage platforms from proactive moderation of harmful content; if the platforms do not know about the content, then under the *Cubby* standard they are less likely to be liable if it is left online.

The current legal regime, in which the First Amendment and Section 230 give platforms substantial breathing room to take down or leave up user content, is far from perfect. Conservatives are understandably concerned about a few dominant platforms unfairly preventing them from speaking to the public, and liberals are understandably concerned about the widespread distribution of harmful but constitutionally protected user content. But I have yet to encounter a substantial change to Section 230 or online platforms' distribution obligations that would be a meaningful net improvement to the current system. Content moderation at such a large scale inevitably requires difficult decisions about whether to leave material up or take it down. Platforms certainly have erred in both directions. But I am even less comfortable with allowing government officials and politicians to influence those decisions.

These concerns are particularly true when it comes to misinformation. For instance, as of mid-2022, Facebook's Community Standards for misinformation were more than 1,500 words, explaining the types of misinformation that it removes and how it arrives at those decisions, including by consulting health organizations on health misinformation and removing "misinformation that is likely to directly contribute to a risk of interference" with the ability of people to vote. Such removals are not and cannot be required by law, but Facebook goes beyond its legal requirements and tries to remove harmful content. Facebook does not get everything right; in part, whether a decision is "right" depends on who is evaluating the decision and when the decision is being evaluated. It might have seemed reasonable in March 2020 to prohibit users' claims that COVID-19 is airborne, but a year later, such a policy would have made little sense.

By allowing private companies to make these decisions, we at least increase the likelihood that individuals will be able to choose among platforms with different moderation policies, some that allow more content and others that are more restrictive. Of course, many of those benefits depend on rigorous competition, which is lacking in social media. This is at least partly a result of the economic concept of network effects: services like social media often are more attractive when they have large numbers of users, as the largest providers offer the opportunity to connect with more people. This makes competition among providers particularly challenging. But social media history shows that even giants are not immune from competition. And there is a chance that within the next few years, another social media company will be a credible rival to TikTok.

Content policies that are set by a small group of companies in a weakly competitive market are far from a utopia. But they are better than uniform policies that the government dictates. Mandated content moderation standards increase homogeneity among platforms and are susceptible to abuse by government officials who want to control what people see online.

One way to address the legitimate concerns about platform power might be through the balance that Newsom struck—prohibiting government restrictions on content moderation while allowing certain disclosure requirements that might increase transparency and public trust. Of course, any such requirements would need to meaningfully address First Amendment concerns about chilling the platforms' ability to moderate content. I question whether even the most transparent policies would ultimately lead to better content moderation, but they might build trust with users.

An even more effective (though partial) solution to the legitimate concerns about centralized platform power lies in one of the primary—and often forgotten—purposes of Section 230: user empowerment. While Section 230's sponsors wanted platforms to feel free to engage in the sort of moderation that Prodigy had done, they also wanted these companies to provide users with tools such as Net-Nanny and SurfWatch, which allowed parents to block inappropriate content on their children's computers. "We want to encourage people like Prodigy, like CompuServe, like America Online, like the new Microsoft network, to do everything possible for us, the customer, to help us control, at the portals of our computer, at the front door of our house, what comes in and what our children see," Congressman Chris Cox, one of Section 230's two authors, said during floor debate on the bill in 1995. "This technology is very quickly becoming available, and in fact every one of us will be able to tailor what we see to our own tastes."[56] And Section 230's opening section states that it is national policy "to encourage the development of technologies which maximize user control over what information is received by individuals, families, and schools who use the Internet and other interactive computer services."[57]

Some of Section 230's policy statements and findings reflect a July 1995 report from a working group organized by the Center for Democracy and Technology, which was looking for solutions to concerns about children's access to online pornography that did not include censorship. User empowerment, the group wrote, was a more effective and constitutionally permissible solution. "Instead of relying on government censorship, or even government-imposed rating systems, parents should be able to block the delivery of certain information to their children," the group wrote.[58]

When Section 230 was signed into law the next year, it was difficult to envision a few large companies having an outsized impact on society as do Google, Facebook, and other social media and online service providers. Although the economics and scale of the Internet are drastically different from 1996, the concept of user empowerment could address many concerns about harmful online content such as false and misleading information, while also resolving concerns about a single company acting as the arbiter of truth. One solution might be to give people the option to screen out content that is flagged by third-party fact-checkers, provided that they also have the option to view that content.

Techdirt editor Mike Masnick proposed a thoughtful framework for modern user empowerment. In a 2019 article, Masnick suggested that the Internet return to being based around nonproprietary protocols rather than centralized platforms. "Rather than relying on a few giant platforms to police speech online, there could be widespread competition, in which anyone could design their own interfaces, filters, and additional services, allowing whichever ones work best to succeed, without having to resort to outright censorship for certain voices," Masnick wrote. "It would allow end users to determine their own tolerances for different types of speech but make it much easier for most people to avoid the most problematic speech, without silencing anyone entirely or having the platforms themselves make the decisions about who is allowed to speak."[59] Masnick proposes a compelling solution that attempts to reduce the concentration of decision-making over online speech while not reverting to a completely unfiltered approach. He correctly recognizes that the protocols-based system faces many challenges, including that they might "tend to be too complicated and too cumbersome to attract a large enough userbase" and that large platforms "are already so large and so entrenched that it would be nearly impossible to unseat them with a protocols-based approach."[60] But such obstacles are not a reason to give up on a protocol-based moderation system, particularly if some platforms buy in to the model. Indeed, later in 2019, Twitter CEO Jack Dorsey tweeted approvingly about Masnick's article, writing that "it reminded us of a credible path forward: hire folks to develop a standard in the open." He made that observation as he announced the launch of the Bluesky project, which was charged with the development of "an open and decentralized standard for social media." Although Dorsey stepped down from his position in November 2021, as of March 2022, the initiative continued under new CEO Parag Agrawal.[61] As of late 2022, it is unclear what the fate of Bluesky is under new Twitter owner Musk. Twitter and other platforms should continue to experiment with decentralized content systems to find solutions that place as much control as possible in the hands of users and provide an alternative to either an entirely unfiltered online experience or one that is controlled by a few large companies.

Another promising example of decentralized social media lies in the Fediverse, which is a network of compatible social media platforms known as "instances" and accessible by increasingly popular apps such as Mastodon. As Alan Z. Rozenshtein noted, breaking away from the "walled gardens" of traditional social media is more in line with email and other protocol-based features of the Internet. "The Internet initially grew around a set of open, decentralized applications, many of which remain central to its functioning today," he wrote.[62] The Fediverse takes control of speech away from a handful of powerful companies.

Although federated services have gained popularity, platforms such as Twitter, Facebook, Instagram, and TikTok remained dominant forces in online speech as of late 2022. Until we experience a more fundamental shift in internet usage, we cannot ignore the role of centralized platforms in the misinformation debate. Intermediaries are key to reducing misinformation and other harmful content. They can do better, but they are only one part of an imperfect solution.

Chapter 14

Accountability

The US legal system does not enable people to entirely avoid consequences of the harms resulting from false speech. But those consequences should be borne not only by the speaker, but also by those who reacted to the speech and hurt others.

The law has long held people at least partly responsible for how they react to false speech. For instance, Gaston Jaillet was held responsible for the losses that he suffered from selling stock, even though he relied on the erroneous Dow Jones report. Of course, these cases often involved plaintiffs who sought to hold accountable the publishers or distributors of false or misleading speech. But this reasoning extends to those who say that they have committed acts that have harmed others because of their belief in misinformation, propaganda, or conspiracy theories. While we can and should place some blame on speakers, we also should expect the recipients of the speech to be discerning. That expectation should lead to holding recipients accountable if they break the law, even if they say that they were motivated by lies that others had told.

Such accountability could at least cause others to think twice before relying on outlandish Internet conspiracies. But what level of responsibility should we impose on the recipients of false speech? Judges in the District of Columbia federal trial court had a chance to answer this question as they presided over the criminal prosecutions of hundreds of people who stormed the Capitol on January 6, 2021. Federal law gives judges discretion in sentencing but requires them to consider factors such as the defendant's history, the deterrence effect of the sentence, whether the sentence reflects the seriousness of the crime, and sentencing disparities among similar defendants.[1] One issue that loomed over many of these sentences is that the defendants were reacting to a systematic effort to discredit the 2020 election results that was fostered by online commentators, conservative media, and politicians, including the president of the United States.

Many of those charged pleaded guilty, but the judges had to sentence them. How should the judges consider, if at all, that they were influenced by a propaganda and misinformation campaign about the election results? This dilemma was pervasive in many sentences. The different approaches to accountability for reactions to false speech can be seen in the sentencing for two of the men who entered the Capitol on January 6 and pleaded guilty to relatively low-level misdemeanors: John Lolos and Russell James Peterson.

John Lolos owns and operates a Washington State security company that promises it will "control who is allowed access to certain areas of your offices or corporate headquarters" and "ensure that the right people have access to the appropriate parts of your buildings and grounds." He also was one of the thousands of supporters of Donald Trump who came to Washington, DC, to attend President Trump's Stop the Steal rally on the morning of January 6 at the Ellipse.[2] At the rally, Trump rattled off election conspiracies and told the rally attendees and thousands of other supporters to "fight like hell" and "walk down Pennsylvania Avenue."[3]

And so Lolos did. According to prosecutors' court filings, he walked with others to the Capitol. Once outside, he text-messaged a friend, "I'm there were [*sic*] storming the Capitol now," along with a photo that he took of a mob of people outside the building.[4] Once he arrived at the Capitol, wearing a black balaclava that partly obscured his face, he crawled through a broken window with others.[5] When he arrived at the Crypt, he chanted and waved a red flag emblazoned with "TRUMP 2020 KEEP AMERICA GREAT" and an American flag.[6] After encountering police in riot gear at the Hall of Columbus, he left the building. While leaving, he yelled, "They left! We did it!" and waved his flag. Afterward, he texted a photograph of himself and added the caption "Me after battle."[7]

Two days later, Lolos boarded a flight at Reagan National Airport but was escorted off the plane for repeatedly yelling, "Trump 2020!"[8] He was arrested the next day, and in August Lolos pleaded guilty to one count of parading, demonstrating, or picketing in a capitol building, a misdemeanor that carries up to six months of incarceration and a fine of up to $5,000.[9] Deciding what sentence to impose fell to Judge Amit Mehta, a former public defender and private law firm partner whom President Barack Obama appointed to the District of Columbia federal court in 2014.[10]

Representing Lolos was Edward B. MacMahon Jr., one of the most renowned criminal defense attorneys in the DC area, perhaps best known for representing Zacarias Moussaoui, the "twentieth hijacker" during the September 11 terrorist attacks. In the brief that MacMahon filed with Mehta before sentencing, he noted the role that Trump's claims about the election played in Lolos's decision to travel to DC. "Mr. Lolos was especially animated by claims of voter fraud which he believed was rampant in the United States," MacMahon wrote. And once Lolos arrived at the rally "at the express invitation of the then President," he intended to "hear speeches and protest the rampant voter fraud that Mr. Lolos heard about on a daily basis after the 2020 presidential election."[11] The claims about election fraud, MacMahon wrote, also played a role in his client's actions at the Capitol. "There is no doubt that Mr. Lolos was upset about perceived voter fraud and he followed the crowd as it made its way to the Capitol," MacMahon wrote.[12] Unlike other January 6 defendants, MacMahon noted, Lolos was not violent, did not vandalize, and did not glorify the events on social media.[13] MacMahon requested that Lolos receive probation with no additional incarceration beyond the two days he served after his arrest.[14]

On November 19, 2021, Mehta held Lolos's sentencing hearing. Although such hearings normally are conducted in a courtroom with the defendant and counsel present, Mehta held this sentencing via Zoom per COVID-19 precautions. Federal Prosecutor Anthony L. Franks argued that Lolos should receive one month of incarceration and pay $500 in restitution. Franks acknowledged that the government did not have evidence that Lolos destroyed property during his 43 minutes in the Capitol. But he noted that Lolos owns a security company. "With his professional background, he shouldn't have stormed the Capitol," Franks said. "He should have turned around when he saw the chaos all around him; the rioters climbing in through broken windows."[15] MacMahon told Mehta that Lolos was among the first January 6 defendants to plead guilty, and that while he had entered the Capitol, he wasn't violent toward police or breaking windows.[16] Nor did he try to enter the Senate or House chambers. MacMahon acknowledged Lolos's behavior on the plane two days later but emphasized that unlike other January 6 defendants, Lolos did not make further comments about the event on social media.[17]

When it came time for Lolos to make his case to Mehta, he presented his story and reasoning in great detail, beginning with what prompted him to come to Washington, DC. "So I saw voter fraud on TV—and I'll get to the specifics—voter fraud in Philadelphia, Chicago, Detroit, Your Honor," Lolos said. "I saw the Republican witnesses getting kicked out of the voting polls, all on video and audio. Then they started videotaping through the windows. Then they blocked that."[18] Lolos explained that he heard of truck drivers attesting about ballots being delivered from New York City to Philadelphia and elsewhere, and he also recounted that 10 or 20 years ago, Lolos had visited the Federal Bureau of Investigation to report that he "had a videotape of the League of Women Voters punching multiple ballots." The FBI, he said, told him that they knew about the video but supervisors were preventing them from acting on it.[19] Once at the January 6 rally in Washington, DC, Lolos said, he was barely able to hear what the speakers were saying. When people began leaving, he reports, other spectators said they were heading to the Capitol to protest voter fraud. "I go, okay, hey, I want to protest voter fraud, too," he said.[20] By the time that he got to the Capitol, he said, the violence that was shown on television had already occurred. He said that he initially saw neither barricades nor law enforcement outside.[21] He entered the building, he said, to talk to the police, and he described his discussions with officers, including Lolos telling an officer that he supports the officer.[22]

Eventually, Mehta interrupted Lolos. "It sounds like to me you are wanting to justify your conduct that day," Mehta said.

"No, I'm not justifying it," Lolos replied. "I'm not portraying myself as a victim. I take full responsibility. I went in there."[23]

MacMahon asked Mehta for a pause to speak with his client, but Lolos declined.

"I don't want to talk anymore, Your Honor," Lolos said. "I want to keep going about this. I'm sorry, Mr. MacMahon, I just want to keep going about this."

Lolos emphasized that he fully took responsibility. "I chose to go in there," Lolos said. "I chose to talk to the police. I chose to go into the Crypt area, no matter what. I chose to listen to the police. I chose to picket and protest. I chose to go up the stairs, Your Honor."[24] But Lolos then emphasized that he did not "barge in" and that he, like others, told the police that he supported them. Lolos said he also did not hear anyone tell the group to leave.

"Why did you think anybody needed to tell you to leave?" Mehta asked.

"Your Honor, I thought that was the designated area that we were going to protest since they told us to come in," Lolos replied.[25]

Mehta was incredulous. "Hang on," Mehta said. "You thought the way to get to a designated protest area was through a broken window?"

"No," Lolos said. "I went in the broken window to talk to law enforcement. That's what's on the video."[26]

Lolos continued to explain his actions both at the Capitol and on the plane, with Mehta appearing to get impatient and repeatedly asking him to wrap up his comments.

After Lolos concluded, Prosecutor Franks asked to briefly address Mehta. Lolos's statements, Franks said, establish why he needs to be incarcerated. "If he gets mad again, he's not deterred," Franks said. "He hasn't taken—he's said that he's taken responsibility, but he asked—he talked about people to the left of him and to the right of him and what other people were doing and that he was going into the Capitol to talk to the police. If something happens again regarding alleged voter fraud, I would proffer that he's going to do this again; he's not going to be deterred by probation."[27] Indeed, after Lolos's long and winding monologue, Mehta would have had a strong argument to impose the one month of incarceration that the government was requesting, or even up to the six-month maximum. But that is not what he did.

Mehta discussed Lolos's success in business and the letters of support that he received, and compared Lolos's case with those of January 6 defendants who had already been sentenced to incarceration. Mehta concluded that Lolos's behavior falls between defendants who received 90 days of home detention and those who received 45 days of incarceration.[28] But that did not end Mehta's analysis. The events of January 6 were not merely a First Amendment–protected protest, Mehta said, but a "criminal effort" that hundreds or thousands of people committed.

But people like Lolos did not plan to enter the Capitol, Mehta said. "The fact remains that he and others were called to Washington, D.C. by an elected official; he was prompted to walk to the Capitol by an elected official," Mehta said.[29] And fueling that call, Mehta said, were lies. "People like Mr. Lolos were told lies, fed falsehoods, and told that our election was stolen when it clearly was not," Mehta said. "And regrettably, people like Mr. Lolos, for whatever reason, who are impressionable and who believe such falsehoods and such lies, took it to heart, and they are the ones who are suffering the consequences."[30]

Mehta noted that he was considering whether to incarcerate Lolos for 30 days, while the people "who created the conditions" that led to the January 6 events had not been held accountable for what they did and said. "In a sense, Mr. Lolos, I think you were a pawn, you were a pawn in a game that was played and directed by people who should have known better, and I think that mitigates your conduct," Mehta said. Mehta found it "disappointing and regrettable" that Lolos continued to say that election fraud occurred. "But at some level, not entirely without reason, because once you hear people who should know better tell you that an election was stolen, and they say it loudly enough and frequently enough, it's not surprising that people will believe it," Mehta said. "And once they believe something, it's very difficult for people to unbelieve what they hear."[31]

Although Mehta believed Lolos was a pawn, Mehta said that he was disappointed because "it still sounds like to me that you believe that what happened that day really was not that big a deal, and that's just wrong."[32] He noted that Lolos was not "sort of compelled to go inside the Capitol building," and Mehta said he did not believe that Lolos thought that he was permitted to be in the Capitol for almost 45 minutes.[33] Considering all of these factors and the need for deterrence, Mehta sentenced Lolos to 14 days in prison—less than half what the government requested.

What is most noteworthy about Mehta's ruling is not whether he sentenced Lolos to two weeks or one month or six months, but the reasoning behind the sentence. And Mehta made it abundantly clear that he believed that Lolos was a victim of the election lies spread by high-profile speakers. Should Mehta's determination that Lolos was a "pawn" for liars be a mitigating factor? A fairness consideration permeates Mehta's analysis. After all, Lolos was exposed to all sorts of claims about election fraud from the media and high-profile politicians. Why should he not rely on their confident assertions that the election was stolen?

But it also is a bit too simplistic to treat Lolos as a helpless recipient of lies. He is a successful businessman and employer. Millions of people heard the false claims about the 2020 election, but he was among the small group that both believed and acted on the claims. Beyond the fairness issue, there is a practical danger in even partly minimizing the damage that someone caused just because they did so in reliance on the lies of another person. The law should strongly discourage people from engaging in harmful actions based on implausible or thinly sourced factual claims. But the law should *encourage* people to carefully evaluate whether claims are false. Telling people such as Lolos that they are pawns of liars works against these goals.

Another January 6 sentencing hearing—which took place before a different judge on the same DC court less than two weeks later—would reveal a different approach, one that focuses more on individual accountability for the reaction to lies.

Russell James Peterson was born to a 17-year-old mother and never knew his father. As his mother fought a drug addiction, he was placed in foster care. His grandmother adopted him when he was 8, but when he was 14, his grandmother died and he returned to foster care, before being emancipated at 16. He became addicted to drugs beginning at age 17, but his wife eventually helped him overcome his addiction.[34] Peterson lost his job as a restaurant cook in 2020 during the pandemic, so he and his wife moved from California to Pennsylvania to live with his mother while looking for a job.[35]

In the weeks after the November 2020 presidential election, Peterson posted on Facebook that he believed the result was due to fraud. For instance, in a December 4, 2020, reply to another user's comment, Peterson wrote, "unfortunately Yes. The only way to restore balance and peace is through war. Too much Trust has been lost in our great nation." Nine days later, he wrote, "Enact Martial Law Mr. President. Allow the citizens to make things right for our country since elected officials refuse too [*sic*]." In a New Year's Eve Facebook reply, he told another user that he will "personally be in DC January 6."[36]

Indeed, he was. A week later, according to federal prosecutors, Peterson drove with his mother and wife to the Stop the Steal rally on January 6, with Peterson wearing a black sweatshirt emblazoned with "YOUR FEELINGS," with an illustration intended to convey "FUCK YOUR FEELINGS."[37] After listening to Trump and other speakers claim election fraud, the trio walked toward the Capitol. But as tear gas was being deployed, his wife, who has asthma, and his mother decided to return to their car, while Peterson proceeded to the Capitol. Body camera footage from police outside the Capitol showed Peterson telling officers, "They want to defund you, we don't! We need you."[38]

Peterson entered the Capitol on the Senate side, where rioters had broken the windows 10 minutes earlier. While in the building, Peterson took to Facebook and livestreamed two videos of rioters. In the first livestream, which showed rioters chanting, "Stop the steal," Peterson said, "So we took the Capitol. The Capitol is ours right now." In the second livestream, during which Peterson is walking near the Capitol Visitor's Center, a fellow rioter says, "we gotta fucking charge the cops," and Peterson says, "If you guys can't tell, there is tear gas in the air. They didn't stop us."[39]

About 90 minutes after he entered the Capitol, Peterson returned to Pennsylvania with his mother and wife. On Facebook later that day, Peterson boasted about his activities at the Capitol. After someone posted, "You think Trump going to come out and be like yea that's my dogg." Peterson replied, "No not for Trump my friend. Rules were changed before the election that went against the constitution of the United States. And has created uncertainty in the future of elections. I know the Government doesn't give too [*sic*] shits about me. I'm trying to change that. I stormed the castle broke into the chambers and smoked a blunt on the couch." The other person replied: "Ahh ok. Keep smoking the. Keep the peace bro. Don't be on no bullshit." And Peterson responded: "I got mased, tear games [*sic*], and lumped up a lil bit. Overall I had fun lol."[40] The next month, the FBI arrested Peterson, and he pleaded guilty to the same misdemeanor to which Lolos had pleaded guilty, exposing him to up to six months of incarceration.[41]

The case went to Judge Amy Berman Jackson, whom President Obama had appointed to the DC federal district court in 2011. A former federal prosecutor, later in her practice career Jackson was a defense attorney who represented former congressman William Jefferson in his corruption trial.[42] Because Peterson pleaded guilty only to a Class B misdemeanor, the sentencing guidelines did not apply. So, Jackson had discretion to sentence him to six months in prison, no time at all, or anywhere in between. His lawyer, Dani Jahn of the DC Federal Public Defender's office, requested that Jackson sentence Peterson to no incarceration, a year of probation, $500 in restitution, and 40 hours of community service.[43] The government, however, requested that Jackson sentence him to two weeks of incarceration and $500 in restitution.[44] In a brief filed before Jackson sentenced Peterson, Jahn acknowledged the gravity and harms of the January 6 riots, including the loss of five lives. But Peterson neither physically harmed the Capitol nor did he cause the riots that day, Jahn wrote. Among the causes, she wrote, were that "the former president, the rally's organizers and speakers, and nefarious, organized groups contributed to the chaos."[45] Jahn noted the inflammatory comments of Trump and other speakers at the Stop the Steal Rally, such as Alabama Congressman Mo Brooks telling "American patriots" to "start taking down names and kicking ass," and Trump's personal attorney Rudy Giuliani calling for "trial by combat."[46]

Peterson's sentencing hearing took place on December 1, 2001, nearly 11 months after he entered the Capitol. Because of pandemic restrictions, Jackson held the sentencing via video conference. Prosecutor Amanda Jawad called January 6 one of "the most serious crimes in our nation's history," and noted that Peterson "was present only a few feet away from some of the violence that occurred outside the Capitol." Jawad acknowledged that "we're not alleging that Mr. Peterson encouraged the violence" and that he "is not the most egregious offender."[47] Jahn discussed her client's "tumultuous upbringing," his battles with addiction, and the economic toll that the pandemic took on him. And she emphasized his decision to stay off social media after January 6. "I think everyone connected to this video conference hearing can attest that social media played a huge role in the events of January 6th, from people that are not members of this criminal case but are elected officials, to those such as Mr. Peterson," Jahn said.[48]

Jackson noted that Jahn had provided a "very powerful and heavily footnoted account" of the statements by Trump and his supporters. "You never tie any of that specifically to your client, so I just want to make sure I understand what are you telling me, and what was the point of that portion of your memo?" Jackson asked.

"Your Honor, the point of that is that you have these other persons who are not charged with criminal conduct who fueled the fire, if you will, to many people, including Mr. Peterson," Jahn replied. "And so, we need to start the conversation at that point. We need to start the conversation with what led all of these people, including Mr. Peterson, to arrive at a peaceful protest, to then lead to the events of January 6, at around 2:23 in the afternoon."[49]

Judge Jackson could have adopted the approach that her colleague, Judge Mehta, took just 12 days before with Lolos's case, and focused on the politicians and commentators who spread lies about election fraud.

But that is not what she did.

After taking a short break, Jackson delivered a lengthy statement explaining how she would approach sentencing Peterson in what she described as "one of the more difficult" cases on her docket. She first examined the circumstances that led to his crime, and at least implicitly rejected Jahn's reliance on the statements of Trump and his supporters. "You did not end up in the Capitol by mistake," Jackson told Peterson. "You were not simply swept along by events. There's no ambiguity about why you were there."[50] Three letters were of particular concern for Jackson: "LOL." Contrary to Peterson's Facebook post, she said, the storming of the Capitol was not funny. "Hundreds of police officers were injured, people lost their lives, the building was defiled, personal property was stolen, public property was damaged, there were threats to kill public officials ranging from Nancy Pelosi to Mike Pence," Jackson said. "No one locked in a room, cowering under a table for hours was laughing."[51]

Peterson's beliefs about the election, Jackson said, were not an excuse. "You did receive a lot of overwhelming, inaccurate information on social media, but you had a choice to reject the lies and not to join the antidemocratic call for martial law," Jackson said.[52] Jackson acknowledged that some speakers at the rally "stoked the flames of fear and discontent" among the audience, but she refused to allow that to serve as an excuse for Peterson or others. "No one was swept away to the Capitol," Jackson said. "No one was carried. The rioters were adults. And this defendant, like hundreds of others, walked there on his own two feet and he bears responsibility for his own actions. There may be others who bear greater responsibility and who also must be held accountable, but this is not their day in court, it is yours."[53] Jackson recognized the challenges that Peterson had confronted throughout his life, and the positive impact that he has had on the lives of others. Jackson said that she did not think he posed a safety threat to the community, but she "can't overlook the fact that I need to deter not only you, but others from doing similar things in the future."[54]

Jackson then announced her decision: 30 days of incarceration—more than twice what the government had requested. More telling than the sentence was the reasoning that she employed in reaching the decision. Unlike Mehta, Jackson was unwilling to place part of the blame for the defendant's actions on the people who lied to him. While this might seem unfair, it is perhaps a more effective long-term strategy for combatting misinformation. The ultimate sentences differed by only a few weeks, but Jackson's rationale in reaching the sentence is the more appropriate way to handle bad acts caused by lies. While lies may very well play a key role in motivating an individual's decision to engage in harmful actions, ultimately the decision to act is made by the individual. By holding people fully accountable for how they respond to lies—particularly if they commit crimes while doing so—we can at least partly motivate them to both scrutinize the veracity of information and moderate their responses to that information.

The potential for lax criminal penalties is not the only reason why people react to misinformation in dangerous and irrational ways. For instance, in a February 2021 analysis of the court records of 31 QAnon followers who committed crimes, the National Consortium for the Study of Terrorism and Responses to Terrorism found that more than two-thirds had "documented mental health concerns" such as paranoid schizophrenia and bipolar disorder, and more than 40 percent had experienced trauma, such as physical or sexual abuse.[55] These and other root causes require far more support than the criminal justice system can meaningfully address.

As with all suggested improvements, accountability of speech recipients will not be a panacea for all the ills that accompany misinformation. But setting strong accountability could be one factor to at least deter some of the damage that stems from falsehoods.

Chapter 15

Demand

Just over a year after the attack on the Capitol, former president Barack Obama traveled to Stanford University, in the heart of Silicon Valley, to deliver an important message: Disinformation and misinformation are threatening our democratic underpinnings.

In his April 21, 2022, speech, Obama outlined how social, geopolitical, and technological changes have made America more vulnerable to the threats posed by misinformation. Obama's warnings were not particularly novel; since the Russian interference in the 2016 presidential election, politicians and commentators had long been warning about the threats of misinformation. But the former president's focus on misinformation underscored the importance of the problem.

Perhaps most noteworthy about his speech was the scope of the solutions that he presented. Obama recognized the strong First Amendment protections, and much of his discussion did not involve restricting the flow of false information. "I believe we have to address not just the supply of toxic information, but also the demand for it," Obama said. Among his solutions on the demand side of the equation was reinvesting in local journalism and rebuilding civic institutions.[1] Obama's inclination to focus on demand for falsehoods is particularly useful in a democratic country in which the supply cannot be easily regulated. As this book has outlined, centuries of US legal precedent counsel against the government defining one "truth" and regulating everything that it believes to be false.

A less legally problematic—and more effective—solution is to focus on the demand side. Ensure that the public has access to rigorously vetted information, but more importantly, provide them with the tools to sort through and assess the information that they receive. All of this requires trust. When the public does not trust government efforts to help fight misinformation, the outcome could be disastrous.

For instance, six days after Obama's speech, during testimony at a House Appropriations subcommittee, Homeland Security Secretary Alejandro Mayorkas announced that two Department of Homeland Security officials took the lead in forming a "misinformation/disinformation governance board."[2] Also, on Wednesday, April 27, 2022, a *Politico* newsletter reported that "DHS is standing up a new Disinformation Governance Board to coordinate countering misinformation related to homeland security, focused specifically on irregular migration and Russia." The board's executive director was Nina Jankowicz, who had worked on disinformation at a nonprofit and had advised the Ukrainian Foreign Ministry.[3]

DHS provided no information about the board's authority, mission, or constraints, other than its terribly creepy name. Conservative media claimed that the new board was the Biden administration's attempt to censor opposing viewpoints. They seized on Jankowicz's past criticisms of Donald Trump and her assessment in October 2020 that the Hunter Biden laptop story was a "tale."

The highest-profile criticism came a day after Mayorkas's testimony, in a long segment on Tucker Carlson's Fox News show on Thursday, April 28, 2022. "So today, to herald the coming of the new Soviet America, the administration announced its own Ministry of Truth," Carlson said, referring to the censorship regime in George Orwell's book *1984.* "This will be called the Disinformation Governance Board."[4] Carlson said that his show contacted DHS to ask how Janko-wicz planned to "censor" information, and DHS denied such plans. It provided little concrete information, telling his show only that the board would focus on Russian propaganda, Ukraine, and human smug-gling. But Carlson had concerns about that as well. "First of all, it's not their job to decide what you learn about the border or Russia or Ukraine," Carlson told his millions of viewers. "It's your job. You're an adult. You can read whatever you want, but of course it's not about that anyway."[5] Many others joined Carlson's vehement concerns that the Biden administration would use the Disinformation Governance Board as a censorship tool. "To our technocrats' dismay, this isn't Eu-rope, where the state can dictate allowable speech and sometimes ar-rests those who don't abide," David Harsanyi wrote in a *New York Post* opinion piece on Friday, April 29, 2022, the day after Carlson's seg-ment. "Here, citizens are the ones who call out the state for peddling misinformation, not the other way around."[6] Also that Friday, Florida Governor Ron DeSantis raised similar fears. "They want to be able to put out false narratives without people being able to speak out and fight back. They want to be able to say things like Russia collusion," he said at a news conference. "And perpetuate hoaxes. And then have people like us be silenced. They want to be able to advocate for COVID lockdowns."[7]

Yet despite three days of nonstop criticism of the "Biden Ministry of Truth," DHS provided few details about what the Disinformation Governance Board actually *would* do. Although DHS never said that the board would censor, by the weekend it had not unambiguously said that the board would *not* censor, nor had it clearly explained the board's duties.

Mayorkas had a chance to at least attempt to restore trust on Sun-day, May 1, 2022, when he appeared on the CNN show *State of the Union.* But that is not what happened. When host Dana Bash asked Mayorkas about the board, he acknowledged that his department "probably could have done a better job of communicating what it does and does not do." Bash asked what the board will do. And his response was just as unclear as his initial announcement.

"So, what it does is, it works to ensure that the way in which we address threats, the connectivity between threats and acts of violence are addressed without infringing on free speech, protecting civil rights and civil liberties, the right of privacy," Mayorkas said. "And the board, this working group, internal working group, will draw from best practices and communicate those best practices to the operators, because the board does not have operational authority."[8] Mayorkas may have thought that he was easing concerns by assuring Bash that the board does not infringe free speech or privacy, but his answer created more questions than answers. What are "best practices" for disinformation? How are these best practices determined? And perhaps most importantly, who are the "operators"?

It was not until late Monday—after nearly a week of high-profile coverage—that DHS released a "fact sheet" that provided examples of how DHS had fought disinformation over the past decade. The statement characterized the board as "an internal working group that was established with the explicit goal of ensuring these protections are appropriately incorporated across DHS's disinformation-related work and that rigorous safeguards are in place." It went on to say that the board also "seeks to coordinate" DHS's efforts with other federal agencies and outside stakeholders.[9] Yet even this fact sheet failed to provide a concrete explanation about the new board's activities and the limits on its authority. And more confusingly, despite the previous week of criticism, it continued to refer to the new working group as the "Disinformation Governance Board." Not surprisingly, after a few weeks of constant confusion and negative publicity, DHS paused and ultimately disbanded the board.[10]

I saw no evidence supporting the speculation that the Disinformation Governance Board was intended to act as a censorship arm of the Biden administration, as many commentators and politicians had predicted. Indeed, DHS had been addressing the threats of false-hoods even during the Trump administration, so this was not a particularly new concept. But I also saw no clear communication from DHS about what the board actually *would* do, so the speculation and concern were justified.

The board's fundamental failures were in two symbiotic values necessary to effectively combat false speech: trust and transparency. The board's name was its first fatal flaw. If, as the fact sheet states, the board's mere purpose is to "coordinate," why would DHS use the word "governance" in the title? Coordination and governance are two *very* different concepts, so it is understandable if members of the public immediately reacted with distrust. The lack of transparency also eroded that trust. The clumsily opaque manner in which DHS announced the board fueled the widespread dissemination of claims that the new entity would function as a Ministry of Truth. Rather than announcing a grand "Disinformation Governance Board" with few details, DHS could have stated from the outset that it was forming an internal working group to continue its efforts to respond to foreign disinformation, while providing specific examples of the types of work that the group would do and articulating clear limits on its authority that would prevent it from ever censoring Americans.

The federal government's botched rollout of the Disinformation Governance Board is a lesson in how the government should not address the demand side of false speech. For example, some research suggests that the public's willingness to accept COVID-19-related public health measures is correlated to trust in government. A comparison of global COVID-19 infections, published in *The Lancet* in February 2022, estimated that if all countries reached the level of trust in government of Denmark (which ranked at about the 75th percentile of trust), about 12.9 percent fewer COVID-19 infections would have taken place worldwide. Trust, the researchers concluded, is a factor that the government can directly influence. "Governments and communities maintain or increase the public's trust by providing accurate, timely information about the pandemic, even when that information is still limited, and by clearly communicating the risk and relevant vulnerabilities," they wrote. "The identity of the messenger in risk communication can also improve or damage trust."[11]

Building trust is no easy task. But candor and humility can help. And that includes acknowledging what the government does not know and when it has gotten something wrong. For instance, at the start of the COVID pandemic in early 2020, the US public health advice was to avoid wearing masks, and much of the government messaging focused on disinfecting surfaces because many public health authorities insisted that the virus was not airborne.[12] Once that was proven incorrect, the government acknowledged it, but its previous insistence in the absolute and unquestionable correctness of its science may have undermined at least some public confidence in future government public health guidance. By the time the vaccine was available in early 2021, at least some people lacked confidence in the government's claims that the vaccines are safe and effective. Some factors in governmental trust—such as economic inequality and broader political dynamics—are difficult to influence through messaging. But government officials could have at least attempted to improve trust by being candid about what was both known and unknown. Such candor is particularly important at the beginning of a public health crisis involving a novel virus, when so much is unknown.

A notable example of building trust through candor and transparency came from Johnson & Johnson's 1982 response to the deaths of seven people who had consumed Tylenol that had been laced with potassium cyanide. Although the company's lawyers advised management to be tight-lipped during the crisis, Johnson & Johnson Chief Executive Officer James E. Burke did not heed their counsel, and gave many candid media interviews.[13] In a *Washington Post* opinion piece early in the COVID-19 outbreak, Roger Lowenstein compared Burke's candor with President Donald Trump's minimization of the threat of COVID-19. "Unlike Burke, who took questions with openness and humility, Trump has been evasive, critical (even of his own officials), self-inflating and often wrong," Lowenstein wrote.[14]

How should the government go about responding to what it views as misinformation? This, too, is a tricky balancing act. Even if the government is not directly prohibiting speech, its declaration of the one absolute truth could raise similar distrust. Indeed, many critics of the Disinformation Governance Board, fearful that it would censor, called it the Ministry of Truth. But the board might deserve that term even though it had no censorship ability. As Orwell described it in *1984*, the Ministry of Truth, "an enormous pyramidal structure of glittering white concrete," displayed Party slogans including, "War Is Peace," "Freedom Is Slavery," and "Ignorance Is Strength." The main job of the Ministry of Truth, Orwell wrote, "was not to reconstruct the past but to supply the citizens of Oceania with newspapers, films, textbooks, telescreen programs, plays, novels—with every conceivable kind of information, instruction, or entertainment, from a statue to a slogan, from a lyric poem to a biological treatise, and from a child's spelling book to a Newspeak dictionary."[15]

The First Amendment does not prohibit the government from producing counterspeech, as long as it is not also censoring the speech that it is criticizing. Instead, the challenge rests in how people will react to government pronouncements of truth. By arrogantly declaring itself the arbiter of the one official truth, the government could risk driving people into baseless conspiracy theories.

That is not to say that the government should avoid correcting what it believes is misinformation. It should. But it should do so with candor, transparency, and humility. Some public health officials' statements failed to meet that standard. For instance, Dr. Anthony Fauci, a National Institutes of Health official who helped lead the COVID-19 response under both Trump and Biden, sometimes seemed to lose patience with what he believed was misinformation about public health precautions and vaccines.

In a June 9, 2021, MSNBC interview, host Chuck Todd asked Fauci about Republican criticism of Fauci's past statements. Fauci acknowledged that at the start of the pandemic, he advised people not to wear masks both because there was a mask shortage and because there was insufficient evidence at the time that masks were effective outside of hospitals. But the data began to show that masks worked, so public health officials changed their stance. "That's what's called, Chuck, the scientific process. You make a recommendation, an opinion and a guideline based on what you know at a given time," Fauci said.[16]

So far, this was a straightforward explanation of public health officials' thought processes. But Fauci did not end there. He told Todd that "people want to fire me or put me in jail for what I have done, namely, follow the science," that he "could go the next half-an-hour going through each and every point that they make." Todd then asked Fauci about the impact on public health of the efforts to attack public health officials.

"It's very dangerous, Chuck, because a lot of what you're seeing as attacks on me, quite frankly, are attacks on science, because all of the things that I have spoken about consistently from the very beginning have been fundamentally based on science," Fauci said. "Sometimes, those things were inconvenient truths for people, and there was push-back against me. So, if you are trying to get at me, as a public health official and a scientist, you're really attacking not only Dr. Anthony Fauci; you're attacking science. And anybody that looks at what's going on clearly sees that. You have to be asleep not to see that. That is what's going on. Science and the truth are being attacked."[17]

Nine of those words—"attacks on me, quite frankly, are attacks on science"—would soon be repeated ad nauseam in conservative media. That evening, Senator John Kennedy, a Louisiana Republican, appeared on Sean Hannity's popular Fox News show to respond to Fauci. Kennedy used most of the segment to ask questions about the origins of COVID-19 in light of new reports. "Maybe coincidence, but

Dr. Fauci needs to address and he needs to hit these things head on, otherwise, it's going to undermine public health, people's confidence in public health, and the American people are going to end up trusting Dr. Pepper more than Dr. Fauci," Kennedy said.[18] And Fauci's nine-word quote was the entire focus of a *New York Post* editorial the next day. "By now, only Martians can be unfamiliar with Fauci's arrogance—not to mention his deceptions, manipulations and, well, lies," the *Post* wrote. "From the effectiveness of masks to the coronavirus lab-leak theory, Fauci has been on every side of the issue, claiming the 'science' backs him up each time. Please."[19]

The reporting about and reaction to Fauci's comments may have taken a toll in the public's trust in him. The Annenberg Public Policy Center found that 65 percent of Americans surveyed trusted his COVID-19 advice in January 2022, a six-point drop from the previous April. And between April 2021 and January 2022, the percentage of Americans surveyed who said that they lacked confidence in him rose from 29 percent to 35 percent.[20] Fauci's flippant reaction to his critics might be understandable from a human perspective after more than a year of battling endless conspiracy theories about COVID-19. But they do not help correct false statements, and they probably do not build trust among many people who are already hesitant about the vaccine and other public health measures. It is not enough to say something like, "I'm a scientist and I know more than you do, and if you don't agree then you are anti-science." Provide evidence in a clear and concise manner, and concede uncertainties.

Yet months after Fauci's interview, his boss, National Institutes of Health Director Francis Collins, appeared on National Public Radio to promote COVID-19 vaccinations ahead of Thanksgiving, and he had harsh words for those who spread "misinformation" about the vaccine's safety. "Isn't this like yelling fire in a crowded theater?" he asked. "Are you really allowed to do that without some consequences?"[21] Implying that those who disagree with the scientists might face legal consequences is perhaps not the best way to build trust and knowledge.

A more humble, open, and effective approach to COVID information can be seen in Denmark. Like much of the rest of the world, Denmark locked down most of its population in March 2020. But its leaders' tone was strikingly different. "We stand on unexplored territory in this situation," Prime Minister Mette Frederiksen said when announcing the lockdown. "Will we make mistakes? Yes, we will."[22] Danish political scientist Michael Bang Petersen, who studied the government's public statements about COVID, wrote that these blunt and often uncertain assessments built trust nationwide. "The buy-in that ensued led to low death rates and laid the groundwork for a vaccination rate of 95% for everyone aged above 50 (and 75% for the population in general)," wrote Petersen, who advised the Danish government.[23] Danish researchers for the HOPE Project wrote that this trust also allowed mitigation strategies without fierce opposition. "Temporary lockdowns happened without great backlash in Denmark," they wrote. "There were never any curfews, and limitations on gatherings in private homes were accomplished through widely accepted recommendations from health authorities, rather than laws."[24] As of November 2021, according to the researchers, 471 per 1 million Denmark residents had died of COVID, compared with 2,303 per 1 million in the United States.[25] While it is impossible to measure exactly how much—if any—impact that government candor and trust had in the discrepancy, at the very least it is difficult to conceive of how such factors would have impeded Denmark's progress.

The Disinformation Governance Board debacle and the reaction to some US public health officials' attempts to dismiss speech as "misinformation" counsels against a heavy-handed government approach that seeks to define the one absolute truth. Such approaches are unlikely to be widely accepted and could backfire by causing even more distrust. Rather than declare itself the arbiter of truth, the government should equip the public to sort through the morass of competing information sources.

In that vein, a transparent, humble, and effective way for the government to combat false speech can be seen in the Department of

Homeland Security. I am referring not to its botched 2022 rollout of the Disinformation Governance Board, but to its 2020 efforts to ensure public confidence in US voting systems during the election season. The DHS division responsible for election security, the Cybersecurity and Infrastructure Security Agency, produced catchy public service announcements that helped people identify foreign misinformation. CISA also launched a "Rumor Control" website that then-CISA head Chris Krebs said was intended "to help you, as an informed voter, distinguish between rumors and facts on election security issues."[26]

Rumor Control was written in plain language and a just-the-facts style that is both accessible and not politically loaded. Each "rumor" is accompanied by a "reality," along with a few paragraphs justifying CISA's statement, and perhaps most importantly concludes with links to primary sources for the claims, such as statutes, risk assessments, and fact sheets from other agencies. For instance, one rumor was "Voting system software is not reviewed or tested and can be easily manipulated." CISA's "reality" for that point was, "Voting systems undergo testing from state and/or federal voting system testing programs, which certify voting system hardware and software." After three paragraphs of analysis, CISA listed nine "useful sources," including on-point election statutes and a link to the US Election Assistance Commission's webpage, which describes its certification process for voting systems.[27]

While DHS's publicity efforts might attract some criticism for arbitrating the truth, the manner in which DHS does so is grounded in facts and not politically caustic. By presenting a plain-language analysis and supporting sources, DHS is helping to set the record straight while minimizing concerns that it is hiding something. The website could not—and did not—convince everyone who believed that the election was rigged. But it at least provided the facts both for the public and the media to inform their conclusions. Despite DHS's efforts, thousands of people still stormed the Capitol on January 6, 2021, having bought into the Big Lie. Although DHS never could provide a panacea for all misguided beliefs about the 2020 election, a botched public information effort likely would have led to far more damage.

DHS's Rumor Control website also is a positive example of providing knowledge to combat false speech because it was transparent and enabled anyone to check the facts on which the department relied. Accuracy is particularly important in any government response to misinformation or disinformation. Consider the interagency Active Measures Working Group, the US effort described in chapter 9 to respond to the 1980s Soviet disinformation campaign that claimed HIV was created by the Pentagon. The working group's erroneous response—though unintentional—provided the Soviets with significant ammunition to undercut all responses from the US government, and also to claim that the United States—and not the Soviet Union—was spreading disinformation. The popular idiom "Measure Twice, Cut Once" applies with great force to any government response to potential falsehoods. To respond to misinformation, it might be wise to measure three or four times.

The government also can build confidence in the information that it provides by earning the public's trust. Rick Hasen articulated this point well when he proposed "competent election administration" as one of his solutions to countering false speech about elections. Among Hasen's suggestions to "run fair and transparent elections" are maintaining accurate voter lists, verifying the identity of mail-in voters, and maintaining a paper record of votes.[28]

Likewise, one way that Trump and his allies tried to convince the public to believe their claims that the election was rigged was to point to some states in which election officials continued to tally votes for many days after the election. For instance, in the swing state of Pennsylvania, Trump was beating Biden on election night but gradually lost his lead as local elections offices tallied mail-in ballots. Biden had a relative advantage in mail-in votes, which state law prohibited election workers from even starting to process until Election Day.[29] States, at the very least, should allow early processing of mail-in and early ballots to prevent a steady trickle of votes for weeks after. Doing so would undercut the ability of people to baselessly speculate that election officials are "finding votes" to change the outcome of an election.

Government response to specific cases of false speech can help, but it is of limited efficacy when the government is constantly playing clean-up crew for the latest information disaster. Rather than merely declaring what is true and false, the government can provide citizens with the tools to make informed judgments about the veracity of information. The United States could look to Finland, which has an extensive effort to help prepare people for the challenges of modern misinformation, disinformation, and other false speech. Finland had for decades dealt with Russian propaganda before the emergence of the modern Internet. But in 2016, Finland launched an education initiative to combat fake news. The initiative teaches politicians, journalists, and students in college and K–12 schools about misinformation. For instance, a tenth-grade class at the French-Finnish School of Helsinki engaged in exercises that required them to investigate claims that were made on social media and study clickbait articles. "What we want our students to do is . . . before they like or share in the social media they think twice—who has written this? Where has it been published? Can I find the same information from another source?" Kari Kivinen, the school's director, told CNN in 2019.[30] But Finnish students begin learning these tools before they enter secondary school. Even primary school students learn about how to sort fact from fiction. "Fairytales work well," Kivinen told *The Guardian* in 2020. "Take the wily fox who always cheats the other animals with his sly words. That's not a bad metaphor for a certain kind of politician, is it?"[31] As Jussi Toivanen, a communications staffer for the Finnish prime minister, told the *Europe Monitor* in 2021, "the first line of defence is the kindergarten teacher."[32] Each year, the Open Society Institute–Sofia compiles a Media Literacy Index of 35 European countries, examining factors such as literacy, trust, and media freedom to gauge citizens' resilience to fake news. In 2021, Finland ranked first.[33]

The United States should learn from Finland's experience and bolster media literacy starting at the elementary school level and extending into adulthood. In its report on Russian interference in the 2016 US election, the Senate Intelligence Committee endorsed such a strategy. "Addressing the challenge of disinformation in the long-term will ultimately need to be tackled by an informed and discerning population of citizens who are both alert to the threat and armed with the critical thinking skills necessary to protect against malicious influence," the committee wrote. "A public initiative—propelled by federal funding but led in large part by state and local education institutions—focused on building media literacy from an early age would help build long-term resilience to foreign manipulation of our democracy."[34]

Besides teaching media literacy, K–12 schools should increase the amount of class time devoted to civics education. By understanding how the government works, people may be at least a bit less susceptible to believing crazy conspiracy theories. For example, if the public has a better understanding of the role of inspectors general and how congressional oversight functions, they may be less susceptible to believing thinly sourced fantastical tales of deep-state plots. One champion of civics education is retired Supreme Court Justice Sandra Day O'Connor. After leaving the court in 2006, she advocated for a reinvestment in civics education. Her advocacy was driven in part by her observation over decades that many people distrusted judges and the concept of the independent judiciary. And she traced that to a lack of understanding of basic civics. In a 2014 interview, she observed that surveys of Americans found that two-thirds did not know any Supreme Court justices' names, and far fewer knew the name of the chief justice. Just over half the states required any high school courses about civics or government, she noted, and at the time only 19 included civics in their statewide education assessment scores. "We know that a good quality civic education or learning does help students develop their skills they need in the 21st century," she said. "They need to think somewhat critically about issues, they need to understand what [it] is to identify a problem and think it through. And they need to engage in some thoughtful and respectful discussion and exchange of ideas with even their peers from different backgrounds."[35] In 2009, O'Connor founded a nonprofit, now known as iCivics, that provides free civics education resources that are taught to millions of students each year.

America has improved its civic knowledge but still has a long way to go, as seen in a survey conducted by the Annenberg Public Policy Center. In 2021, only 56 percent of those surveyed could name all three branches of government, and 20 percent could not name any. Although there is still substantial room for improvement, those statistics are better than they were in 2006, the first year that the center conducted the survey, when only 33 percent could name all three branches, and 36 percent could not name any.[36] Fifty-nine percent of the respondents in 2021 reported having taken a high school civics class, which the study's authors said is "associated with correct answers to civics knowledge questions."

Bolstering the American public's understanding of basic governmental functions allows them to better assess claims about election fraud, government public health efforts, and other topics that are susceptible to misinformation. "A recent surge in voter participation has been accompanied by dangerous degrees of misinformation and tension, even rising to violence," concluded a 2021 report about civics education, funded by the National Endowment for the Humanities and US Department of Education. "Dangerously low proportions of the public understand and trust our democratic institutions. Majorities are functionally illiterate on our constitutional principles and forms. The relative neglect of civic education in the past half-century is one important cause of our civic and political dysfunction."[37] If people are more informed about how, for instance, law enforcement works in the United States, they may be more skeptical of a media commentator or politician's baseless claims that the Federal Bureau of Investigation organized the January 6 attack on the Capitol.

One solution in the US Senate would be a step in the right direction. The Civics Secures Democracy Act, introduced in 2021 by Democrat Chris Coons and Republican John Cornyn, would provide $1 billion a year for civics education at the federal and state level, and would increase the amount of assessments of students' civics knowledge.[38] While even that proposal attracted some opposition from people who feared that the civics education would be politically biased, it is possible to deliver nonpartisan civics education that provides people with the long-term tools to critically evaluate conspiracy theories and other claims about government operations.

Absent more federal support, states should invest more heavily in civics education. For instance, New Jersey was in the minority of states that did not require middle schools to teach civics. In 2021, the state legislature changed that by unanimously passing a law that requires civics education in all public middle schools and directs Rutgers University to develop a curriculum for the courses. "An understanding of civics strengthens our democracy by ensuring an understanding of the role that everyone plays in the future of their community, our state, and our nation," Governor Phil Murphy said in a statement when he signed the bill into law.[39]

Adequate funding for public, university, and K–12 libraries also can help to equip Americans with the tools to better distinguish facts from falsehoods. "Information that is deliberately faked with malicious or mercenary intent is deeply offensive to librarians and our professional ethics, and it spurs our passion and our mission to promote information literacy," Lisa Rose-Wiles, a librarian at Seton Hall University, wrote in 2018. "The ability to evaluate information and use it wisely lies at the heart of information literacy."[40] Since the emergence of PizzaGate and QAnon, many librarians across the United States have developed information literacy training programs for their students and communities.[41] For instance, Aquinas College in Grand Rapids,

Michigan, requires students to take a one-credit class, in a computer classroom, about information literacy. "I wanted my students to learn more about fake news, but also to be aware of misinformation in general, the biases of media outlets, and their own confirmation bias; understand that professional journalists in the 'mainstream media' have a code of ethics, which means their reporting is factual and sourced; and develop strategies for evaluating the information that comes their way on social media and elsewhere," Aquinas librarian Shellie Jeffries wrote in an article about the course. Among the students' homework assignments was to critically investigate the factual support for a news item that they found on social media.[42]

And the government can only go so far in helping to shore up people's knowledge and ability to tell fact from fiction. Institutional media such as broadcasters and newspapers have long tried to provide facts to the general public. Of course, many media outlets have failed in that quest, sometimes in high-profile ways, but at least journalists belong to a profession that attempts to provide readers and viewers with the truth. Unfortunately, both online news organizations and traditional news outlets such as newspapers and broadcasters have struggled financially over the past two decades. According to a Pew Research Center analysis, between 2008 and 2020, US newsroom employment fell 26 percent.[43] Between 2005 and 2021, more than 2,000 local newspapers shut down, creating "news deserts."[44] It is hard to have a complete discussion about how false speech takes hold without examining the steep decline in sources for professionally gathered and vetted information. As veteran journalist Margaret Sullivan wrote in the *Washington Post*, while public trust in large mainstream media has declined dramatically, people continue to trust their local news outlets. "Yet these are the very same outlets that are rapidly disappearing," Sullivan wrote. "That's especially worrisome at a time when conspiracy theories and misinformation are rampant."[45]

In her 2021 book *Saving the News*, law professor Martha Minow makes a strong argument that the First Amendment's free speech and press protections anticipate a healthy and robust and independent news media. Among the most compelling of Minow's many potential solutions is for the government to provide tax benefits for local nonprofit news outlets. Such benefits for a public good such as journalism would not be unprecedented; Minow points to postal subsidies that newspapers long received. "Public and nonprofit media options—aided by direct and indirect public support—can fill news deserts and other gaps left by profit-oriented companies," she wrote. "Public and nonprofit media also provide crucial competition and can stimulate for-profits to win viewers by doing better."[46] As Professor David Ardia has noted, "government support for news is as old as the nation itself," dating back to the Post Office Act of 1792, which subsidized the mailing of newspapers.[47] While many of the economic problems that the news media face are largely out of the government's control, policy makers should recognize the vital role of an independent press in equipping people with the tools to sort fact from fiction. While tax credits or direct subsidies alone are unlikely to restore local news media to their glorious monopoly days, the policies may at least reduce further erosion in local news sources.

Even policies that lead to the creation of new local news sources do not guarantee that people will flock to them and spend less time reading sketchy information sources that they found on Facebook. News organizations, like politicians, need to build trust. There is no easy way to do so, but community outreach likely helps, as seen in the greater trust that people have for their local news outlets compared to nationwide media. In the late nineties and early aughts, many regional newspapers established "ombudsman" positions in their newspapers, usually experienced journalists who serve as the public point of contact for readers with questions or complaints about coverage. Many ombudsmen even wrote columns that were critical of their paper's news coverage. And part of the solution to building knowledge is in the hands of the government and can be fostered by the First Amendment. As Ardia observed, federal laws that provide the public with access to government information, such as the Freedom of Information Act, are riddled with exceptions that often do not adequately promote government transparency. A series of US Supreme Court cases from the 1980s create a limited First Amendment right to access to courts. Ardia makes a strong case for robust public access to government information. "From the perspective of self-governance, there is no more important a category of information than information *about the government*," Ardia wrote.[48]

No easy solution will ensure that Americans will have the knowledge to sort fact from fiction. But the government could help by building public trust, providing tools for people to use when confronted with a growing number of information sources, and creating an environment for institutions like libraries and news organizations to thrive.

Conclusion

Less than seven months after he fired shots in Comet Ping Pong, Edgar Maddison Welch arrived in the District of Columbia federal courtroom of District Judge Ketanji Brown Jackson. He had already pleaded guilty to interstate transportation of a firearm and assault with a dangerous weapon, and on the morning of June 22, 2017, Jackson was presiding over his sentencing hearing.[1]

Earlier that month, Welch's lawyers had filed with Jackson a one-page letter that Welch had handwritten in neat cursive. In it, he apologized for his "foolish and reckless" choice. "I felt very passionate about the possibility of human suffering, especially the suffering of a child, and was prompted to act without taking the time to consider the repercussions of my actions, or the possible harm that might come from them," Welch wrote.[2]

Welch had requested 18 months in prison, but federal prosecutor Demian Shipe Ahn argued that the extraordinary harms warranted 4.5 years. At the sentencing hearing, Ahn sought to place ultimate responsibility on Welch, and not on the online conspiracy theorists who had propagated PizzaGate. Ahn urged Jackson to consider the need to deter such vigilantes, pointing to one victim's fear that Welch or someone like him would return to the restaurant. "It is that real fear that this Court's sentence must stress," Ahn said. "In this era of Internet rumors and endless online incitement, the Court can't do anything about that. There's First Amendment protections for people who speak online on all variety of topics. But the Court can address and its sentence must address deterrence against similar people who would take that online information, make it real, bring a gun into somebody else's place of business or home, and threaten or harm other people."[3]

Jackson recognized that "this is no ordinary assault case," so there was little precedent to guide her. "I'm truly very sorry that you find yourself in this position because you do seem like a nice person who, in your mind, was trying to do the right thing," Jackson said. "Unfortunately, those good intentions are not enough to excuse your reckless behavior and the damage, the real damage that it caused."[4]

Jackson sentenced him to four years in prison. While Jackson expressed some sympathy for Welch, her ultimate sentence was 2.5 years more than what Welch had requested and only six months less than the government's recommendation, suggesting that she was unwilling to give Welch a free pass simply because he had believed in misinformation. This was the right approach, and might cause others to think twice before reacting to lies in dangerous and unlawful ways.

Among the victims who spoke at the sentencing hearing was James Alefantis, Comet Ping Pong's owner. He discussed the toll that PizzaGate had taken on him and his employees. But he struck a positive note. "I do hope that one day, in a more truthful world, every single one of us will remember . . . that day as an aberration, a symbol of a time of sickness when some parts of our world went mad, when news was fake and lies were seen as real and our social fabric had frayed," Alefantis said. "So as I stand before you today, I am hopeful. I am hopeful that those who provoke fear, that traffic in lies and perpetuate conspiracy will awake to the tangible harms that result from their actions. I am hopeful that one day reason will prevail before a shot rings out again in a place of warmth and love and community gathering."[5]

Unfortunately, Alefantis's optimistic vision has not yet materialized. Within months of Welch's sentencing hearing, the PizzaGate conspiracies metastasized into QAnon, fanning the flames of fantastical claims that Democrats and members of the "deep state" were satanists running child sex-trafficking rings. Five years later, during her Supreme Court confirmation hearings, Judge Jackson would find herself on the receiving end of conspiracy theories about her supposed leniency on child predators, and some of that animus could be traced to Pizza-Gate and QAnon. And that was only one of many examples of false speech circulating online and creating real-world harms.

Alefantis's reference to the times when "news was fake" reflected a concern throughout 2016 about "fake news" propagated by Russia and domestic conspiracy theorists. But even that term was quickly co-opted by those who were trying to challenge media and government reports. On December 10, 2016, President-Elect Donald Trump first tweeted "FAKE NEWS" to push back on a CNN report.[6] By July 2017, Trump had tweeted about "fake news" more than 60 times to rebut claims about Russia collusion, management problems at the White House, and crowd sizes at his events. He also generally attacked unfriendly media outlets as fake news.[7] The term seemed to apply to any news that Trump did not like. Some of it might have been accurate, and some of it might not have been. But that wasn't the point of Trump's criticism.

Although Trump viewed many media outlets as fake news, the legal strictures on his authority prevented him from doing much more than taunting reporters and media executives. Trump could not send journalists or social media commentators to prison just because they have criticized him. This is a feature of the US legal system that we often take for granted. But it also is something that we gradually erode with censorial proposals that address the problem of today without considering the abuse of tomorrow.

I do not argue that the First Amendment and other legal protections always prevent the government from imposing consequences for false speech. Criminal fraud laws, perjury prohibitions, advertising regulations, and defamation lawsuits are among the ways that Americans have long faced consequences for their falsehoods. *United States v. Alvarez* holds that false speech is not categorically exempt from First Amendment protection. The Supreme Court has recognized that some false speech, including some types that have not yet reached the Supreme Court, may be unprotected. But the court set a high bar for such a finding.[8] And the harms created by the rapid distribution of falsehoods on the Internet should not change this calculus. As the Supreme Court wrote in 2011, "whatever the challenges of applying the Constitution to ever-advancing technology, the basic principles of freedom of speech and the press, like the First Amendment's command, do not vary when a new and different medium for communication appears."[9]

Of course, the Supreme Court always could lower that bar, either by trying to distinguish modern misinformation threats from other cases, or by overruling precedent (as Thomas and Gorsuch are open to with *New York Times v. Sullivan*). A creative prosecutor or plaintiff's lawyer, or a frustrated bench of five Supreme Court justices, may be all that's needed to carve out health misinformation or claims about corrupt election administration from First Amendment protection. Likewise, state high courts could modify their protections for substantial truth or opinion, or reformulate torts such as negligence to better enable people to sue based on their reactions to false speech. And state legislatures could amend or repeal their fair report privileges and anti-SLAPP statutes.

I recognize the potential for such change, but I wrote this book to urge lawyers, judges, and legislators to act with great caution before rolling back protections for allegedly false speech, and to carefully consider solutions other than censorship. While piercing these safeguards is particularly tempting in the age of misinformation, it is vital to keep in mind the reasons that judges and lawmakers have protected false speech since the nation's founding. Leaders in Russia and China and Bangladesh and Burkina Faso and so many other countries also had justifications for expanding criminal and civil penalties for purported falsehoods. And once they obtained the power to impose consequences, they chilled dissent and other valuable speech.

While we'd like to think that such censorial abuse never would happen in the United States, that is not the case. It *could* happen here. But it *doesn't currently* happen because of the First Amendment and other speech safeguards that some are eager to tear down to combat the misinformation crisis of the day.

And that is why I have such a visceral reaction when a media commentator, litigator, or politician advocates for new speech restrictions by reflexively invoking the fire in the crowded theater. They may have compelling reasons to seek new legal restrictions on speech: a public health crisis, conspiracy theories that undermine democracy, and many other urgent problems that they believe are exacerbated by false or misleading speech. Or they might have nefarious motives, such as to stifle criticism or consolidate political power.

But the motivations of the proponents of new censorship should not determine whether courts or legislators should adopt their proposals. Even speech restrictions developed by people with the purest of intentions eventually could be misused by others down the road. If you pass a law that imposes liability for "health misinformation," today that might apply to claims that vaccines have microchips. But in a few years, a different presidential administration might try to apply that same restriction to any criticisms of the government's public health efforts.

Fire in a crowded theater brushes aside the exceedingly careful scrutiny that courts have applied to speech restrictions for the past century.

Fire in a crowded theater ignores the ways government leaders in the United States and other countries can—and have—used censorship powers to squelch and punish dissent.

Fire in a crowded theater disregards the many times when speech that is believed to be false on day one might be more (or less) credible on day two, after healthy debate and discussion.

Fire in a crowded theater neglects that much of what is branded "misinformation" is often just lousy opinion and not an assertion of fact.

Fire in a crowded theater overlooks the limited efficacy of government censorship in combatting falsehoods.

Fire in a crowded theater sets unrealistic expectations for what the government could accomplish by regulating speech.

Fire in a crowded theater discounts the power of counterspeech and providing listeners and readers with the tools to better identify false statements.

Misinformation, disinformation, propaganda, unintentional white lies, intentional whoppers, and all flavors of falsity pose real challenges for America. We must finally leave the crowded theater and do the hard work of finding solutions that empower rationality and preserve the free speech tradition that has defined the country.

"That at any rate is the theory of our Constitution," Oliver Wendell Holmes Jr. wrote in the 1919 dissent in *Abrams v. United States*, first articulating his marketplace of ideas theory. "It is an experiment, as all life is an experiment."[10]

Acknowledgments

This book would not have been possible without the many people who served as sounding boards, reviewed drafts, and helped me track down information about free speech cases decided over the past century. Among those who helped me are Danielle Citron, Ari Cohn, Mike Godwin, Eric Goldman, James Grimmelmann, Joe Hatfield, Jeffrey Hermes, Jeff Jarvis, Orin Kerr, Kate Klonick, Genevieve Lakier, Mike Masnick, Roger McConchie, Michael Norwick, Catherine Ross, Alan Rozenshtein, Matthew Schafer, Jared Schroeder, Scott Shapiro, Barbara Wall, and Kyu Ho Youm. The extraordinarily talented and patient librarians at the Library of Congress Law Library and Manuscript Room helped me track down records for Supreme Court cases.

Thanks to my superagent, Jane Dystel, and her colleague Miriam Goderich for helping shape my idea into a project, and to Laura Davulis and her talented colleagues at Johns Hopkins University Press for bringing this book to print. I am grateful to Mila Gauvin, Elsa Schulz, and Liz Seif for excellent research assistance and cite-checking, to Ashleigh McKown for outstanding editing, and to Hannah de Keijzer for proofreading. And thanks to my family, Crystal Zeh, Julia, Chris, and Betty Kosseff, and Eileen Peck, for their support.

As always, I am grateful to my colleagues and midshipmen at the Naval Academy for challenging my views and discussing the complicated technical and legal realities of online speech.

Notes

Introduction

1. Affidavit in Support of a Criminal Complaint, United States v. Welch, 16-cr-232 (D.D.C. Dec. 12, 2016), at ¶¶8, 23.
2. *Id.* at ¶6.
3. *Id.* at ¶¶8–14.
4. Jane Pauley and Ted Koppel, *Are the News Stories We Americans Read, See, or Hear Fact or Fiction*, CBS SUNDAY MORNING (Dec. 18, 2016).
5. United States v. Stevens, 559 U.S. 460 (2010).
6. Schenck v. United States, 249 U.S. 47, 52 (1919).
7. Thomas Healy, THE GREAT DISSENT: HOW OLIVER WENDELL HOLMES CHANGED HIS MIND—AND CHANGED THE HISTORY OF FREE SPEECH IN AMERICA 91 (2013). *See also* Carlton F. W. Larson, *"Shouting 'Fire' in a Theater": The Life and Times of Constitutional Law's Most Enduring Analogy*, 24 WM. & MARY BILL RTS. J. 181, 189 (2015): "Of all the sources upon which Holmes might have drawn when writing *Schenck*, Wertz's closing argument in the *Debs* case is by far the most plausible."
8. Brandenburg v. Ohio, 395 U.S. 444, 447 (1969).
9. United States v. Miselis, 972 F.3d 518, 533 (4th Cir. 2020).
10. *See* Jeff Kosseff, *America's Favorite Flimsy Pretext for Limiting Free Speech*, THE ATLANTIC (Jan. 4, 2022).
11. *The Definition of Lying and Deception*, STANFORD ENCYCLOPEDIA OF PHILOSOPHY (2015).

Part I. Why the Law Protects Falsehoods

1. Gitlow v. New York, 268 U.S. 652 (1925).
2. *See* Near v. Minnesota, 283 U.S. 697, 713 (1931): "In determining the extent of the constitutional protection, it has been generally, if not universally, considered that it is the chief purpose of the guaranty to prevent previous restraints upon publication."
3. *See* New York Times Co. v. Sullivan, 376 U.S. 254 (1964).

Chapter 1. Marketplace

1. Thomas Healy, THE GREAT DISSENT: HOW OLIVER WENDELL HOLMES CHANGED HIS MIND—AND CHANGED THE HISTORY OF FREE SPEECH IN AMERICA (2013).
2. Abrams v. United States, 250 U.S. 616, 619–20 (1919).
3. *Id.* at 620.
4. Brief for Plaintiffs in Error, Abrams v. United States, No. 316, 12–13 (Sept. 23, 1919).
5. *Id.* at 2.
6. *Id.* at 11, 42.

7. *Id.* at 45.

8. *Id.* at 619.

9. *Id.* at 627 (Holmes, J., dissenting).

10. *Id.* at 627–28.

11. *Id.* at 628–29.

12. *Id.* at 630.

13. *Id.*

14. Stanley Ingber, *The Marketplace of Ideas: A Legitimizing Myth*, 1984 Duke L. J. 1, 3 (1984).

15. John Milton, *Areopagitica* (accessed Dec. 3, 2022), https://www.gutenberg.org/cache/epub/608/pg608-images.html.

16. Vincent Blasi, *Holmes and the Marketplace of Ideas*, 2004 Sup. Ct. Rev. 1, 19 (2004) (quoting Feb. 28, 1919, letter from Holmes to Laski).

17. John Stuart Mill, On Liberty (1859), at 19.

18. *Id.*

19. Blasi, *supra* note 16, at 19.

20. *Id.* at 13n41.

21. *Id.* at 46.

22. John H. Wigmore, *Abrams v U.S., Freedom of Speech and Freedom of Thuggery in War-Time and Peace-Time*, 14 Ill. L. R. 539, 552 (1920).

23. Whitney v. California, 274 U.S. 357, 376 (1927) (Brandeis, J., concurring).

24. United States v. Rumely, 345 U.S. 41, 56 (1953) (Douglas, J., concurring).

25. Based on a LEXIS database search that I conducted in March 2022.

26. Lamont v. Postmaster General, 381 U.S. 301, 308 (1965) (Brennan, J., concurring).

27. Keyishian v. Board of Regents, 385 U.S. 589, 603 (1967) (cleaned up).

28. Consolidated Edison Co. v. Public Service Commission, 447 U.S. 530, 537–38 (1980).

29. James Weinstein, *What Lies Ahead? The Marketplace of Ideas, Alvarez v. United States, and First Amendment Protection of Knowing Falsehoods*, 51 Seton Hall L. Rev. 135, 141 (2020).

30. Declaration of Brian Bowcock, Exhibit A to Government's Reply in Support of Its Request for Imposition of Community Service, United States v. Alvarez, 07-cr-1035 (C.D. Cal July 17, 2008), at ¶ 4.

31. FBI 302 report of interview with Melissa Anne Campbell, Exhibit C to Government's Reply in Support of Its Request for Imposition of Community Service, United States v. Alvarez, 07-cr-1035 (C.D. Cal July 17, 2008), at 1 [hereinafter Campbell 302].

32. *Big Creek Hydroelectric System*, California Water Boards (last updated Sept. 15, 2022), https://www.waterboards.ca.gov/waterrights/water_issues/programs/water_quality_cert/big_creek/.

33. Campbell 302, at 1.

34. *Id.* at 2.

35. *Statistics & FAQS*, Congressional Medal of Honor Society (accessed Nov. 6, 2022), https://www.cmohs.org/medal/faqs.

36. Campbell 302, at 2.

37. *Id.*

38. *Id.* at 3.

39. *Id.*

40. *Id.* at 4.

41. 151 Cong. Rec. S12688 (Nov. 10, 2005).

42. FBI 302 Report of June 23, 2007, Walnut Valley Water District Board Meeting, Ex. B to Motion to Dismiss Indictment, United States v. Alvarez, 07-cr-1035 (C.D. Cal Dec. 21, 2007).

43. *Alvarez Again Denies Claim He Got Medal,* Los Angeles Daily News, Sept. 27, 2007.

44. Motion to Dismiss Indictment, United States v. Alvarez, 07-cr-1035 (C.D. Cal Dec. 21, 2007), at 3.

45. Kenneth Ofgang, *Senate Confirms R. Gary Klausner as Judge of U.S. District Court,* Metropolitan News Express, Nov. 18, 2002.

46. (In Chambers) Order Denying Defendant's Motion to Dismiss, United States v. Alvarez, 07-cr-1035 (C.D. Cal Apr. 9, 2008), at 3.

47. Reporter's Transcript of Proceedings, United States v. Alvarez, 07-cr-1035 (C.D. Cal May 5, 2008).

48. Declaration of Brian Bowcock, Exhibit A to Government's Reply in Support of Its Request for Imposition of Community Service, United States v. Alvarez, 07-cr-1035 (C.D. Cal July 17, 2008), at ¶2.

49. Reporter's Transcript of Proceedings, United States v. Alvarez, 07-cr-1035 (C.D. Cal July 21, 2008), at 8–9.

50. *Id.* at 5–6.

51. *Id.* at 10–13.

52. *Id.* at 10.

53. Appellant's Opening Brief, United States v. Alvarez, Case No. 08-50345 (9th Cir. Feb. 11, 2009).

54. Government's Answering Brief, United States v. Alvarez, No. 08-50345 (9th Cir. April 24, 2009), at 10.

55. *Id.* at 11–12.

56. The audio for this oral argument was obtained from the Ninth Circuit's website (accessed Nov. 6, 2022), https://www.ca9.uscourts.gov/media/audio/?20091104%20 12:01:00/08-50345/.

57. Gertz v. Robert Welch, 418 U.S. 323, 340 (1974).

58. United States v. Alvarez, 617 F.3d 1198, 1213 (9th Cir. 2010).

59. *Id.* at 1216.

60. *Id.* at 1217.

61. *Id.* at 1223 (Bybee, J., dissenting).

62. Shikha Dalmia, *Searching for Alex Kozinski,* Reason (July 2006).

63. *Id.*

64. Niraj Chokshi, *Federal Judge Alex Kozinski Retires Abruptly after Sexual Harassment Allegations,* N.Y. Times, Dec. 18, 2017.

65. United States v. Alvarez, 638 F.3d 666 (9th Cir. 2011) (Kozinski, J., concurring in denial of rehearing en banc).

66. *Id.* at 674–75.

67. *Supreme Court Procedure,* SCOTUSblog (accessed Nov. 6, 2022), https://www .scotusblog.com/supreme-court-procedure/.

68. Cert Petition, United States v. Alvarez at 13.

69. The dialogue from the oral argument comes from a recording and transcript provided by the Oyez Project (accessed Nov. 6, 2022), https://www.oyez.org/cases/2011 /11-210.

70. United States v. Alvarez, 567 U.S. 709, 719 (2012) (plurality).

71. *Id.* at 727.
72. *Id.* at 728.
73. *Id.* at 732 (Breyer, J., concurring).
74. *Id.* at 734.
75. *Id.* at 737–38.
76. Brief of Professors Eugene Volokh and James Weinstein as *Amici Curiae* in Support of Petitioner, United States v. Alvarez, No. 11-210 (Dec. 6, 2011), at 22–24.
77. *See* Weinstein, *supra* note 29 at 148; United States v. Alvarez, 567 U.S. 709, 719 (2012) (plurality).
78. *Id.* at 734 (Breyer, J., concurring).
79. *Id.* at 744–45 (Alito, J., dissenting).
80. *Id.* at 745.
81. H.R. 258 (113th Cong.).
82. Weinstein, *supra* note 29, at 167.
83. Robert A. Sedler, *The "Law of the First Amendment" Revisited*, 58 Wayne L. Rev. 1003, 1021 (2013).
84. Richard Delgado and Jean Stefancic, *Images of the Outsider in American Law and Culture: Can Free Expression Remedy Systemic Social Ills?*, 77 Cornell L. Rev. 1258, 1287 (1992).
85. Ingber, *supra* note 14, at 25–26.
86. *Id.* at 26.
87. *Id.* at 48.
88. Paul H. Brietzke, *How and Why the Marketplace of Ideas Fails*, 31 Val. U. L. Rev. 951, 962 (1997).
89. Dawn Nunziato, *The Marketplace of Ideas Online*, 94 Notre Dame. L. Rev. 1519, 1560 (2019).
90. *Id.* at 1561.
91. Bianca Rodriguez, *The 10 Most Followed Celebrities on Instagram in 2022*, Marie Claire, Mar. 31, 2021.

Chapter 2. Democracy
1. *About Alexander Meiklejohn*, Amherst College (accessed Nov. 7, 2022), https://www.amherst.edu/campuslife/careers/post-graduation-planning-for-first-generation-and-or-low-income-students/meiklejohn-fellows/about-alexander-meiklejohn.
2. Alexander Meiklejohn, Free Speech and Its Relation to Self-Government (1948), at 88.
3. *Id.*
4. *Id.* at 91.
5. Alexander Meiklejohn, *What Does the First Amendment Mean?*, 20 U. Chi. L. Rev. 461, 464 (1953).
6. Alexander Meiklejohn, *The First Amendment Is an Absolute*, 1961 Sup. Ct. Rev. 245, 255 (1961).
7. David S. Ardia, *Beyond the Marketplace of Ideas: Bridging Theory and Doctrine to Promote Self-Governance*, 16 Harv. L. & Pub. Pol. Rev. 101, 166 (2022).
8. Harry Kalven Jr., *The New York Times Case: A Note on the Central Meaning of the First Amendment*, 1964 Sup. Ct. Rev. 191, 221n125 (1964).
9. Curtis Publishing Co. v. Butts, 388 U.S. 130 (1967).
10. Post Pub. Co. v. Hallam, 59 F. 530, 531–33 (1893).
11. *Id.* at 532.
12. *Id.* at 532–33.

13. *Berry Paid Expenses of Theo. Hallam in the Sixth (Ky.) District Contest for the Nomination of a Democrat for Congress*, CINCINNATI POST, Oct. 14, 1892; Post Pub. Co. v. Hallam, 59 F. 530, 533 (1893).
14. Post Pub. Co. v. Hallam, 59 F. 530, 533 (1893).
15. *Id.* at 539–40.
16. *Id.* at 539.
17. *Id.* at 531.
18. *Id.* at 540.
19. *Id.*
20. *Id.*
21. *Id.* at 540–41.
22. *Id.* at 541.
23. *Id.*
24. *See William Howard Taft*, WHITE HOUSE (accessed Nov. 7, 2022), https://www .whitehouse.gov/about-the-white-house/presidents/william-howard-taft/.
25. *Letter from William H. Taft to Gustavus H. Wald*, UNIVERSITY OF CINCINNATI LIBRARY (Oct. 21, 1901).
26. The article was obtained from the front page of the August 20, 1904, edition of the *Topeka State Journal*.
27. Coleman v. MacLennan, 98 P. 281, 282 (1908).
28. Kans. Const. Bill of Rights § 11.
29. Coleman, 98 P. at 283.
30. *Id.*
31. *Id.* at 283–84.
32. *Id.* at 284.
33. *Id.* at 285.
34. *Id.*
35. *Id.*
36. *Id.* at 288.
37. *Id.* at 289.
38. *Id.* at 292.
39. *Id.*
40. *Libel of a Candidate for Election to a Public Office*, 22 HARV. L. REV. 445, 446 (1909).
41. John L. Garrou, *Constitutional Law—Defamation—Misstatements of Fact about Public Figure Privileged*, 44 N.C. L. REV. 442 (1966).
42. Petition for a Writ of Certiorari to the Supreme Court of Alabama, New York Times v. Sullivan, No. 606-39 (Nov. 21, 1962), at 69.
43. *Id.* at 72.
44. Petition for a Writ of Certiorari to the Supreme Court of Alabama, New York Times v. Sullivan, No. 606-39 (Nov. 21, 1962), at Appendix C(1).
45. *Id.*
46. *Id.*
47. New York Times v. Sullivan, 376 U.S. 254, 258 (1964).
48. Brief for the Petitioner, New York Times v. Sullivan, No. 39 (Sept. 6, 1963), at 18.
49. *Id.* at 19–20.
50. New York Times v. Sullivan, 376 U.S. 254, 258–59 (1964).
51. Brief for the Petitioner, New York Times v. Sullivan, No. 39 (Sept. 6, 1963), at 19–21.
52. Derryn E. Moten, *Alabama's Racism Was a Powerful Tool for Gov. John Patterson*, MONTGOMERY ADVERTISER, June 7, 2021.

53. Bruce L. Ottley, John B. Lewis, and Younghee J. Ottley, *New York Times v. Sullivan: A Retrospective Examination*, 33 DePaul L. Rev. 741, 760 (1984).
54. *Id.* at 759 (quoting *Not the First Lie about South*, Alabama J., Apr. 9, 1960).
55. Brief for the Petitioner, New York Times v. Sullivan, No. 39 (Sept. 6, 1963), at 21–22.
56. *Id.* at 22.
57. *Id.* at 22–23.
58. *Id.* at 23.
59. *Id.*
60. New York Times v. Sullivan, 144 So.2d 25, 28 (Ala. 1962).
61. *Id.* at 44.
62. *Id.* at 40.
63. Petition for a Writ of Certiorari to the Supreme Court of Alabama, New York Times v. Sullivan, No. 606-39 (Nov. 21, 1962), at 12.
64. Brief for Respondent in Opposition, New York Times v. Sullivan, No. 606-39 (Dec. 15, 1962), at 18.
65. *Id.* at 23.
66. Brief for the Petitioner, New York Times v. Sullivan, No. 39 (Sept. 6, 1963), at 54n*.
67. Brief of the American Civil Liberties Union and the New York Civil Liberties Union as Amicus Curiae, New York Times v. Sullivan, No. 39 (Sept. 8, 1963), at 28 (internal quotation marks and citations omitted).
68. New York Times v. Sullivan, 376 U.S. 254, 268 (1964).
69. *Id.* at 269.
70. *Id.* at 270.
71. *Id.* at 271–72.
72. *Id.* at 273.
73. *Id.* at 275.
74. *Id.* at 276.
75. *Id.* at 277.
76. *Id.* at 278–79.
77. *Id.* at 279.
78. *Id.* (internal quotation marks and citation omitted).
79. *Id.* at 280.
80. *Id.* at 282.
81. *Id.* at 293 (Black, J., concurring).
82. *Id.* at 299 (Goldberg, J., concurring in the result).
83. Curtis Publishing Co. v. Butts, 388 U.S. 130, 134 (1967) (plurality opinion).
84. Gertz v. Robert Welch, 418 U.S. 323 (1973).
85. Floyd Abrams, Preface to New York Times v. Sullivan: The Case for Preserving an Essential Precedent (2022), at iv.
86. Lee C. Bollinger, *Free Speech and Intellectual Values*, 92 Yale L. J. 438, 439 (1983).
87. Gerald J. Baldasty and Roger A. Simpson, *The Deceptive "Right to Know": How Pessimism Rewrote the First Amendment*, 56 Wash. L. Rev. 365, 377–78 (1981).
88. William J. Brennan Jr., *The Supreme Court and the Meiklejohn Interpretation of the First Amendment*, 79 Harv. L. Rev. 1, 14 (1965).
89. Dave Heller and Katharine Larsen, *English Libel Law and the SPEECH Act: A Comparative Perspective*, in New York Times v. Sullivan: The Case for Preserving an Essential Precedent (2022), at 169–70.
90. Hill v. Church of Scientology of Toronto, [1995] 2 S.C.R. 1130, ¶ 137.

91. *See* Mitchell Drucker, *Canadian v. American Defamation Law: What Can We Learn from Hyperlinks*, 38 CAN.-U.S. L. J. 141, 148–49 (2013).
92. *See* Grant Vogeli, COURT COSTS—AN OFTEN OVERLOOKED PART OF LITIGATION (2018).
93. *See* Michael Norwick, *The Empirical Reality of Contemporary Libel Litigation*, in NEW YORK TIMES V. SULLIVAN: THE CASE FOR PRESERVING AN ESSENTIAL PRECEDENT (2022), at 122.
94. For a comprehensive overview of state anti-SLAPP laws, *see* Austin Vining and Sarah Matthews, *Overview of Anti-SLAPP Laws*, REPORTERS COMMITTEE FOR FREEDOM OF THE PRESS (accessed Jan. 6, 2023), https://www.rcfp.org/introduction-anti-slapp-guide/.
95. *Id.*
96. N.Y. Civ. Rights. L. 76-a.
97. *See* Jeff Kosseff and Matthew Schafer, *How States and Congress Can Prepare for a Looming Threat to Freedom of Speech*, LAWFARE (July 5, 2022).

Chapter 3. Sunlight

1. Brian J. Steffen, *The Falsity Burden of Private Libel Plaintiffs since Philadelphia Newspapers, Inc. v. Hepps*, 16 COMM & L. 57, 69–70 (1994).
2. Cowley v. Pulsifer, 137 Mass. 392, 392–93 (Mass. 1884).
3. *Id.* at 393–94 (quoting Rex v. Wright, 8 T.R. 293, 298).
4. Cowley v. Pulsifer, 137 Mass. 392, 394 (Mass. 1884).
5. *Id.*
6. *Id.*
7. Samuel Arthur Dawson, FREEDOM OF THE PRESS: A STUDY OF THE LEGAL DOCTRINE OF "QUALIFIED PRIVILEGE" (1924), 115.
8. Kathryn Dix Sowle, *Defamation and the First Amendment: The Case for a Constitutional Privilege of Fair Report*, 54 N.Y.U. L. REV. 469, 474 (1979).
9. Yohe v. Nugent, 321 F.3d 35, 38 (1st Cir. 2003).
10. *Id.* at 38–39.
11. *Id.* at 38.
12. *Id.* at 39.
13. *Id.*
14. Memorandum of Decision, Yohe v. May, Case 1:00-cv-10802 (D. Mass. Mar. 27, 2001) (quoting ELM Medical Laboratory, Inc. v. RKO General, Inc., 403 Mass. 779, 782 (1998).
15. *Id.*
16. Brief of Plaintiff Appellant, Harry Yohe, Yohe v. Nugent, No. 01-2131 (1st Cir. April 8, 2002), at 7.
17. Brief of Defendants-Appelles Kate Walsh and Nashoba Publications, Yohe v. Nugent, No. 01-2131 (1st Cir. May 8, 2002), at 12.
18. Yohe v. Nugent, 321 F.3d 35, 43 (1st Cir. 2003).
19. *Id.* (internal citations omitted).
20. *Id.*
21. *Id.* at 44.
22. *Id.*
23. *Id.* at 45.
24. *See generally* Dan Laidman, *When the Slander Is the Story—The Neutral Reportage Privilege in Theory and Practice*, 17 UCLA ENT. L. REV. 74 (2010).

25. Edwards v. National Audubon Society, 556 F.2d 113, 116 (2d Cir. 1977).
26. *Id.* at 116–17.
27. *Id.* at 117.
28. *Id.* at 118.
29. *See Biographical Information: Charles Miller Metzner*, CourtListener (accessed Nov. 7, 2002), https://www.courtlistener.com/person/2230/charles-miller-metzner/.
30. Edwards v. National Audubon Society, 423 F. Supp. 516, 519 (S.D.N.Y. 1976).
31. Edwards v. National Audubon Soc'y, 556 F.2d 113, 120 (2d Cir. 1977).
32. *Id.*
33. *Id.*
34. *Id.*
35. *Id.* at 122.
36. Arnold H. Lubasch, *$61,000 Libel Award against Times and Audubon Official Overturned*, N.Y. Times (May 26, 1977).
37. Donna Lee Dickerson, *Fashioning a New Libel Defense: The Advent of Neutral Reportage*, 3 Comm. & L. 77, 86 (1981).
38. Dickey v. CBS, 583 F.2d 1221, 1226 (3d Cir. 1978).
39. Brief of Appellees, Wolfe v. Glenn, Docket Nos. 633 EDA 2001 and 707 EDA 2001 (Pa. Super. Ct. June 29, 2001), at 11.
40. *Id.* at 12.
41. *Id.*
42. Norton v. Glenn, 860 A.2d 48, 50–51 (Pa. 2004).
43. *Id.* at 51.
44. *Id.* at 57.
45. *Courts Action Stifles Vigorous Reporting*, Seattle Times, Apr. 17, 2005.
46. Philadelphia Newspapers v. Hepps, 475 U.S. 767, 769 (1986).
47. *Id.* at 770–71.
48. *Id.* at 776–77.

Chapter 4. Truth

1. *Criminal Defamation Laws Are 19th Century Holdover*, News Media and the Law (Spring 2001).
2. *Document 4: Blackstone Commentaries of the Laws of England 151*, in The Founders' Constitution (Philip B. Kurland and Ralph Lerner, eds., 1986), https://press-pubs .uchicago.edu/founders/documents/amendI_speechs4.html.
3. David Lange, *The Speech and Press Clauses*, 23 UCLA L. Rev. 77, 97 (1975).
4. Thomas Fleming, *Verdicts of History IV: "A Scandalous, Malicious, and Seditious Libel,"* American Heritage (Dec. 1967) [hereinafter *Verdicts of History*].
5. New York Times v. Sullivan, 376 U.S. 254, 273–74 (1964) (quoting Sedition Act of 1798, 1 Stat. 596).
6. *Id.* at 274.
7. US House of Representatives, History, Art, and Archives, The Sedition Act of 1798.
8. *Verdicts of History.*
9. *Id.*
10. The Law Practice of Alexander Hamilton (Julius Goebel Jr., ed., 1964), at 777. [hereinafter Law Practice].
11. *Verdicts of History.*
12. Eugene Volokh, *Alexander Hamilton, the Truth, and Freedom of the Press*, Volokh Conspiracy (June 28, 2016); Law Practice, at 777.

13. *Verdicts of History;* Law Practice, at 778.
14. Law Practice, at 775.
15. *Id.* at 779; *Ambrose Spencer,* New York Courts Legal History (accessed Jan. 5, 2023), https://www.nycourts.gov/history/legal-history-new-york/luminaries-supreme-court/spencer-ambrose.html.
16. Law Practice, at 785.
17. *Verdicts of History;* Law Practice, at 785–86.
18. Edward S. Corwin, *Freedom of Speech and Press under the First Amendment: A Resumé,* 30 Yale L. J. 48, 52 (1920); Law Practice, at 787–88.
19. Kate Elizabeth Brown, *Rethinking People v. Croswell: Alexander Hamilton and the Nature and Scope of "Common Law" in the Early Republic,* 32 Law & Hist. Rev. 611, 619 (2014).
20. Paul McGrath, *People v. Croswell: Alexander Hamilton and the Transformation of the Common Law of Libel,* Judicial Notice (Summer 2011) [hereinafter Judicial Notice], at 11.
21. *Verdicts of History;* Law Practice, at 789.
22. Law Practice, at 790.
23. *Verdicts of History.*
24. Law Practice, at 792–93.
25. *Id.* at 795–96.
26. *See* Roy Robert Ray, *Truth: A Defense to Libel,* Minn. L. Rev. (1931), at 43.
27. The Speeches at Full Length of Mr. Van Ness, Mr. Caines, the Attorney-General, Mr. Harrison, and General Hamilton in the Great Cause of the People against Harry Croswell on an Indictment for a Libel on Thomas Jefferson, President of the United States (1804), at 32.
28. *Id.* at 63.
29. *Id.* at 64.
30. *Id.* at 67–68.
31. *Id.* at 69.
32. *Id.* at 70.
33. Genevieve Lakier, *The Invention of Low-Value Speech,* 128 Harv. L. Rev. 2166, 2180–85 (2015); Morris D. Forkosch, *Freedom of the Press: Croswell's Case,* 33 Fordham L. Rev. 415, 438 (1965).
34. *Verdicts of History.*
35. *Id.*
36. People v. Croswell, 3 Johns. Cas. 337, 377–78 (N.Y. 1804).
37. *Id.* at 378.
38. *Id.* at 391.
39. *Id.* at 392.
40. *Id.* at 395.
41. *Id.* at 402–3.
42. Judicial Notice, at 17.
43. *Id.*
44. *See* Kyu Ho Youm, *The Impact of People v. Croswell on Libel Law,* Journalism Monographs (June 1989), at 11.
45. *Id.* at 15 (quoting C. Lawhorne, Defamation and Public Officials 60 (1971)).
46. Marc A. Franklin, *The Origins and Constitutionality of Limitations on Truth as a Defense in Tort Law,* 16 Stan. L. Rev. 789, 792 (1964) [hereinafter *Origins and Constitutionality*].

47. A. Jay Wagner and Anthony L. Fargo, CRIMINAL LIBEL IN THE LAND OF THE FIRST AMENDMENT (2015), at 34.

48. *See Origins and Constitutionality*, at 790–91 ("English defamation law has for centuries consistently treated truth as a complete defense to a civil defamation action, and the American states early adopted the English Rule"); Kyu Ho Youm, *The Impact of People v. Croswell on Libel Law*, JOURNALISM MONOGRAPHS (June 1989), at 4.

49. *See Garrison v. Louisiana*, 379 U.S. 64, 74 (1964). "We held in *New York Times* that a public official might be allowed the civil remedy only if he establishes that the utterance was false and that it was made with knowledge of its falsity or in reckless disregard of whether it was false or true."

50. Franklin, *Origins and Constitutionality*, at 792.

51. *Presidents of the Continental Congresses and Confederation Congress, 1774–1789*, US HOUSE OF REPRESENTATIVES: HISTORY, ART, AND ARCHIVES (accessed Nov. 9, 2022), https://history.house.gov/People/Continental-Congress/Presidents/.

52. *See, e.g.*, Turner v. KTRK Television, 38 SW 3d. 103, 115 (Tex. 2000).

53. Edward Hutheson, *Flood History: An Overview of the 1889 Tragedy*, JOHNSTOWN AREA HERITAGE ASSOCIATION (accessed Nov. 9, 2022), https://www.jaha.org/attractions/johnstown-flood-museum/flood-history/; *Statistics about the Great Disaster*, JOHNSTOWN AREA HERITAGE ASSOCIATION (accessed Nov. 9, 2022), https://www.jaha.org/attractions/johnstown-flood-museum/flood-history/facts-about-the-1889-flood/.

54. Jackson v. Pittsburg Times, 152 Pa. 406 (1893).

55. *Id.*

56. *Id.*

57. *Id.*

58. *Colonel Frederick Hill Collier*, ANTIETAM ON THE WEB (accessed Nov. 9, 2022), https://antietam.aotw.org/officers.php?officer_id=248.

59. Jackson v. Pittsburg Times, 152 Pa. 406 (1893).

60. *Id.*

61. *Id.*

62. *Id.* at 418.

63. *Id.*

64. Brian McCollum, *Eminem's "Slim Shady LP" Turns 20: An Oral History of the Album That Created a Superstar*, DETROIT FREE PRESS, Feb. 23, 2019.

65. "Brain Damage" written by Jeff Bass, Mark Bass, and Marshall Mathers. Published by Eight Mile Style, LLC, and Martin Affiliated, LLC, administered by Bridgeport Music Inc. Used with permission.

66. *Eminem Blows Up*, Exhibit B to Brief on Appeal of Defendant-Appellee Marshall Bruce Mathers, III, Bailey v. Mathers, No. 252123 (Ct. App. Mich. Dec. 16, 2004), at 2–3.

67. *Id.*

68. *Id.*

69. Brief on Appeal of Defendant-Appellee Marshall Bruce Mathers, III, Bailey v. Mathers, No. 252123 (Ct. App. Mich. Dec. 16, 2004), at 2–3.

70. *Id.* at 3.

71. Deposition of Marshall Mathers, III, Exhibit E.(4) to Brief on Appeal of Defendant-Appellee Marshall Bruce Mathers, III, Bailey v. Mathers, No. 252123 (Ct. App. Mich. Dec. 16, 2004), at 63.

72. Bailey v. Mathers, 33 Media L. Rep. 2053 (Ct. App. Mich. 2005) (internal quotation and citations omitted).

73. Deposition of DeAngelo Bailey, Exhibit E.(2) to Brief on Appeal of Defendant-Appellee Marshall Bruce Mathers, III, Bailey v. Mathers, No. 252123 (Ct. App. Mich. Dec. 16, 2004), at 44–49.

74. *Id.* at 49–58.

75. Deposition of Marshall Mathers, III, Exhibit E.(4) to Brief on Appeal of Defendant-Appellee Marshall Bruce Mathers, III, Bailey v. Mathers, No. 252123 (Ct. App. Mich. Dec. 16, 2004), at 7–8.

76. *Id.* at 8.

77. *Id.* at 9.

78. *Id.* at 10.

79. *Id.* at 13–14.

80. *Id.* at 16–17.

81. *Id.* at 17–18.

82. *Id.* at 48–53.

83. *Id.*

84. *Id.* at 53.

85. *Id.* at 62–63.

86. Complaint, Mathers v. Roseville School District, Macomb County Circuit Court No. 82-4266-NO (Nov. 23, 1982), Exhibit E.(1) to Brief on Appeal of Defendant-Appellee Marshall Bruce Mathers, III, Bailey v. Mathers, No. 252123 (Ct. App. Mich. Dec. 16, 2004), at ¶¶5–8.

87. *See Deborah A. Servitto*, BLOOMBERG (accessed Nov. 9, 2022), https://www.bloomberg.com/profile/person/18601903.

88. Bailey v. Mathers, 31 Media L. Rep. 2575 (Macomb Cty. Cir. Ct. Oct. 17, 2003).

89. *Id.*

90. *Id.*

91. *Id.*

92. *Id.*

93. Appellant Brief, Bailey v. Mathers, No. 252123 at 8–9 (Ct. App. Mich. Sept. 16, 2004).

94. Bailey v. Mathers, 33 Media L. Rep. 2053 (Ct. App. Mich. 2005).

95. Mariel Concepcion, *Eminem Discusses Being Bullied and His Rhyming Process*, BILLBOARD (Oct. 11, 2010).

Chapter 5. Uncertainty

1. Abrams v. United States, 250 U.S. 616, 630 (1919) (Holmes, J., dissenting).

2. Frederick Sontag, *Uncertain Truth* (1995), at ix.

3. John MacFarlane, *Future Contingents and Relative Truth*, 53 PHIL. Q. 212 (July 2003).

4. Robert Linn, THE LAST CHANCE DIET (1976), at xv.

5. *Id.* at 64.

6. *Id.* at 73.

7. *Id.* at xv.

8. Smith v. Linn, 48 Pa. D. & C.3d 339, 341 (1988).

9. *Id.*

10. Bonnie L. Cook, *William W. Vogel, 92, Former President Judge of the Montgomery County Court*, PHILADELPHIA INQUIRER, Sept. 9, 2019.

11. *Judges Smith, Corso Will Run Unopposed*, MORNING CALL, Nov. 3, 1985.

12. Smith v. Linn, 48 Pa. D. & C.3d 342 (1988).

13. *Id.* at 350.

14. *Id.* at 351.

15. *Id.* at 351–52.

16. *Id.*at 352–53.

17. Smith v. Linn, 386 Pa. Super. 392 (1989).

18. Smith v. Linn, 587 A.2d 309 (Pa. 1991).

19. *See, e.g.,* Philip Ball and Amy Maxmen, *The Epic Battle against Coronavirus Misinformation and Conspiracy Theories*, NATURE (May 27, 2020).

20. *See, e.g., Franklin County Woman Has Covid-19*, CHICAGO DAILY HERALD, Mar. 27, 2020. "Officials urge the public to practice social distancing of at least six feet from others, wash hands frequently, disinfect common surfaces and stay home."

21. *See, e.g.,* Fadel Allassan, *Surgeon General Defends Reversal on Face Mask Policy*, AXIOS (July 12, 2020).

22. Tomé Morrissy-Swan, *Arsenic, Tapeworms, and Cigarettes: The Ten Weirdest Fad Diets of All Time*, THE TELEGRAPH, Jan. 12, 2018.

23. Dorit R. Reiss and John Diamond, *Measles and Misrepresentation in Minnesota: Can There Be Liability for Anti-Vaccine Misinformation That Causes Bodily Harm?*, 56 SAN DIEGO L. REV. 531, 539 (2019).

24. Garry Abrams, *Mushrooms That Kill: Fungi Fan Looks Back at a Brush with Death after He and Friend Dined on a "Perfect" Death Cap*, L.A. TIMES, Apr. 18, 1988.

25. *Id.*

26. THE ENCYCLOPEDIA OF MUSHROOMS (1979).

27. Appellants' Opening Brief, Winter v. G.P. Putnam's Sons, 89-16308 (9th Cir. Jan. 22, 1990), at 3.

28. *Id.* at 6.

29. *Id.* at 13.

30. Winter v. GP Putnam Sons, 938 F.3d 1033, 1035 (9th Cir. 1991).

31. *Id.*

32. *Id.* at 1036.

33. *Id.* at 1037.

34. *Id.* at 1037n9.

35. Complaint (attached to Notice of Removal) ¶¶ 4–5, Brandt v. Weather Channel, 4:98-cv-10060 (S.D. Fla. Aug. 3, 1998) [hereinafter Brandt Complaint]; Tony Chamberlain, *Forecast Can Get You in Some Hot Water*, BOSTON GLOBE, Aug. 8, 1999; Martin Wisckol, *Bodies of Two Fishermen Found in Keys*, SOUTH FLORIDA SUN-SENTINEL, June 3, 1997.

36. Brandt Complaint ¶¶ 6–12; Wisckol, *supra* note 35.

37. Brandt Complaint ¶ 8.

38. Brandt v. Weather Channel, 204 F.3d 1123 (11th Cir. 1999) (affirming without opinion).

39. Defendant The Weather Channel's Motion to Dismiss and Memorandum in Support at 10, Brandt v. Weather Channel, 4:98-cv-10060 (S.D. Fla. Sept. 9, 1998).

40. *Id.*

41. *Id.* at 10–11 (quoting Tumminello v. Bergen Evening Record, 454 F. Supp. 1156, 1160 (D.N.J. 1978).

42. Plaintiffs' Memo of Law and Response to the Defendant's Motion to Dismiss at 2–5, Brandt v. Weather Channel, 4:98-cv-10060 (S.D. Fla. Oct. 8, 1998).

43. *Id.* at 5–6 (emphasis in original).
44. Susan Spencer-Wendel, *Retired Federal Judge James C. Paine, Dies at 85*, PALM BEACH POST, Mar. 8, 2010.
45. Brandt v. Weather Channel, 42 F.Supp.2d 1344, 1346 (S.D. Fla. 1999).
46. *Id.*
47. Brown v. United States, 790 F.2d 199, 204 (1st Cir. 1986).

Chapter 6. Opinion

1. 4 ANNALS OF CONG. 934 (1794). For a discussion of the importance of this debate to modern First Amendment jurisprudence by a former Supreme Court Justice, see William O. Douglas, *The Right of Association*, 63 COLUM. L. REV. 1361, 1382–83 (1963).
2. *Letter from Thomas Jefferson to William Duane, 25 July 1811*, FOUNDERS ONLINE, https://founders.archives.gov/documents/Jefferson/03-04-02-0052; *see also* Jeremy J. Ofseyer, *Speech or Opinion—Two Objects of First Amendment Immunity*, 2002 UTAH L. REV. 843, 876 (2002): "Jefferson and Madison were especially concerned with diversity of opinion on matters of political and religious doctrine. Jefferson saw diverse political opinion as the natural reflection of the diversity of human nature."
3. United States v. Associated Press, 52 F. Supp. 362, 372 (S.D.N.Y. 1943).
4. Gertz v. Robert Welch, 418 U.S. 323, 339–40 (1974).
5. *See* Mark Jurkowitz, Amy Mitchell, Elisa Shearer, and Mason Walker, *U.S. Media Polarization and the 2020 Election: A Nation Divided*, PEW RESEARCH CENTER (Jan. 24, 2020).
6. Herring Networks v. Maddow, 8 F.4th 1148, 1152 (9th Cir. 2021).
7. *Id.*
8. *Id.* at 1153.
9. *Id.*
10. Complaint for Defamation and Damages, Herring Networks v. Maddow, 19CV1713 (S.D. Cal. Sept. 9, 2019) at ¶¶ 24–26.
11. *Id.* at ¶¶ 30–31.
12. *Id.* at ¶¶ 38–39.
13. *Id.* at ¶ 52.
14. Cal. Civ. Proc. Code 425.16(b)(1).
15. Memorandum of Points and Authorities in Support of Defendants' Special Motion to Strike Plaintiff's Complaint, Herring Networks v. Maddow, 19CV1713 (S.D. Cal. Oct. 21, 2019), at 7–8.
16. Milkovich v. Lorain Journal, 497 U.S. 1, 18 (1990).
17. *Id.* at 3–7.
18. *Id.* at 18.
19. *Id.* at 18–19.
20. *Id.* at 19–20 (cleaned up).
21. *Id.* at 21.
22. Memorandum of Points and Authorities in Support of Defendants' Special Motion to Strike Plaintiff's Complaint, Herring Networks v. Maddow, 19CV1713 (S.D. Cal. Oct. 21, 2019), at 13.
23. *Id.* at 15–16.
24. Declaration of Professor Stefan Th. Gries in Support of Herring Network Inc.'s Opposition to Defendants' Motion to Strike, Herring Networks v. Maddow, 19CV1713 (S.D. Cal. Dec. 2, 2019), Exhibit B, at 17.

25. Declaration of Charles Herring in Support of Plaintiff's Opposition to Defendants' Special Motion to Strike, Herring Networks v. Maddow, 19CV1713 (S.D. Cal. Dec. 2, 2019), at Exhibit A.

26. Transcript of Motion Hearing, Herring Networks v. Maddow, 19CV1713 (S.D. Cal. May 19, 2020), at 2–5.

27. *Id.* at 5–10.

28. *Id.* at 11.

29. *Id.* at 13.

30. *Id.* at 15.

31. Herring Networks, Inc. v. Maddow, 445 F. Supp. 3d 1042, 1050 (S.D. Cal. 2020) (internal citation and quotation marks omitted). Although Bashant considered the text of the *Daily Beast* article and the Maddow show transcript, she found that procedural rules barred her from considering the exhibits that Herring submitted, such as the linguist's report.

32. *Id.* at 1053.

33. Video: 20-55579 Herring Networks, Inc. v. Rachel Maddow (U.S. Court of Appeals for the Ninth Circuit 2021), at 7:49.

34. *Id.* at 8:35.

35. *Id.* at 9:18.

36. *Id.* at 10:30.

37. *Id.* at 26:59.

38. Herring Networks v. Maddow, 8 F.4th 1157, 1161 (9th Cir. 2021).

39. *Id.* at 1157–58.

40. *Id.* at 1160.

41. *Id.* at 1160–61.

42. *Id.* at 1161.

43. ONY v. Cornerstone Therapeutics, 720 F.3d 490, 492–94 (2d Cir. 2013).

44. *Id.* at 493.

45. *Id.* at 493–94.

46. *Id.* at 494.

47. *Id.* at 494–95.

48. *Id.* at 494.

49. *Id.* at 495.

50. *Id.*

51. ONY v. Cornerstone Therapeutics, No. 11-CV-1027S (W.D.N.Y. May 17, 2012) at 16, 17.

52. *Id.* at 19.

53. *Id.* at 20.

54. Brief for Plaintiff-Appellant, ONY v. Cornerstone, 12-2414 (2d Cir. Sept. 21, 2012), at 22.

55. ONY v. Cornerstone Therapeutics, 720 F.3d 490, 496 (2d Cir. 2013).

56. *Id.*

57. *Id.* at 497.

58. *Id.* at 497–98.

Chapter 7. Responsibility

1. Martin H. Redish, *Value of Free Speech*, 130 U. Pa. L. Rev. 591, 593 (1982).

2. *Id.* at 620–21.

3. Papers on Appeal from Order (Complaint), Jaillet v. Cashman (N.Y. Jan. 19, 1923), at 8.

4. *Id.* at 10.
5. Eisner v. Macomber, 252 U.S. 189, 219 (1920).
6. Papers on Appeal from Order (Complaint), Jaillet v. Cashman (N.Y. Jan. 19, 1923), at 9.
7. *Id.* at 10.
8. *Id.* at 8.
9. *Ticker's Error on Stock Dividend Brings $2,218 Claim*, LANSING STATE J., Mar. 12, 1920.
10. Jaillet v. Cashman, 115 Misc. 383, 384 (N.Y.S. 1921).
11. *Id.*
12. Jaillet v. Cashman, 202 A.D. 805 (N.Y. App. Div. 1922).
13. Brief for Appellant, Jaillet v. Cashman (N.Y.), at 28.
14. *Id.*
15. *Id.* at 29.
16. Brief for Defendant-Respondent, Jaillet v. Cashman (N.Y.), at 20.
17. *Id.* at 24.
18. Jaillet v. Cashman, 139 N.E. 714 (N.Y. 1923).
19. *Former Governor Curry Dies*, ALBUQUERQUE J., Apr. 12, 1932.
20. Curry v. Journal Pub. Co., 68 P.2d 168, 169 (N.M. 1937).
21. Brief of Appellants, Curry v. Journal Pub. Co. (N.M.), at 2.
22. *Id.* at 3.
23. *Id.*
24. Curry v. Journal Pub. Co, 68 P.2d 168, 170 (N.M. 1937).
25. *Id.* at 172–73.
26. *Id.* at 173 (internal citation omitted).
27. *Id.* at 174.
28. *Id.* at 176.
29. Daniel v. Dow Jones & Co., 137 Misc.2d 94, 95 (N.Y. Civ. Ct. 1987).
30. *Id.*
31. Wolfgang Saxon, *Lewis Friedman; Judge, 56, Heard Complex Cases*, N.Y. TIMES, Feb. 20, 1998.
32. Daniel v. Dow Jones & Co., 137 Misc.2d 94, 95 (N.Y. Civ. Ct. 1987).
33. *Id.*
34. *Id.* at 97.
35. *Id.* at 97–98.
36. *Id.* at 99.
37. *Id.* at 101.
38. *Id.* at 102.
39. Complaint and Jury Demand, Rosenberg v. Harwood, Case No. 100916536 (Third Dist. Ct. Utah Sept. 10, 2010), at ¶¶ 23–25.
40. *Id.* at ¶¶ 26–28.
41. *Id.* at ¶¶ 20–41.
42. Memorandum of Points and Authorities of Defendant Google, Inc. in Support of Motion to Dismiss, Complaint and Jury Demand, Rosenberg v. Harwood, Case No. 100916536 (Third Dist. Ct. Utah Dec. 2, 2010), at 10–11.
43. Memorandum Decision, Rosenberg v. Harwood, Case No. 100916536 (Third Dist. Ct. Utah May 27, 2011).
44. *Id.*
45. *Id.*

Chapter 8. Efficacy

1. Alexis De Tocqueville, DEMOCRACY IN AMERICA (Henry Reeve, trans., 1835), available at https://www.gutenberg.org/files/815/815-h/815-h.htm.
2. Susan B. Anthony List v. Ohio Elections Commission, 45 F. Supp. 3d 765, 771 (S.D. Ohio 2014).
3. *Id.*
4. Kasie Hunt, *Driehaus Sues to Stop Abortion Attacks*, POLITICO (Oct. 7, 2010).
5. Susan B. Anthony List v. Ohio Elections Comm'n, 45 F. Supp. 3d 765, 771 (S.D. Ohio 2014).
6. *Id.* at 769.
7. *Id.* at 770.
8. *Id.* at 776.
9. *Id.* at 776–77 (internal quotation marks and citations omitted).
10. *Id.* at 777–78.
11. *Id.* at 778.
12. Brief of Appellants-Defendants Ohio Elections Commission and Its Members, Susan B. Anthony List v. Driehaus, Case No. 2014-4008 (6th Cir. Feb. 11, 2015), at 16.
13. Susan B. Anthony List v. Driehaus, 814 F.3d 466, 474 (6th Cir. 2016) (internal quotation marks and citations omitted).
14. *Id.*
15. *Id.* at 475.
16. *Id.*
17. *Id.*
18. 281 Care Committee v. Arneson, 766 F.3d 774, 777–78 (8th Cir. 2014).
19. *Id.* at 778.
20. *Id.* at 787.
21. *Id.* at 789.
22. *Id.* at 793.
23. *Id.* at 796.
24. Commonwealth v. Lucas, 472 Mass. 387, 403 (2015).
25. *Id.* at 404.

Chapter 9. The Scope of the Problem

1. Steven Vosloo, *Digital Misinformation/Disinformation and Children*, UNICEF (Aug. 24, 2021).
2. Michael J. O'Brien and Izzat Alsmadi, *Misinformation, Disinformation and Hoaxes: What's the Difference?*, THE CONVERSATION (Apr. 21, 2021).
3. Olivia Goldhill, *Truth Is the Dangerous New Propaganda Tool*, QUARTZ (Oct. 18, 2019). "An emphasis on fact-checking and crackdown on bot networks over the past three years means false statements are more likely to be flagged, which weakens their impact. Misleading but technically true statements, by contrast, escape repercussions."
4. Renee DiResta, *It's Not Misinformation. It's Amplified Propaganda*, THE ATLANTIC (Oct. 9, 2021).
5. *Propaganda*, CAMBRIDGE ADVANCED LEARNER'S DICTIONARY (4th ed. 2013).
6. Indictment, United States v. Internet Research Agency, 1:18-cr-32 (Feb. 16, 2018), at ¶ 4.
7. Richard Gunther, Erik C. Nisbet, and Paul Beck, *Trump May Owe His 2016 Victory to "Fake News," New Study Suggests*, THE CONVERSATION (Feb. 15, 2018).
8. Linda Qiu, *Trump Has Amplified Voting Falsehoods in Over 300 Tweets since Election Night*, N.Y. TIMES, Nov. 16, 2020.

9. Nick Corasaniti, Reid J. Epstein, and Jim Rutenberg, *The Times Called Officials in Every State: No Evidence of Voter Fraud*, N.Y. TIMES, Nov. 10, 2020.

10. Christina A. Cassidy, *Far Too Little Vote Fraud to Tip Election to Trump, AP Finds*, ASSOCIATED PRESS (Dec. 14, 2021).

11. William Cummings, Joey Garrison, and Jim Sergent, *By the Numbers: President Donald Trump's Failed Efforts to Overturn the Election*, USA TODAY, Jan. 6, 2021.

12. Steve Holland, Jeff Mason, and Jonathan Landay, *Trump Summoned Supporters to "Wild" Protest, and Told Them to Fight. They Did*, REUTERS (Jan. 6, 2021).

13. Alan Feuer, Michael S. Schmidt, and Luke Broadwater, *New Focus on How a Trump Tweet Incited Far-Right Groups before Jan. 6*, N.Y. TIMES, Mar. 29, 2022.

14. Bill McCarthy, *Misinformation and the Jan. 6 Insurrection: When "Patriot Warriors" Were Fed Lies*, POLITIFACT (June 30, 2021).

15. Claudia Deane, Kim Parker, and John Gramlich, *A Year of U.S. Public Opinion on the Coronavirus Pandemic*, PEW RESEARCH CENTER (Mar. 5, 2021).

16. *KFF COVID-19 Vaccine Monitor: Media and Misinformation*, KAISER FAMILY FOUNDATION (Nov. 8, 2021).

17. Soroush Vosoughi, Deb Roy, and Sinan Aral, *The Spread of True and False News Online*, SCIENCE (Mar. 9, 2018).

18. James Vincent, *Why We Need a Better Definition of "Deepfake,"* THE VERGE (May 22, 2018).

19. *Id.*

20. Bobby Chesney and Danielle Citron, *Deep Fakes: A Looming Challenge for Privacy, Democracy, and National Security*, 107 CAL. L. REV. 1753, 1755–56 (2019).

21. *Id.* at 1757.

22. Will Rahn and Dan Patterson, *What Is the QAnon Conspiracy Theory*, CBS NEWS (Mar. 29, 2021).

23. *Id.*

24. Lois Beckett, *QAnon: A Timeline of Violence Linked to the Conspiracy Theory*, THE GUARDIAN, Oct. 16, 2020.

25. Josh Hawley (@HawleyMO), Twitter, https://twitter.com/HawleyMO/status/1504221926662844418?s=20&t=14u-eQPCwmzjd65xAD5W0g (Mar. 16, 2022).

26. Ian Millhiser, *Josh Hawley's Latest Attack on Ketanji Brown Jackson Is Genuinely Nauseating*, Vox (Mar. 18, 2022).

27. Andrew McCarthy, *Ho-Hum: The Cases Senator Hawley Cites Show Judge Jackson Is an Unremarkable Sentencer in Child-Porn Cases*, NATIONAL REVIEW (Mar. 21, 2022).

28. David D. Kirkpatrick and Stuart A. Thompson, *QAnon Cheers Republican Attacks on Jackson. Democrats See a Signal*, N.Y. TIMES, Mar. 24, 2022.

29. Marjorie Taylor Greene (@RepMTG), Twitter, https://twitter.com/repmtg/status/1511150070367985664?lang=en (Apr. 4, 2022).

30. Laurie Kellman, *GOP Turns Fury on Schiff over Russian Collusion Claims*, ASSOCIATED PRESS (Mar. 25, 2019).

31. *All the Adam Schiff Transcripts*, WALL ST. J., May 12, 2020.

32. *Id.*

33. Will Hurd, AMERICAN REBOOT (2022), at 63.

34. Emma-Jo Morris and Gabrielle Fonrouge, *Smoking-Gun Email Reveals How Hunter Biden Introduced Ukrainian Businessman to VP Dad*, N.Y. POST, Oct. 14, 2020.

35. *Q&A: How Trump Seized on a Dubious Biden-Ukraine Story: The Origins of the Story Also Trace Back to Trump Lawyer Rudy Giuliani, Who Has Pushed Unfounded Claims about Biden and His Son, Hunter Biden*, ASSOCIATED PRESS (Oct. 15, 2020).

36. The Situation Room, transcript, CNN (Oct. 16, 2020).
37. Audrey Conklin, *Facebook Official Who Said Platform Is Reducing Distribution of Hunter Biden Story Has Worked for Top Dems*, Fox News (Oct. 14, 2020).
38. Kari Paul, *Facebook and Twitter Restrict Controversial New York Post Story on Joe Biden*, The Guardian, Oct. 14, 2020.
39. Brian Flood, *Twitter's Double Standard Emerges after NY Post Hunter Biden Story Blocked, Other Media Get Pass, Critics Say*, Fox News (Oct. 15, 2020).
40. Katie Benner, Kenneth P. Vogel, and Michael S. Schmidt, *Hunter Biden Paid Tax Bill, but Broad Federal Investigation Continues*, N.Y. Times, Mar. 16, 2022.
41. Andrew Prokop, *The Return of Hunter Biden's Laptop*, Vox (Mar. 25, 2022).
42. Joseph Bernstein, *Bad News*, Harper's Magazine (Sept. 2021).
43. *Id.*
44. *See* Mike Masnick, *Most Information about Disinformation Is Misinformation*, Techdirt (Aug. 30, 2021). "There are problems with education, with social safety nets, with healthcare (especially mental healthcare). There are problems with income inequality and corruption. There are tons of problems out there, and many of these manifest themselves through false information that people share online. But saying that the 'disinformation' is the problem—rather than a way in which the underlying problem shows itself—misses the point entirely."
45. Izabella Kaminska, *A Lesson in Fake News from the Info-Wars of Ancient Rome*, Financial Times, Jan. 17, 2017.
46. Kenneth Scott, *The Political Propaganda of 44–30 B.C.*, in Memoirs of the American Academy in Rome, vol. 11 (1933), 7–49.
47. Philip Davidson, Propaganda and the American Revolution, 1763–1783 (1941), at 237.
48. David Uberti, *The Real History of Fake News*, Colum. J. R., Dec. 15, 2016.
49. Adam Hochschild, Bury the Chains: The British Struggle to Abolish Slavery (2005), at 263.
50. *Proceedings and Debates of the House of Representatives of the United States, at the Second Session of the Sixth Congress, Begun at the City of Washington, Monday, November 17, 1800*, 10 Annals of Cong. 781, 970 (1799–1801).
51. Adrienne LaFrance, *In 1858, People Said the Telegraph Was "Too Fast for the Truth,"* The Atlantic (July 28, 2014), quoting *LATEST BY TELEGRAPH; The Overland Pacific Mails—The Cass-Yrissari Treaty—Utah Affairs*, N.Y. Times, Aug. 19, 1858.
52. *Id.*
53. Douglas Selvage and Christopher Nehring, *Operation Denver: KGB and Stasi Disinformation Regarding AIDS*, Wilson Center (July 22, 2019).
54. *Id.*
55. *Id.*
56. David Robert Grimes, *Russian Fake News Is Not New: Soviet Aids Propaganda Cost Countless Lives*, The Guardian, June 14, 2017.
57. Terry Gross, *Inside the Russian Disinformation Playbook: Exploit Tension, Sow Chaos*, Fresh Air (Nov. 15, 2018).
58. Thomas Boghardt, *Soviet Bloc Intelligence and Its AIDS Disinformation Campaign*, 53 Stud. Intelligence 1, 15 (Dec. 2009).
59. *Id.*
60. *Id.* at 18.

Chapter 10. When Regulation or Liability Is Not the Answer

1. Mike Masnick, *Senator Gillibrand Says We Don't Have to Regulate Speech, Just Misinfo. Who Wants To Tell Her?*, Techdirt (May 26, 2022), video posted to MSNBC.com.
2. Press release, *Inslee Statement on Efforts to Stop Violence Fueled by Election Lies* (Jan. 6, 2022).
3. Brandenburg v. Ohio, 395 U.S. 444, 447–48 (1969).
4. Scott Shackford, *Washington's Governor Wants to Prevent Another January 6 with Unconstitutional Censorship*, Reason (Jan. 10, 2022).
5. Austin Jenkins, *Washington Gov. Inslee Says Lying about Elections Should Be a Crime*, KUOW (Jan. 6, 2022).
6. S.B. 5843, 67th Leg., Reg. Sess. (Wash. 2022).
7. *Id.*
8. *Senate State Government and Elections Committee*, TVW (Jan. 28, 2022), https://tvw .org/video/senate-state-government-elections-committee-2022011526/?eventID =2022011526, at 00:17:09.
9. *Id.* at 00:32:04.
10. *Id.* at 00:31:43.
11. Joseph O'Sullivan, *Bill That Would Make It a Crime for Some to Lie about Election Results Dies in WA Senate*, Seattle Times, Feb. 15, 2022.
12. Hess v. Indiana, 414 U.S. 105, 107 (1973).
13. *Id.* at 108–9 (cleaned up).
14. 281 Care Committee v. Arneson, 766 F.3d 774, 794 (8th Cir. 2014).
15. Press release, *Klobuchar, Luján Introduce Legislation to Hold Digital Platforms Accountable for Vaccine and Other Health-Related Misinformation* (July 22, 2021).
16. Ryan Knutson, *Sen. Klobuchar Says Congress Is Losing Patience with Tech Giants*, Wall St. J., Oct. 20, 2021.
17. *See* Jeff Kosseff, The Twenty-Six Words That Created the Internet (2019), 270–71.
18. *See* Reno v. American Civil Liberties Union, 521 U.S. 844 (1997); FCC v. Pacifica, 438 U.S. 726 (1978); Miami Herald Publishing v. Tornillo, 418 U.S. 241 (1974).
19. 47 U.S.C. § 309.
20. 47 C.F.R. § 73.1217.
21. In re Amendment of Part 73 Regarding Broadcast Hoaxes, 7 FCC Rcd 4106, 4106 (June 12, 1992).
22. *Id.* at 4107.
23. *Id.* at 4108.
24. Joel Timmer, *Potential FCC Actions Against "Fake News": The News Distortion Policy and the Broadcast Hoax Rule*, 24, Comm. L. & Pol'y 1, 30–31 (2019).
25. Free Press, Emergency Petition for Inquiry into Broadcast of False Information on COVID-19 (2020), at 3–4.
26. *Id.* at 5.
27. *Id.* at 6.
28. *Id.* at 7.
29. Letter of Michelle M. Carey, Chief, Media Bureau, and Thomas M. Johnson Jr., General Counsel, to Jessica J. González and Gaurav Laroia, Free Press, Federal Communications Commission, DA 20-385, at 1 (Apr. 6, 2020), https://docs.fcc.gov /public/attachments/DA-20-385A1.pdf.
30. *Id.* at 2.
31. *Id.* at 3.

32. *Id.* at 4.
33. Complaint, Cohoon v. Konrath, Case 2:20-cv-00620 (E.D. Wisc. Apr. 16, 2020), ¶ 10 [hereinafter "Complaint"].
34. *Id.* ¶ 16.
35. *Id.* ¶¶ 17–18.
36. *Id.* ¶ 19.
37. *Id.* at Ex. 2.
38. *Id.* ¶ 23.
39. *Id.* at Ex. 3.
40. *Id.* ¶¶ 26–27.
41. *Id.* ¶ 28.
42. *Id.* ¶ 29.
43. *Id.* ¶ 30.
44. *Id.* ¶ 33.
45. *Id.* ¶¶ 34–35.
46. *Id.* ¶¶ 36, 38.
47. *Id.* ¶ 37 and Ex. 5.
48. *Id.* ¶ 40.
49. Defendants' Brief in Support of Motion for Summary Judgment, Cohoon v. Konrath, Case 2:20-cv-620 at 2 (E.D. Wisc. Apr. 24, 2020) [hereinafter "Summary Judgment Brief"].
50. Complaint ¶¶ 42–45.
51. *Id.* at Ex. 7.
52. *Id.* at Ex. 8.
53. *Id.* at Ex. 9.
54. *Id.*
55. Summary Judgment Brief, at 23–28.
56. Bruce Vielmetti, *Senate Approves Ludwig for Federal Court Seat in Milwaukee*, MILWAUKEE JOURNAL SENTINEL, Sept. 9, 2020.
57. Order Granting Plaintiff Declaratory Judgment, Cohoon v. Konrath, Case 2:20-cv-620 at 2 (E.D. Wisc. Sept. 24, 2021), at 5–6.
58. *Id.* at 6 (quoting United States v. Alvarez, 567 U.S. 709, 717 (2012)).
59. *Id.* at 6–7.
60. *Id.* at 7.
61. Cass Sunstein, LIARS: FALSEHOODS AND FREE SPEECH IN AN AGE OF DECEPTION (2021).
62. *Id.*
63. *Id.*
64. Jamie Whyte, *Polluting Words: Is There a Coasean Case to Regulate Offensive Speech?*, INTERNATIONAL CENTER FOR LAW AND ECONOMICS WHITE PAPER (Sept. 2021), at 19–20.
65. Hadas Gold, *Donald Trump: We're Going to "Open Up" Libel Laws*, POLITICO (Feb. 26, 2016).
66. Michael M. Grynbaum, *Trump Renews Pledge to "Take a Strong Look" at Libel Laws*, N.Y. TIMES, Jan. 10, 2018.
67. McKee v. Cosby, 139 S. Ct. 675, 675 (2019) (Thomas, J., concurring).
68. *Id.* at 676.
69. *Id.* at 682.

70. Matthew Schafer, *A Response to Justice Thomas*, in NEW YORK TIMES V. SULLIVAN: THE CASE FOR PRESERVING AN ESSENTIAL PRECEDENT (2022), at 77–78.

71. Tah v. Global Witness Publ'g, 991 F.3d 231, 254–55 (D.C. Cir. 2021) (Silberman, J., dissenting in part).

72. *Id.* at 255–56.

73. Berisha v. Lawson, 141 S. Ct. 2424 (2021).

74. *Id.* at 2425 (statement of Thomas, J., dissenting from denial of certiorari).

75. *Id.*

76. *Id.* at 2427 (statement of Gorsuch, J., dissenting from the denial of certiorari) (cleaned up).

77. *Id.* at 2428.

78. *Id.* at 2429.

79. *See* Gertz v. Robert Welch, 418 U.S. 323, 344 (1974).

80. *See Translation of Provisions for the Administration of Internet News Information Service 2017*, STANFORD CENTER FOR INTERNET AND SOCIETY (June 1, 2017), https://wilmap.stanford.edu/entries/provisions-administration-internet-news -information-service-2017.

81. Maria Repnikova, *China's Lessons for Fighting Fake News*, FOREIGN POLICY (Sept. 6, 2018).

82. *Id.*

83. *Id.*

84. FREEDOM HOUSE, FREEDOM IN THE WORLD 2022, CHINA (2022).

85. Anton Troianovski, *Russia Takes Censorship to New Extremes, Stifling War Coverage*, N.Y. TIMES, Mar. 4, 2022.

86. Tiffany Hsu and Michael M. Grynbaum, *"Minute-to-Minute Triage": Weighing News Against Safety in Russia*, N.Y. TIMES, Mar. 15, 2022.

87. Bangladesh, Translation of Digital Security Act, 2018, Act No. XLVI of 2018, at §21.

88. *Bangladesh: New Law Will Silence Critics*, HUMAN RIGHTS WATCH (Sept. 24, 2018).

89. *Bangladesh: Crackdown on Social Media*, HUMAN RIGHTS WATCH (Oct. 19, 2018).

90. Amnesty International, NO SPACE FOR DISSENT (July 2021), at 4.

91. Translation of Title I of Book III of the Penal Code of 2018 in Henri Barbeau, *Burkina Faso: Parliament Amends Penal Code*, LIBRARY OF CONGRESS (Sept. 20, 2019).

92. Press release, Committee to Protect Journalists, *Burkina Faso Parliament Passes Legal Revisions Criminalizing False News, Reporting on Terrorism* (July 3, 2019).

93. Peter Cunliffe-Jones, Alan Finlay, and Anya Schiffrin, *Punitive Laws Are Failing to Curb Misinformation in Africa. Time for a Rethink*, THE CONVERSATION (June 24, 2021).

94. *Id.*

95. Alexander Damiano Ricci, *French Opposition Parties Are Taking Macron's Anti-Misinformation Law to Court*, POYNTER (Dec. 4, 2018).

96. Angelique Chrisafis, *French MPs Criticise "Hasty and Ineffective" Fake News Law*, THE GUARDIAN, June 8, 2018.

Chapter 11. When Regulation or Liability Might Be an Answer

1. United States v. Alvarez, 567 U.S. 709, 721 (2012).

2. *Id.*

3. Alison Durkee, *After Court Lets Fox News Challenge Move Forward, Here's Where Dominion and Smartmatic's Defamation Suits Stand Now—And Who Could Be Next*, FORBES (Mar. 9, 2022).

4. Opinion, U.S. Dominion, Inc., v. Fox News Network, C.A. No.: N21C-03-257 (Del. Super. Ct. Dec. 16, 2021), at 6–7, 15–16.
5. *Id.* at 7.
6. *Id.* at 8–9.
7. *Id.* at 10.
8. *Id.* at 11.
9. *Id.* at 12.
10. *Id.*at 12–13.
11. *Id.* at 28–29.
12. *Id.* at 14–15.
13. Complaint, U.S. Dominion, Inc. v. Fox News Network, N21C-03-257 (Del. Super. Ct. Mar. 26, 2021), at 4.
14. Defendant's Brief in Support of Its Rule 12(b)(6) Motion to Dismiss for Failure to State a Claim, U.S. Dominion, Inc. v. Fox News Network, N21C-03-257 (Del. Super. Ct. May 18, 2021), at 1.
15. Opinion, U.S. Dominion, Inc., v. Fox News Network, C.A. No.: N21C-03-257 (Del. Super. Ct. Dec. 16, 2021), at 6–7, 40–42.
16. *Id.* at 42–43.
17. *Id.* at 43.
18. *Id.* at 47.
19. *Id.* at 48.
20. *Id.* at 51.
21. *Id.*
22. Mike Masnick, *Since When Is It Illegal to Just Mention a Trademark Online*, Techdirt (Jan. 5, 2005).
23. Rich v. Fox News Network, 939 F.3d 112, 117 (2d. Cir. 2019).
24. *Id.* at 117–18.
25. *Id.* at 118.
26. *Id.* at 119.
27. *Id.* at 119–20.
28. *Id.* at 120.
29. *Id.* at 122 (internal quotation marks and citation omitted).
30. *Id.* at 122.
31. *Id.* at 125–26.
32. *Id.* at 127.
33. *Id.* at 130.
34. Michael Isikoff, *Fox Paid Seven Figures to Settle Lawsuit over Bogus Seth Rich Conspiracy Story*, Yahoo News (Nov. 24, 2020).
35. For an argument in favor of general tort liability for news organizations that disseminate health misinformation, *see* John Culhane, *Fox News Could Be Sued If Its Anti-Vax Statements Caused People to Die*, Slate (July 23, 2021). "These purveyors of misinformation are either lying, or acting in reckless disregard of truth versus falsity by not doing even the most basic research to check out what they're spewing, And it's also considered a misrepresentation to state a half-truth, leaving out vital information needed to place a statement in context."
36. United States v. Stevens, 559 U.S. 460 (2010).
37. Virginia Pharmacy Board v. Virginia Consumer Council, 425 U.S. 748, 761 (1976).
38. Central Hudson Gas & Electric Corp. v. Public Service Commission of New York, 447 U.S. 557, 566 (1980).

39. 15 U.S.C. § 45(a)(1).

40. FTC Policy Statement on Deception (Oct. 14, 1983).

41. H.R. 133, 116th Cong., Sec. 1401 (2020).

42. Complaint for Civil Penalties, Permanent Injunction, and Other Relief, United States v. Nepute, 4:21-cv-437 (E.D. Mo. Apr. 15, 2021).

43. National Institute of Family and Life Advocates v. Becerra, 138 S.Ct. 2361, 2367 (2018).

44. *Id.* at 2372.

45. *Id.*

46. *Id.* at 2373.

47. *Id.* at 2375–76.

48. Kathleen M. Sullivan, *The Intersection of Free Speech and the Legal Profession: Constraints on Lawyers' First Amendment Rights*, 67 FORDHAM L. REV. 569, 569 (1998).

49. Matter of Giuliani, 197 A.D.3d 1, 6 (N.Y. App. Div. 2021).

50. *Id.* at 4.

51. *Id.* at 7.

52. *Id.*

53. United States v. Alvarez, 567 U.S. 709 (2012) (plurality opinion).

54. 18 U.S.C. 1001.

55. United States v. Alvarez, 567 U.S. 709 (2012) (plurality opinion).

56. People v. Leader, 2021 IL App (2d) 190589-U (Ill. Ct. App., 2d Dist., Mar. 11, 2021) (unpublished) at *5 (quoting 720 ILCS 5/26-1(a)(4)).

57. *Id.* at *7.

58. Minnesota Voters Alliance v. Mansky, 138 S. Ct. 1876 (2018).

59. Rick Hasen, CHEAP SPEECH 110 (2022).

Part III. Empowering Rationality

1. Lyrissa Barnett Lidsky, *Nobody's Fools: The Rational Audience as First Amendment Ideal*, 2010 U. ILL. L. REV. 799, 819 (2010).

Chapter 12. Counterspeech and Self-Help

1. Harry Kalven Jr., *If This Be Asymmetry, Make the Most of It!*, CENTER MAG. (May/June 1973), at 36, quoted in David Kohler, *Self Help, the Media and the First Amendment*, 35 HOFSTRA L. REV. 1263 (2007).

2. Kohler, *supra* note 1, at 1263–64.

3. *Id.*

4. Gertz v. Robert Welch, 418 U.S. 323, 344 (1974).

5. Press release, Quinnipiac University, *Inflation Tops Russia-Ukraine War as Most Urgent Issue in U.S., Quinnipiac University National Poll Finds; 52% Disapprove of GOP Senators' Handling of Ketanji Brown Jackson Hearings* (Mar. 30, 2022).

6. Reno v. ACLU, 521 U.S. 844, 850 (1997).

7. Robert D. Richards and Clay Calvert, *Counterspeech 2000: A New Look at the Old Remedy for "Bad" Speech*, 2000 BYU L. REV. 553, 556 (2000).

8. Susan Crawford, *Whiter Libel*, SUSAN CRAWFORD BLOG (July 5, 2006), http://scrawford.blogware.com/blog/_archives/2006/7/5/2086324.html, archived at https://web.archive.org/web/20080907175231/.

9. Pew Research Center, INTERNET/BROADBAND FACT SHEET (Apr. 7, 2021).

10. *See* David L. Hudson Jr., *Retraction*, THE FIRST AMENDMENT ENCYCLOPEDIA (accessed Jan. 6, 2023), https://www.mtsu.edu/first-amendment/article/1012/retraction.

11. Robert M. Ackerman, *Bringing Coherence to Defamation Law through Uniform Legislation: The Search for an Elegant Solution*, 72 N.C. L. REV. 291, 323 (1994). "Retraction statutes enacted by individual states have generally passed constitutional muster when their effect has been merely to eliminate punitive damages in libel or slander actions."
12. Arizona Rev. Stat. 12-653.02.
13. Dealer Computer Servs. v. Fullers'White Mt. Motors, No. CV07-00748-PCT-JAT, 2008 U.S. Dist. LEXIS 83311 (D. Ariz. Oct. 17, 2008).
14. OCGA § 51-5-11.
15. Mathis v. Cannon, 556 S.E.2d 172, 176 (Ga. Ct. App. 2001).
16. *Id.*
17. Mathis v. Cannon, 573 S.E.2d 376, 377 (Ga. 2002).
18. *Id.* at 385.
19. *Id.* (quoting *Gertz*, 418 U.S. at 344).
20. *Id.* at 389 (Hunstein, J., dissenting).
21. Statement of Offence, United States v. Pruitt, 21-cr-23 (D.D.C. June 3, 2022) at ¶¶ 10–16.
22. Government's Sentencing Memo, United States v. Pruitt, 21-cr-23 (D.D.C. Aug. 19, 2022) at Ex. 4.
23. *Id.*
24. *The Principles of the Truth-O-Meter: PolitiFact's Methodology for Independent Fact-Checking*, POLITIFACT (Feb. 12, 2018).
25. Jon Greenberg, *Greene Twists Logic and Facts in Pedophilia Charge against GOP Senators*, POLITIFACT (Apr. 6, 2022).

Chapter 13. Intermediaries

1. Adi Robertson, *What Elon Musk's Twitter "Free Speech" Promises Miss*, THE VERGE (Apr. 15, 2022).
2. Twitter, COVID-19 MISINFORMATION REPORT (July 14, 2021).
3. Manhattan Community Access Corp. v. Halleck, 139 S. Ct. 1921, 1926 (2019).
4. *Id.* at 1928 (cleaned up).
5. *Id.* at 1934.
6. Prager University v. Google, 951 F.3d 991, 995 (9th Cir. 2020).
7. *Id.* at 995–96.
8. *Id.* at 998.
9. Genevieve Lakier, *Informal Government Coercion and the Problem of "Jawboning,"* LAWFARE (July 26, 2021).
10. Bantam Books, Inc. v. Sullivan, 372 U.S. 58, 61 (1963).
11. *Id.* at 66–67.
12. Blum v. Yaretsky, 457 U.S. 991 (1982).
13. Lakier, *supra* note 9.
14. Vivek H. Murthy, US Surgeon General, CONFRONTING HEALTH MISINFORMATION (July 2021).
15. Brief for Appellant the Miami Herald Publishing Company, *Miami Herald Publishing v. Tornillo*, No. 73-797 (Feb. 28, 1974), at 2.
16. Miami Herald Publishing v. Tornillo, 418 U.S. 241, 245–46 (1974).
17. *Id.* at 247–48.
18. *Id.* at 254.
19. *Id.* at 256.
20. *Id.* at 258.

21. 475 U.S. 1 (1986).
22. 515 U.S. 557 (1995).
23. Turner Broadcasting System v. FCC, 512 U.S. 622, 656 (1994).
24. *Id.* at 646.
25. *See generally* Eugene Volokh, *Treating Social Media Platforms Like Common Carriers?*, 1 J. FREE SPEECH LAW 1 (2021) (summarizing arguments on both sides).
26. Reno v. ACLU, 521 U.S. 844, 885 (1997).
27. Biden v. Knight First Amendment Inst., 141 S.Ct. 1220 (Thomas, J., concurring).
28. NetChoice v. Florida, —F.4th—, No. 21-12355 (11th Cir. 2022), at 7; quoting *Governor Ron DeSantis Signs Bill to Stop the Censorship of Floridians by Big Tech*, RON DESANTIS (May 24, 2021), https://www.flgov.com/2021/05/24/governor-ron-desantis-signs-bill-to-stop-the-censorship-of-floridians-by-big-tech/.
29. *Id.* at 10.
30. *Id.* at 11.
31. *Id.* at 12–13.
32. *Id.* at 14.
33. *Id.* at 23.
34. *Id.* at 25.
35. *Id.* at 43.
36. *Id.* at 59 (cleaned up).
37. *Id.* at 60.
38. *Id.* at 63.
39. *See, e.g.,* Cathy Gellis, *The Problem with the Otherwise Very Good and Very Important Eleventh Circuit Decision on the Florida Social Media Law*, TECHDIRT (May 23, 2022).
40. Netchoice v. Paxton, 49 F.4th 439, 445–46 (5th Cir. 2022).
41. *Id.* at 446.
42. *Id.* at 494.
43. *Id.* at 459.
44. *Id.* at 478–79.
45. Stratton Oakmont, Inc. v. Prodigy Services Co., 23 Media L. Rep. 1794 (N.Y. Sup. Ct. May 24, 1995).
46. Cubby v. CompuServe, 776 F.Supp. 135 (S.D.N.Y. 1991).
47. 47 U.S.C. § 230(c)(1).
48. Zeran v. America Online, 129 F.3d 327, 330 (4th Cir. 1997).
49. 47 U.S.C. § 230(c)(2).
50. *See* Elizabeth Banker, *A Review of Section 230's Meaning and Application Based on More Than 500 Cases*, INTERNET ASSOCIATION (July 2020).
51. Netchoice v. Paxton, 49 F.4th 439, 468 (5th Cir. 2022).
52. 47 U.S.C. § 230(c)(2) (emphasis added).
53. *See* Anshu Siripurapu, *Trump and Section 230: What to Know*, COUNCIL ON FOREIGN RELATIONS (Dec. 2, 2020).
54. *Joe Biden: Former Vice President of the United States, Editorial Board Interview*, NEW YORK TIMES, Jan. 17, 2020.
55. *See* Matal v. Tam, 137 S.Ct. 1744 (2017) (concluding that a prohibition on registering disparaging trademarks violates the First Amendment); CONGRESSIONAL RESEARCH SERVICE, SECTION 230: AN OVERVIEW (Apr. 7, 2021), at 51. "Because Section 230 provides immunity for private speech activities and similarly cannot be framed as advancing a government message, *Tam* could suggest that viewpoint-based conditions on Section 230 immunity are unconstitutional."

56. Cong. Rec. H. 8470 (Aug. 4, 1995).

57. 47 U.S.C. § 230(b)(3).

58. *Parental Empowerment, Child Protection and Free Speech in Interactive Media*, CENTER FOR DEMOCRACY AND TECHNOLOGY (July 24, 1995).

59. Mike Masnick, *Protocols, Not Platforms: A Technological Approach to Free Speech,* KNIGHT FIRST AMENDMENT INSTITUTE, FREE SPEECH FUTURES SERIES (Aug. 21, 2019).

60. *Id.*

61. Kate Conger, *Twitter Wants to Reinvent Itself, by Merging the Old with the New*, N.Y. TIMES, Mar. 2, 2022.

62. Alan Z. Rozenshtein, *Moderating the Fediverse: Content Moderation on Distributed Social Media* 2, J. FREE SPEECH L. (forthcoming 2023).

Chapter 14. Accountability

1. 18 U.S.C. § 3553.

2. Government's Sentencing Memorandum, United States v. Lolos, Case No. 1:21-cr-242 (D.D.C. Nov. 10, 2021), at 2 [hereinafter Gov. Sentencing Memo].

3. *Read Trump's Jan. 6 Speech, a Key Part of Impeachment Trial*, NATIONAL PUBLIC RADIO (Feb. 10, 2021).

4. Gov. Sentencing Memo, at 5–6.

5. *Id.* at 6–7.

6. *Id.* at 8–9.

7. *Id.* at 10.

8. *Id.* at 12.

9. *Id.*

10. District Judge Amit Mehta, US District Court for the District of Columbia.

11. Defendant's Memorandum in Aid of Sentencing, United States v. Lolos, Case No. 1:21-cr-242 (D.D.C. Nov. 12, 2021), at 2–3.

12. *Id.* at 3.

13. *Id.* at 4.

14. *Id.* at 2.

15. Transcript of Sentencing Via Zoom Proceedings, United States v. Lolos, 21-CR-243 (D.D.C. Nov. 19, 2021), at 16.

16. *Id.* at 25.

17. *Id.* at 28.

18. *Id.* at 30–31.

19. *Id.* at 31.

20. *Id.* at 31–32.

21. *Id.* at 32.

22. *Id.* at 35.

23. *Id.* at 36.

24. *Id.*

25. *Id.* at 37.

26. *Id.* at 38.

27. *Id.* at 46–47.

28. *Id.* at 50–53.

29. *Id.* at 55.

30. *Id.* at 55–56.

31. *Id.* at 56.

32. *Id.* at 56–57.

33. *Id.* at 57.
34. Defendant's Sentencing Memorandum, United States v. Peterson, 21-cr-309 (D.D.C. Nov. 23, 2021), at 8.
35. *Id.* at 8–9.
36. Government's Sent'g Memorandum, United States v. Peterson, 21-cr-309 (D.D.C. Nov. 23, 2021), at 3–4.
37. *Id.* at 4–5.
38. *Id.* at 6–8.
39. *Id.* at 8–11.
40. *Id.* at 13–14.
41. *Id.* at 14–15.
42. Samantha Hawkins, *Former Baltimore Colleagues Eager to See What Federal Judge Does in Roger Stone Case*, MARYLAND MATTERS (Feb. 20, 2020).
43. Defendant's Sent'g Memorandum, United States v. Peterson, 21-cr-309 (D.D.C. Nov. 23, 2021), at 10.
44. Government's Sentencing Memorandum, United States v. Peterson, 21-cr-309 (D.D.C. Nov. 23, 2021), at 6–8.
45. Defendant's Sent'g Memorandum, United States v. Peterson, 21-cr-309 (D.D.C. Nov. 23, 2021), at 6–7.
46. *Id.* at 1–2.
47. Sent'g Transcript, United States v. Peterson, 21-cr-309 (D.D.C. Dec. 1, 2021), at 5–8.
48. *Id.* at 12–13.
49. *Id.* at 13–14.
50. *Id.* at 16–17.
51. *Id.* at 19.
52. *Id.* at 21.
53. *Id.* at 22.
54. *Id.* at 26.
55. National Consortium for the Study of Terrorism and Responses to Terrorism, QANON OFFENDERS IN THE UNITED STATES (Feb. 2021).

Chapter 15. Demand

1. Barack Obama, *Disinformation Is a Threat to Our Democracy* (Apr. 21, 2022), https://barackobama.medium.com/my-remarks-on-disinformation-at-stanford-7d7af7ba28af.
2. Bridget Johnson, *DHS Standing Up Disinformation Governance Board Led by Information Warfare Expert*, HOMELAND SECURITY TODAY (Apr. 27, 2022).
3. POLITICO PLAYBOOK (Apr. 27, 2022).
4. *Tucker: Nina Jankowicz Is the Most Ridiculous of All in Biden's Ministry of Truth*, FOX NEWS (Apr. 28, 2022).
5. *Id.*
6. David Harsanyi, *Team Biden's Plan to Flag "Disinformation" Is Both Laughable—and Dangerous*, N.Y. POST, Apr. 29, 2022.
7. *DeSantis on Biden Disinformation Governance Board: It's a "Belated April Fool's Joke" and "Rejects Bureau in Florida,"* CBS MIAMI (Apr. 29, 2022).
8. State of the Union, transcript, CNN (May 1, 2022).
9. *Fact Sheet: DHS Internal Working Group Protects Free Speech and Other Fundamental Rights When Addressing Disinformation That Threatens the Security of the United States*, DEPARTMENT OF HOMELAND SECURITY (May 2, 2022).

10. Geneva Sands, *DHS Shuts Down Disinformation Board Months after Its Efforts Were Paused,* CNN (Aug. 24, 2022).

11. COVID-19 National Preparedness Collaborators, *Pandemic Preparedness and COVID-19: An Exploratory Analysis of Infection and Fatality Rates, and Contextual Factors Associated with Preparedness in 177 Countries, from Jan 1, 2020, to Sept 30, 2021,* 399 LANCET 1489–512 (Feb. 1, 2022).

12. *See* Maria Cramer and Knvul Sheikh, *Surgeon General Urges the Public to Stop Buying Face Masks,* N.Y. TIMES, Feb. 29, 2020.

13. Roger Lowenstein, *This Company Wrote the Textbook for Managing a Public Health Emergency. First Rule: Transparency,* WASH. POST, Mar. 16, 2020.

14. *Id.*

15. George Orwell, 1984 (1949).

16. *MSNBC Interview with Dr. Anthony Fauci,* POLITICAL TRANSCRIPT WIRE (June 9, 2021).

17. *Id.*

18. *Hannity on Biden's Priorities ahead of Meeting with Putin,* FOX NEWS (June 10, 2021).

19. *The Week in Whoppers: Fauci's Arrogance, Twitter's Double Standard and More,* N.Y. POST, June 10, 2021.

20. *Confidence Declines in CDC and Dr. Anthony Fauci,* ANNENBERG PUBLIC POLICY CENTER (Jan. 27, 2022).

21. *NIH Director Says Pandemic's Toll Is Now on the Shoulders of the Unvaccinated,* ALL THINGS CONSIDERED (Nov. 21, 2021).

22. Michael Bang Petersen, *COVID Lesson: Trust the Public with Hard Truths,* NATURE (Oct. 12, 2021).

23. *Id.*

24. Rebecca Adler-Nissen, Sune Lehmann, and Andreas Roepstorff, *Denmark's Hard Lessons about Trust and the Pandemic,* N.Y. TIMES, Nov. 14, 2021.

25. *Id.*

26. Travis Andersen, *Federal Election Security Boss: "No Foreign Cyber Actor Can Change Your Vote,"* BOSTON GLOBE, Oct. 26, 2020.

27. *Rumor Control,* CYBERSECURITY AND INFRASTRUCTURE SECURITY AGENCY (last updated November 2, 2022), https://www.cisa.gov/rumorcontrol.

28. Rick Hasen, CHEAP SPEECH (2022), 83–84.

29. *See* Benjamin Siegel and Alex Hosenball, *Why Pennsylvania Is Still Counting Votes after Election Day,* ABC NEWS (Nov. 3, 2020); Holly Otterbein, *"The Math Is Pretty Simple": Trump's Lead Shrinks in Pennsylvania,* POLITICO (Nov. 4, 2020).

30. Eliza Mackintosh, *Finland Is Winning the War on Fake News. What It's Learned May Be Crucial to Western Democracy,* CNN (May 2019).

31. Jon Henley, *How Finland Starts Its Fight against Fake News in Primary Schools,* THE GUARDIAN, Jan. 29, 2020.

32. Ruturaj Patil, *An Evolving Fight: Finland's Success in Tackling Misinformation and What the World Can Learn,* EUROPE MONITOR (Sept. 24, 2021).

33. OPEN SOCIETY INSTITUTE–SOFIA, MEDIA LITERACY INDEX (2021).

34. REPORT OF THE SELECT COMMITTEE ON INTELLIGENCE, UNITED STATES SENATE ON RUSSIAN ACTIVE MEASURES CAMPAIGNS AND INTERFERENCE IN THE 2016 U.S. ELECTION, vol. 2, p. 81.

35. *Interview at Association for Supervision and Curriculum Development Conference,* SANDRA DAY O'CONNOR INSTITUTE DIGITAL LIBRARY (Feb. 27, 2014).

36. *Americans' Civics Knowledge Increases during a Stress-Filled Year*, ANNENBERG PUBLIC POLICY CENTER (Sept. 14, 2021).
37. *Educating for American Democracy: Excellence in History and Civics for All Learners*, iCIVICS (Mar. 2, 2021).
38. S.879 (117th Cong.).
39. Press release, Governor Phil Murphy, *Governor Murphy Signs Legislation to Expand Civics Instruction in Schools* (July 23, 2021).
40. Lisa Rose-Wiles, *Reflections on Fake News, Librarians, and Undergraduate Research*, 57 REF. & USER SVCS. Q. 200 (2018).
41. *See* Jorge Revez and Luis Corujo, *Librarians against Fake News: A Systematic Literature Review of Library Practices (Jan. 2018–Sept. 2020)*, 47 J. OF ACADEMIC LIBRARIANSHIP Issue 2 (2021).
42. Shellie Jeffries et al., *Says Who? Librarians Tackle Fake News*, 78 COLLEGE & RESEARCH LIBRARIES NEWS 538 (2017).
43. Mason Walker, *U.S. Newsroom Employment Has Fallen 26% since 2008*, PEW RESEARCH CENTER (July 13, 2021).
44. Margaret Sullivan, *What Happens to Democracy When Local Journalism Dries Up?*, WASH. POST, Nov. 11, 2021.
45. *Id.*
46. Martha Minow, SAVING THE NEWS (2021).
47. David S. Ardia, *Beyond the Marketplace of Ideas: Bridging Theory and Doctrine to Promote Self-Governance*, 16 HARV. L. & PUB. POL. REV. 101, 142 (2022).
48. *Id.* at 160.

Conclusion

1. Transcript of Sentencing, United States v. Welch, 16-cr-232 (D.D.C. June 22, 2017), at 19.
2. Exhibit 1 to Sentencing Memorandum, United States v. Welch, 16-cr-232 (D.D.C. June 13, 2017).
3. Transcript of Sentencing, United States v. Welch, 16-cr-232 (D.D.C. June 22, 2017), at 19, 50–51.
4. *Id.* at 78–79.
5. *Id.* at 40.
6. Erik Ortiz, *Trump Pushes Back on "Apprentice" Ties: I Will Devote "Zero Time" to TV Show*, NBC NEWS (Dec. 10, 2016).
7. Haley Britzky, *Everything Trump Has Called "FAKE NEWS,"* AXIOS (July 9, 2017).
8. *See* United States v. Alvarez, 567 U.S. 709 (2012). "Although the First Amendment stands against any freewheeling authority to declare new categories of speech outside the scope of the First Amendment, the Court has acknowledged that perhaps there exist some categories of speech that have been historically unprotected . . . but have not yet been specifically identified or discussed . . . in our case law. Before exempting a category of speech from the normal prohibition on content-based restrictions, however, the Court must be presented with persuasive evidence that a novel restriction on content is part of a long (if heretofore unrecognized) tradition of proscription" (cleaned up).
9. Brown v. Entertainment Merchants Ass'n, 564 U.S. 786, 790 (2011) (internal quotation marks and citation omitted).
10. Abrams v. United States, 250 U.S. 616, 630 (1919) (Holmes, J., dissenting).

Index

"Slurs, Insults Drag Town into Controversy" (*Chester County Daily Local*),
78–79
Smartmatic, 210–15
Smith, Milan D., Jr., 25–27, 127–28
Smith, Patricia, 108–12
Smith v. California, 59–60
Smith v. Linn, 108–12
Sneed, Joseph Tyree, 114
social media: counterspeech and self-help
on, 235–36; COVID posts on, 191–96;
federal content moderation and, 259–63;
First Amendment rights of, 250–59;
health misinformation on, 185–87; as
intermediaries in misinformation distribution, 245–68; limits of content moderation on, 263–68; marketplace of
ideas and, 41–42; medical misinformation on, 110–12; misinformation and
disinformation on, 171–73; news
organizations and newspapers compared to, 253–54; state action doctrine
and, 247–49
Sontag, Frederick, 106–7
Sotomayor, Sonia, 29–30, 33
Soviet Union, disinformation campaign
by, 176–78, 293
Sowle, Kathryn Dix, 69
Spencer, Ambrose, 85–86, 88
Sputnik News, 122–23
Stanford Encyclopedia of Philosophy, 7
Starbird, Kate, 165
Star Chamber (England), 83, 88
state action doctrine, social media content
intervention and, 246–47
state laws: civics education promotion and,
297; election integrity and, 293–94; fair
report privileges and, 73; false speech
regulation and, 180–85; federal law
violations by, 261–63; free speech obligations and, 138–39; libel claims and,
85–86, 89–90; protection of political
statements and, 147–56; retraction
statutes, 237–40; right of reply statutes,
251–52; social media content regulation
in, 254–59
State of the Union (CNN program), 284
Stefancic, Jean, 38–39
Steffen, Brian J., 66
Stolen Valor Act, free speech protections
and, 20–38, 149, 157

Stone, Andy, 173
The Storm conspiracy, 167
strategic lawsuits against public participation (SLAPP), 124; laws against, 64–65,
304
Stratton Okmont v. Prodigy, 260, 262–63
Streisand effect, 215–16
strict scrutiny test, free speech and,
149–50, 153
substantial truth doctrine: civil libel cases
and, 91–105; libel law and, 58–65;
uncertainty and, 106–7
Sullivan, Kathleen, 223
Sullivan, L. B., 54–65
Sullivan, Margaret, 298–99
Sunstein, Cass, 196–98
Supreme Court (US): commercial speech
protections and, 221–27; defamation
claims and, 90, 201–4; election integrity
cases and, 183, 226–27; free speech
jurisprudence and, 4–5, 9, 12–13, 304–6;
libel cases before, 199–204; marketplace
of ideas and, 17–18; neutral reportage
privilege and, 80–82; newspaper defamation suits and, 124–25; *New York
Times v. Sullivan* and, 57–65; right of
reply statutes and, 251–52; self-help in
First Amendment rulings, 232–33;
social media cases and, 254; state action
doctrine and platform intervention
and, 246–49; Stolen Valor Act ruling
by, 23–38; tax on stock dividends and,
135–39
Supreme Court of Canada, 63–64
SurfWatch, 265
Susan B. Anthony List v. Driehaus,
148–53
sworn testimony, free speech protections
and, 224–25

Taft, William Howard, 48–49, 52, 57–59
Tah v. Global Witness Publishing, 199–201
Taylor, Roger, 20
Techdirt, 215
technology, misinformation and, 176–78
Teilborg, James A., 237
telephone companies, social media com-
pared to, 256–57
Third Circuit Court of Appeals, 78
third-party fact-checkers, 266
Thirteenth Amendment, 3